For one of the age's beauties,
Grace Boyd, who has been
a sparkling and gracious
friend for lo these many
years

John Weld

December 1990

FLY AWAY HOME

Fly Away Home

JOHN WELD

MISSION PUBLISHING · SANTA BARBARA · 1991

Design and typography by Jim Cook

Published by Mission Publishing
Post Office Box 1440
Santa Barbara, California 93102

LIBRARY OF CONGRESS CATALOGING-IN-PUBLICATION DATA

Weld, John, 1905-
   Fly away home: memoirs of a Hollywood stuntman / John Weld.
      p.   cm.
   ISBN 0-9625696-1-5, cloth
      1. Weld, John, 1905-   2. Authors, American—20th century—
Biography.   3. Stunt men and women—United States—
Biography.   4. Hollywood (Los Angeles, Calif.)—Biography.
I. Title.
PS3545.E5155Z464   1991
813'.54—DC20   90-43674
[B]   CIP

To Katy Weld

The books we need are the books
that are ice-axes to break up
the frozen sea within ourselves.

FRANZ KAFKA

CHAPTER ONE

ONE SPRING MORNING in 1899, Nelle Farrow, a blooming and sprightly seventeen, came out of the drugstore in Hendersonville, North Carolina, and, as she passed the barber shop, a handsome stranger in linen suit, starched-collared shirt, stick-pinned necktie and bright-banded straw hat emerged therefrom. They almost collided and for a moment stood face to face, the young man audibly drawing in his breath. In the manner of a properly brought up young lady, Nelle smiled but gave no indication she was impressed.

"I'm sorry," the young man said, doffing his hat and bowing slightly.

"I beg your pardon," Nelle said, not without a trace of feigned hauteur; and slightly lifting her long skirt, she went on.

The young man stood motionless, watching her walk out of his life. Impulsively he hastened back into the barber shop and asked, "Who is that girl?"

Looking out the window, the barber said, "Why, that's Miss Nelle, one of the Farrow girls."

"Prettiest thing I ever did see," the young man said and, sighing, went back out the screen door.

Instead of going homeward, as she had been bent, Nelle crossed the street for another sidelong glance at the handsome stranger. She saw him re-emerge from the barbershop and, showing no interest in him, went into the grocery store. When she came out he was standing on the corner. Had she headed homeward she would have gone in the opposite direction, but she went his way.

"We meet again," he said, doffing his hat. Nelle stopped, suppressing a smile. "Would you be so kind as to help me?"

"Why, yes—I guess so—if I can."

"My name is Harry Weld. I'm from New York. I very much want to make your acquaintance."

Controlling her fluster, Nelle said, "I'm afraid that would be improper."

"Perhaps we have a mutual friend. Do you know Mister Calhoun who runs the furniture store? I sell furniture to him and he will vouch for me."

"I know Mister Calhoun."

"Then please come—let him introduce us."

Mr. Calhoun did so, and thus their romance began. They were married a year later, though much against her parents' wills because he was a Yankee. That is how my sister and I came into being.

I WAS THE first male born to my mother's family in three generations and my appearance produced such rejoicing that it would have been appropriate if three wise men had appeared on asses. My maternal grandmother, immoderately proud of her heredity, wanted me to bear the name of an illustrious ancestor; and my paternal grandmother, also proud of her ancestry, wanted me to bear one of hers, so I was christened with two middle names—Willoughby and Blasingame— considerably more than I needed.

My father died of typhoid fever in 1905, when I was six months old, so I never knew him. I have been told that he was a gallant blade with an effervescent personality. A photograph of him and Mother when they were married shows him to be tall and slender with curly dark hair parted in the middle, a watch chain across his waistcoat and a boutonniere in his jacket lapel. Some of my weaknesses and strengths must have come from his genes, but never having known him I am unable to define them. From him I must have gotten my penchant for elegance, to show off, anything to be liked and admired. If he had lived I doubtless would have lived a more normal life. As a child I probably would not have been sent hither and yon; I might have graduated from college, perhaps from Harvard, and become a doctor, a teacher or a preacher. I'm sure I never would have gone to Hollywood and become a stunt man in the movies, as I did. When I was twenty years old one of his sisters told me I was his "spitting image." He left no estate. When he died he was employed by a life insurance company but had no life insurance. His mother insisted that his remains be buried in the family plot in Brooklyn, but she had to send money to get them there. Mother was left with two children, my sister Elinor, aged two-and-a-half, and me, and no funds.

It was considered degrading for a lady in the proud but impoverished South to work for a living, but Nelle had no choice. She became proficient at typing and shorthand and got a job as a secretary for the Mutual Life Association in Atlanta.

While Mother worked, Elinor and I were attended by our maternal grandmother. She was an authoritative, strong, high-toned lady. Her father had been a medical doctor and before the Civil War had owned a large South Carolina plantation and a passel of slaves. Whatever wealth he had possessed had been lost in the war. He died before I was born. Lacking riches, Grandmother leaned heavily on antecedents. *The Social Register* and Emily Post's *Book of Etiquette* were as important in her library as the Bible. Day after day she pounded into my sister Elinor and me rules of social behavior. Among my earliest memories of her is her telling me: "You are an aristocrat. Always remember that. And see that you conduct yourself accordingly." She so relentlessly drummed manners into me that to this day I rise to give a lady my seat.

One of the men in the office where Mother worked, Robert Curtis Lewis, was of medium height, stout and, though hirsute, slightly bald. He pursued her and eventually she married him. I'm sure she did so for Elinor's and my sakes, though he did not adopt us. From the beginning he and I did not get along well. I was jealous of him and we were always vying for Mother's affection. When I was five he was transferred to Birmingham, Alabama, whither we moved. The abode we settled into was the upper story of a duplex on Thirtieth Street just off Highland Avenue. In the building's basement I met a man who became like a father to me. He was black and his name was Brown. He was not Mister Brown or George Brown or Ambrose Brown, he was just plain Brown although occasionally an insensitive person would call him Boy. His skin was purplish-black and his teeth were so large and white—all, that is, except one of the front ones, which was gold—that when he smiled his entire countenance seemed to light up.

The first time I encountered him he greeted me effusively: "Well, now, howdy-doody? You mus' be one of the newcomers. What's yo' name?"

"John. They call me Jack."

"John's a Biblical name. Glad to meet you. Where you come from?"

"Atlanta."

"Welcome to Birmin'ham."

He was so ingratiating that whenever he came I would go to the basement to be with him. Always he would greet me warmly: "How is yawl, Honey-chile?" or "What is you up to, Massa John?" And when I went to him with one of my discoveries, a beetle, say, or a butterfly, he would profess strong enthusiasm. "Well, now, do tell! Ain't that some'm!" or he would exclaim, "Well, shut my mouth!" or "I'm a suck-egg mule!" He was humble but had a strong sense of pride. I never heard him say a deprecatory word or lose his temper. He would come early in the morning to feed the fires, usually before the white folks got out of bed, and would return in the late afternoon to bank them. Once I offered to help carry out ashes, but he said, "No. This kinda work ain't for the likes of you, Massa John. You is somebody. When you is somebody you don't go 'round dirtin' yo' hands. I'ze got a speculation you was born with a caul."

"What's a caul?"

"Why, honey-chile, a caul is a heavenly cap which some folks is wearin' when they's born. The Lord put it there to show that you is extra, that you is a big-wig."

I began to think I was wearing a halo. "What makes you think that?" I asked.

"Why, son, I can tell. I'ze got the power. I can transmogrify. I won't be surprised if you becomes President."

Tending furnaces was his moonlighting job. His main job was preaching. One day he asked me what I was going to be when I grew up. "I'm gonna be a preacher jes' like you," I said.

"What chew know 'bout the Bible?"

"I know about Jesus and I know about Moses and I know about Ruth and Naomi."

"You know 'bout Lividicus?"

I shook my head. His gold-and-ivory smile lit his black face. "If you is gwinna be a preacher you gotta know 'bout Lividicus an' you gotta know 'bout Deuteronomy." It gave him joy to use long words, not for their meanings so much as because they musicalized his speech.

One day he took me to his church, a white clapboard building of the simplest construction. One of his duties, aside from being its preacher, was to clean the place. There was a belfry over the front door and I wanted to pull the rope to ring the bells, but he asked me not to, saying it would "pontificate" people. "Folks'll think we's callin' 'em to church." He set me to arranging the hymnals right side up in their proper places while he swept the floor. When we had finished the chores, I said, "I wish you'd preach a sermon."

"Why, son," Brown said, "a preacher cain't jes' rare back an' preach no sermon without no congregation."

"Can't I be the congregation?"

"Well, I'll jes' dish you up a smidgen of hellfire an' damnation." And shuffling up the aisle in his cut-toed, down-at-heel shoes, he went to the pulpit, gripped the lectern with both hands and stood for a few moments gathering his thoughts. When finally he began to speak he took as his text the story of Daniel, knowing it would interest a child. His style was stentorian. His voice was strong. It would rise then subside to a confidential tone. For emphasis he would slap or pound the lectern or caress it. He paraphrased the story with such phrases as "And it came to pass" and "Verily I says unto you."

For Christmas that year I was given a bicycle and was so thrilled that I hastened through breakfast and pedaled for hours. Back in our neighborhood I proudly showed the bike to a group of boys and let them ride it. Among them was a black boy who had gotten a scooter for Christmas. Leaving the scooter with me, he took off on the bike and never came back. I was heart-broken. Losing the bicycle was devastating enough, but having it stolen by a black boy made the pain more excruciating. When I told Brown what had happened, he said, "That was a mean thing for that boy to do, but don't judge all black people by him. There's bad apples in every barrel. Look on the bright side: but for you that boy would never have gotten a bicycle. You was his Santa Claus."

THAT FALL my sister Elinor and I matriculated at Lakeview School, she in the third grade, I in the first. After school one day, I went with several older boys to a swimming hole nearby in Shades Creek. The other boys quickly disrobed and dove or belly-flopped into the water. I got undressed, but never having been in water over my head, stood indecisively watching them thrash about. "Come on in!" they shouted and when one said, "What are you—a sissy?" I jumped in. Water closed over me and instinctively I pushed up from the bottom to get a breath, then went down again. I kept doing this until I finally reached the bank. Scrambling out, I shamefully dressed and went home. Mother forthwith arranged for me to get swimming lessons at the Birmingham Athletic Club where I learned to swim and dive, not realizing that water sports were to be important in my life.

For my seventh birthday Mother gave me another bicycle. Going full speed downhill the front wheel struck a pothole and I went heels over head and suffered a concussion. Robert Lewis said, "He hasn't got the sense God gave a nanny goat."

I did seem to be accident prone. In our neighborhood we played a game called "Cavalry": smaller boys would straddle the shoulders of larger ones and try to unseat one another. In falling, my right arm was broken at the elbow. It was a complicated break and took months to restructure. Roller skates became the vogue. I skated sidewalks, jumped curbs, rolled lickity-split down hills and latched onto automobiles, always showing off.

Mother was keenly aware of the conflict between her husband and me and, as soon as summer came she sent me to her sister Sarah and her husband, William Wilmerding. Uncle Billy was a medical doctor.

The Wilmerdings lived on a farm in North Carolina several miles from the town of Selma. Uncle Billy met me at the railroad station in a buggy drawn by a gray horse named Nostradamus and drove me through miles of tobacco to the residence. The thing I most vividly remember about the house was the party-line telephone hanging on the wall near the kitchen. The Wilmerding's rings were two short and one long. The phone rang almost constantly, more often than not for Uncle Billy. A woman was suffering the torments of childbirth, a man had axed a foot or a child was whooping.

The majority of people who lived in this remote area were black sharecroppers and every day Uncle Billy would hitch Nostradamus and go forth to administer to the sick, the halt and the pregnant. Frequently he took me with him, thereby affording me some of the treasured times of my life. A tall, handsome man, he regarded life as a miracle to be enjoyed. "The fact that we're here, you and I," he said while we rolled along, "is miracle enough, because the odds of us getting here were several hundred million to one." And he went on to explain pro-creation.

I noticed that he treated whites and blacks with equal care and tenderness. When I mentioned this to him, he said, "One should judge people and respect them according to their characters not their colors. Black people are as good as white people, but they have a longer, more uphill way to go in this world. We should do what we can to encourage and help them."

One morning before breakfast he was summoned to a sharecropper's shack to attend a young black girl giving birth.

Though Aunt Sadie objected—saying, "He'll be in the way. At childbirth mothers don't want lookers-on,"—he took me with him.

"It'll add to his education," he said.

The milk-chocolate girl was pretty, about fourteen and looked as if she had swallowed a watermelon. Two older black women were with her, giving sympathy and encouragement. Hot water was boiling when we arrived and the girl was in severe discomfort, but it was almost two hours before the baby began emerging. I was benumbed to see it come out head first. It looked like a sheathed rat. Uncle Billy helped ease it out, removed the placenta and, holding the kidlet by the ankles, spanked it into consciousness. It was a girl.

At other such times, when there was no one else to lend a hand, he asked me to help by fetching this or that. He may have thought to kindle in me an interest in medicine, which he did; but what he did more emphatically was to set me an example of humanitarianism.

One day as we rode along, I asked, "Why do you do your doctoring 'way out here, Uncle Billy?"

"Well, son, for one thing, there's no other doctor in these parts and people are sorely in need of medical assistance. For another, I'm researching a disease called pellagra. It's prevalent hereabouts. Pellagra's a disease people get when they don't eat the proper foods."

Uncle Billy's patients, and indeed all of the populace, looked upon him as a combination physician, counselor and judge; and because of the reverence in which he was held he had to be careful not to overstep the bounds of propriety. To live up to the public's image of him, he restrained his temper, did not use profanity or show indecision. During the day he usually eschewed his patients' hospitality, but toward the late afternon he would accept their offers of corn whiskey or hard cider. By the time we headed homeward he often was quite mellow. Under the influence of the stimulants he would discard his professional mien and sing such songs as *Abdul the Bulbul Amir* or *Polly Wolly Doodle*, while we rode through cooling evenings with Nostradamus' hoofs keeping the beat for his rich baritone. And always when we got home the buggy would be loaded with comestibles—vegetables, bread, eggs, fruit and sometimes a pie or cake—payment for his professional services. Infrequently the reward was money.

Uncle Billy was gentle, strong, fair and unselfish. There was no evil in him, no hate, no bitterness, no rancor. He and Brown did more to build my psychic structure than any teachers I have known.

CHAPTER TWO

B ECAUSE GRANDMOTHER WAS forever pointing out life's sinful pitfalls, I got the impression that adults were moral and only children were wicked. The revelation that this assumption was untrue came to me when I was ten years old. On my way home from school I was approached by a buxom, middle-aged woman dressed and hatted in black, wearing dark glasses and carrying a cane.

"Young man," she said, "I'd like you to help me. As you see, I am blind and I would like you to be my guide. I earn a living selling needles. I will pay you twenty-five cents an hour."

"How long will it take?" I asked.

"Oh, maybe two or three hours."

Touched by her handicap, I acceded to her request and we set out, her hand on my shoulder. As we went from house to house she made her pitch, claiming I was her son and saying she had several other children to support. She also stressed her poverty by mentioning her "dear departed husband." No one she approached turned her away empty-handed, and frequently she aroused such sympathy that people gave her money and did not take the needles.

At first I was fascinated, but presently I began to suspect that the lady was an impostor, a con-artist. Guilt rose in me and, after continuing with her for another block, I contrived an excuse to leave her.

At once her attitude changed. Whereas she had treated me with motherly kindness, she abruptly became inimical. "You can't leave me yet!" she exclaimed. "What am I to do?"

"I'm sorry," I said, "I've got to get home."

"You don't expect me to pay you, do you?"

"As you like," I said.

She took from her big black bag a bulging coin purse and snapped it open. "Go ahead," she said testily. "Take a quarter."

I hesitated. It occurred to me that, if she were blind and I took a larger coin, she would not know the difference. Grandmother's indoctrination—"Aristocrats never lie, cheat or steal!"—dissuaded me. I chose a quarter, said, "Thank you, m'am," and left her.

That experience shattered my concept about grown-ups. If they were not to be trusted, it had to be a perilous world.

During my eighth year I got a job delivering the *Birmingham Age-Herald* in the Negro section. I began reading the news and feature stories. It was then that the urge to write began gnawing at my consciousness. It wasn't long before I wrote what I considered a poem about an encounter I had with a dog which tried to bite me while I was delivering papers. I rhymed dog with God, mad with rag, bite with fright and hit with stick. It must have been awful, but the *Age-Herald* printed it. Seeing my name in print so intoxicated me that I decided to become a poet.

In 1916, when I was eleven, I wanted to join a Boy Scout troop but was rejected because the admission age was twelve. The Scout Master, sensing my disappointment, said that if I could get my parents' consent I could go on the troop's jamboree as its mascot. Mother readily gave her consent.

The encampment was on the Coosa River and I was assigned a cot in a tent with three other boys, one of whom, aged sixteen, was endeavoring to become an Eagle Scout. To earn a merit badge, he climbed up to dive from a cliff about fifty feet high, but after reaching the top decided it was too high and came down the way he had gone up.

I felt strongly that I could do the dive and saw an opportunity to win esteem. The next swimming period I climbed the cliff to have a look and was appalled by the height. Those below began yelling for me to dive while the Scout Master, using a megaphone, shouted for me to come down. I was undecided. I considered jumping but thought that would not be impressive. When the Scout Master started up to get me I took a deep breath and dove. I hit the water well, expecting applause. Instead I was severely reprimanded, the Scoutmaster saying, "That was a stupid thing to do! You could have broken your back!"

The dive helped build my confidence and uplifted my ego. It was not until years later that I came upon Dostoyevsky's definition: *The essence of heroism lies in seeking out risks you do not have to take.*

I did not become a member of that scout troop because the next summer, when I was old enough, Mother sent me to Colona, a flag-stop village in the southwestern corner of Colorado. Her Aunt Anna had married a rancher there and she thought ranch life would strengthen and toughen me.

CHAPTER THREE

ON THE WAY TO Colona I rode a narrow-gauge Denver and Rio Grande train which snaked its way through the Royal Gorge perilously close to the tumbling, rumbling Gunnison River. Towering granite cliffs leaned ominously overhead. I was awed by the immensity and grandeur of the earth and mesmerized by the static music of the steel wheels. Sitting on the observation platform watching the twin ribbons of rails recede, it seemed that I was being carried to another world.

I was the only passenger to de-train at Colona. It was in the Uncompahgre Valley and hemmed in by an array of fourteen-thousand-foot mountains. Aunt Anna, her husband Richard Collin and his sixteen-year-old son, Theodore, greeted me. Aunt Anna was a buxom, big-framed woman with an abundance of brown-and-white hair piled under a cloth bonnet. She wore a calico dress and high-button shoes. It was obvious that she had not married Richard Collin for his looks. He had but one eye, and eloquently written in his deeply-lined face was a story of hardship and toil. Nor had she married him for his personality.

He was acerbic, indrawn and deficient in humor and grace. On the plus side he had land and cattle and was strong, hardworking and temperate. She had gotten what she wanted—security. Both had been married before. He had come to Colorado in the 1880's in search of gold and, before taking up ranching, had freighted supplies by mule train from Pueblo to the almost inaccessible mines around Ouray. It was during this period that he had lost the eye. He had a glass replacement which he wore when attending church; at other times he went about with the eyelid limp in its cavity. Theodore was a slender, pale-eyed youth with sloping shoulders and big hands and feet. His long, dusty hair partially covered his ears.

We rode in a wagon the mile and a half to the house. On the ground floor were a parlor, kitchen and dining room. Upstairs were four bedrooms. The toilet was a backhouse. One bathed in a galvanized tub in the kitchen.

After I had been shown my bed. Theodore led me to the corral and a sorrel gelding with a white face and stockings. "This is your horse," Theodore said. "His name is Rex."

Had then and there the Lord carried me away I would have died at the height of elation. My wildest fantasy was being fulfilled. Theodore bridled and saddled Rex, helped me mount, adjusted the stirrups, and, after he had saddled and mounted another horse, we set out at a brisk trot, I squeezing the saddlehorn, my thin buttocks bouncing.

"Let go the saddlehorn," Theodore instructed me. "You're choking it to death."

With that awkward, tenderfooted beginning it would seem unlikely that within a week I would be riding Rex as if I had been born on his back, but such was the case. Eventually Aunt Anna sent Mother a snapshot of me hanging from the horse, head down, a knee crooked around the saddlehorn. On the back in her handwriting was the caption: *Little Jackie, always the show-off.*

Aunt Anna not only kept house and its contents clean and in order, she did the cooking, the dishwashing and the laundry; milked the cows, separated the cream, churned the butter; tended the vegetable garden, picked and canned fruits and vegetables; mended clothing, fed, beheaded and plucked chickens; gathered eggs and did a score of other chores such as emptying the slopjars. And from the day I arrived I was assigned to help her. When I wasn't occupied around the house I assisted Theodore and Uncle Richard with the cattle, cleaned stables, curried horses and kept the mangers full of hay. In our free time Theodore and I trapped muskrats along the creek which ran through the ranch. We would skin them, dry the pelts and mail them to an address in Saint Louis. Incredibly, back would come money. Getting paid for doing something that was fun seemed too good to be true. Meanwhile I ate prodigiously and drank half a gallon of milk every day.

"Where the hell does he put it all?" Uncle Richard asked Aunt Anna. "There'll be nothing left to feed the other pigs." This was uttered without humor. Within a few weeks of consuming Aunt Anna's cooking my nose stopped running and I began gaining weight and height. By the end of summer I had developed into a sturdy, though still skinny cowboy.

With the coming of fall, Theodore and I started going to the Colona school, the best part of which was riding to and from it on horses. The school had eight grades taught by a young woman, Agnes Nesbitt, and a man, Charles Chambers, who was also the superintendent.

What criteria were used to place me in the eighth grade I never knew. Apparently Mr. Chambers thought I was too advanced to go into the sixth grade and there were no other children in the seventh. In any case I found myself in the senior class with Theodore, Hiram McNeill, a husky lad, and three girls, all of whom were two to four years older than I.

Soon after school started I undertook to write the town news. I would gather the gossip and print the items in block letters on lined paper. In that ranch community little was unknown, but printed gossip has a shock value that is lacking in the spoken word. For example, it was generally known that Miss Nesbitt was sweet on Mr. Chambers, but it was titillating to see it in print. I named the paper *The Colona Bugle*, laboriously lettered the copies and sold them for five cents each.

With Mr. Chambers' guidance we started a scout troop. He became the Scout Master and designated me his assistant. The troop was made up of some eleven or twelve boys, three from as far away as Uncompahgre. We spent a great deal of time tying knots, saluting with three fingers and memorizing the Scout oath. We also did a lot of marching.

The United States had recently entered the first World War and marching seemed patriotic. To raise money for uniforms we produced a Scout play which we presented in the school's upstairs assembly hall. I played the lead and frequently forgot my lines, but we made money enough to purchase uniforms.

Wanting to become an Eagle Scout as expeditiously as possible, I enlisted Hiram McNeil in a navigational project which I thought would push us a long way toward that goal. I proposed to him that we build a raft and float it down the Uncompahgre River to Montrose, where it joined the Gunnison, then go on to Delta, a town some forty miles away. Hiram agreed to accompany me and we planned to shove off the following Saturday morning. We worked all week after school making a raft of freshly-cut sapling birches lashed together with lariats.

Shortly after dawn of the appointed day we met at the river with our blanket packs and gunny sacks. Hiram had thought to bring along a compass, although inasmuch as we would be following the course of the river going down and the road coming back it was unlikely we would have any use for it. Nevertheless for adventurers it seemed an appropriate instrument. I had borrowed Theodore's twenty-two rifle, and of course Hiram and I had our Scout axes and Bowie knives. I had also brought a tablet and a pencil with which to keep a log of the journey. We were both wearing our Scout uniforms and, it being early spring, I had taken the precaution of putting on two suits of winter underwear. The river was high and the current strong, and there were still patches of snow on the banks.

Launching the raft proved more difficult than we had anticipated. She was about twelve feet long and seven feet wide and much too heavy for us to lift, so we used our steering poles to work her waterward. Once we got half of her in the water we took the precaution of tying her to a tree so that she would not float away before we were ready to board her. I noted that the part of her that was in the water floated more than half submerged but dismissed it as being inconsequential. It never occurred to us that freshly cut logs are not buoyant. To us, wood was wood and a raft was a raft. We tossed on our gear. I untied the line, and simultaneously the two of us gave the craft a shove and stepped aboard. To our dismay she slowly, almost reluctantly sank. The water came above our ankles, and there she stabilized. Meanwhile the current had caught her and now as she swung around I lost my balance. When I clutched Hiram for support we both sat down in the icy water. In frantically trying to save our gear we lost our steering poles and found ourselves being borne swiftly downstream without control. We watched fearfully as a boulder ahead of us loomed larger. The raft struck it sidewise and tilted, dumping us into the river. I remember seeing my stiff-brimmed Scout hat float off ahead of me. Fortunately at that point the strong current swept bankward, carrying Hiram and me with it. Eventually we were able to hang onto overhanging limbs and climb out of the water. On the bank we did our best to get a fire started by rubbing two sticks together, as we had been taught, but the wood was damp and our hands so cold that the effort was ineffectual. Because our clothing was soaked and began to freeze in the cold wind we disrobed to our underwear and hung garments over rocks and bushes, then proceeded to run up and down the river bank to get warm. We were so engaged when Theodore, who had watched us shove off, came to our rescue and started a fire.

Because of that, my first shipwreck, Hiram and I got teased unmercifully. But what hurt me most was the loss of the rifle Theodore had lent me. I had to buy him another from my share of our muskrat money.

While on the ranch I learned a lot about sex from cattle, hogs, dogs and watching a stallion mount a mare, but the most ridiculous sexual act I ever saw was performed by a dim-witted hired-hand named Sam. He had coitus with a swayback mare named Emily. He must have chosen her for her docility rather than her beauty because she was a palooka and a plug, perhaps twenty years old. I watched while he haltered her to a cottonwood and, standing on the tailgate of a spring-wagon, tugged her rump into position. All the while he was doing this he kept calling her endearing names, presumably to make her more amenable to the seduction. There was the matter of holding Emily's tail to one side, and this task fell to my lot. Emily did not like her fly-swatter restricted and kept swishing the appendage out of my hands. Eventually though, she sensed I was determined, and she desisted. Throughout the carnality she remained complacent. She just stood patiently in the shade of the cottonwood with eyes closed. Either she was enjoying it or was not fully aware of what Sam was doing.

When Sam had finished I asked him if a centaur might be the result of the debauch, but not knowing what I was talking about he didn't get the joke.

Because of my impetuosity and boisterousness, I was the cause of acrimony at times between Aunt Anna and Uncle Richard. Aunt Anna considered me well-mannered and perhaps even smart, but not so Uncle Richard. He thought I was a smart-aleck and when I fell out of a cherry tree and had to be taken to a doctor in Montrose to have a broken arm set, he swore to Almighty God he was going to send me home.

The straw that broke my welcome with the Collins was my sliding down the chaff-exhaust of the threshing machine and getting wedged in the blades of the cutting wheel. What so upset Uncle Richard, I think, was the timing. It happened at gloaming. After a hard day's work in the field he had just settled down for an hour of reading before retiring.

Theodore and I, having helped with the supper dishes, played a desultory game of dock-on-the-rock, then wandered over to the newly-arrived threshing machine. It was the first such contraption I had ever seen and excited my imagination. Its elephantine snout, which spewed the chaff, particularly intrigued me and I climbed up to examine it. What prompted me to do what next I did, heaven knows. The only likely explanation is that Theodore must have dared me. Anyway, there was a rope handy which I tied about my waist. Then, with Theodore braced and hanging onto the rope's other end, I crawled head first into the pipe, the diameter of which was just wide enough to admit me. The metal inside was smooth, worn slick by the wheat-straw, and it was easy to hunch myself forward a few inches at a time. I intended to go only a short way, for thereafter the pipe sloped sharply downward, but, when I screamed to Theodore and he began pulling, the rope broke and I slid downward, slowly at first, then with a whoosh into the cutting mechanism. My hands and head became wedged between blades. I could not move.

My outcries of anguish might have been heard in Montrose and Ouray. I was in pain, but more distressing than the pain was the realization that I had been stupid. Uncle Richard and the threshing crew came a-running. They spent some time trying to get a hook affixed to me so that I could be drawn out the way I had gone in. When this effort proved fruitless they began working by lantern light to disassemble the machine. It took several hours to free me. No one got to bed until well after midnight.

I soon received a letter from Mother summoning me home and enclosing a check for my railroad fare to Birmingham. I was in the country store when I read the letter, and I told the storekeeper, the post-mistress, and the big black retriever who slept beside the pot-bellied stove that I was going home; I told Mildred Hotchkiss, who entered the store as I was rushing out, and I hollered the exciting news into the blacksmith shop before leaping into the saddle. Coming toward me at a distance was a little girl and I stopped to tell her, too. Before galloping on I dug into a pocket and brought forth all the money I had, a dime, and this I pressed into her hand. I wanted everyone to share my happiness.

AMONG MY EFFECTS there is a photograph of that Colona grammar school graduating class: the three girls, Theodore, Hiram and myself. We boys are in Scout uniforms standing behind the seated girls, all of whom are wearing identical organdy dresses and wide, stiff ribbons in their hair. Everyone looks uncomfortable. I am the only one who is smiling, and my smile is self-conscious and cocky. As valedictorian of the class, I was the big man on campus.

CHAPTER FOUR

THAT FALL, apparently to please my stepfather, I was sent to Horner's Military Academy in Charlotte, North Carolina. At age thirteen, I was the youngest and smallest boy in the school. I remember being shocked that my roommate, a sophomore, smoked cigarets. I remember the merciless hazing and my first attempt at shaving. I remember the tall, stern headmaster, Colonel Horner, reprimanding me for gazing at the legs of a dining-room waitress. That year I won first prize in the manual of arms contest, mainly, I think, because the rifle was large and I was small.

The next year I went to Castle Heights Military Academy in Lebanon, Tennessee. Meanwhile I had grown about three inches and had acquired a prominent Adam's apple. Upon my arrival I was temporarily housed with a teacher, Major Ball. He was short and stout with small hands, wore thick-lensed pince-nez and was neat to the point of prissiness. He had a heavily-bearded face which he shaved twice a day and his fat lips were unusually red. His cordovan puttees, shoes and Sam Browne belt were always highly polished, his whip-cord uniform spic and span. Neither his voice nor his manner was effeminate, but he had an unmanly way of walking on the balls of his feet. There were two bunks in his quarters, arranged one above the other, and I assumed I was to sleep in the upper one; but come bedtime he allowed as how it was a cold night and suggested I share his bed. The proposal was repugnant but, respectful of authority, I complied. During the night I was awakened by an embrace and shocked to find the man's penis between my thighs. I tried to move away, but he clung to me until he had ejaculated; whereupon he got up, mumbling an apology, inferring he had been dreaming, and climbed into the upper bunk.

The next day I moved in with a rotund mooncalf named Cathcart from Yazoo City, Mississippi. His parents, for some God-forbidden reason, had christened him Cuthbert, but with the indelicacy of youth he became known as Fatso. He was a freshman; I, a sophomore. He was a year and a half older, was shorter and weighed twice as much as I. His parents had sent him to the school with the hope that by some miracle he would be transformed into an estimable man.

We got along well as roommates. For some reason, perhaps because I talked a lot, he thought I was smart. His greatest weakness I recognized because it was one of mine—a yearning to be liked. It grieves me to report that I shamelessly took advantage of this propensity.

Our most onerous chore in preparing our room for daily inspection was emptying the chamber pots. They had to be carried to the main lavatory, emptied, rinsed and wiped. I made a deal with him to help write his assignments if he would take on that task. Throughout the year he religiously did this.

Fatso's great talent was: he was a farter. He was trying to become the school bugler and when he practiced I noticed that, almost with every toot, a comparable sound would come from his other end. I prevailed upon him to put on a Toot and Poot show. He would blow the toots and I would light the poots.

For the performance I rounded up four cadets and persuaded them to pay twenty-five cents each to see what I glorified as the greatest and most amazing act of all time. From the school kitchen I procured matches and got Fatso to bare his bottom and lay face down across his bunk with the horn. "Okay," I said, "go ahead," and he started tooting and pooting.

My first tries at igniting a fart failed, but by moving the match close and closer, I finally produced a slender spurt of blue flame. Thereafter we did it several times, every toot louder and every poot more illuminating. Everyone was delighted, Fatso, most of all. It was my first experience in show business and whetted my appetite for it.

Words about our fantastic spectacle went the rounds and reached the powers-that-be. Fatso and I were summoned by Colonel Rice, the headmaster. When we entered his office he was busy at his desk. We stood at attention. Finally he looked up. "They tell me you've been playing with matches in your room."

Fatso looked at me. I said, "Not exactly, sir."

"What do you mean, not exactly?"

"It was an experiment, sir."

"Don't you realize you might have burned the building down?"

Right then Fatso farted. I said, "We were trying to cure Cuthbert's indigestion."

The Colonel uttered a "Humpf," and addressed Fatso: "What seems to be wrong with you?"

"I sometimes let out a lot of wind," Fatso said. "My ma thinks it's beans."

The Colonel: "Go see the doc'. Quit eating beans. Cut down on your intake. You're too fat. If I hear of you playing with matches again you'll both be sent home."

As Fatso and I saluted and turned to go, he let out a lulu. It was a fine finale.

FATSO AND I roomed together throughout my three years at the Academy. I was his mentor, sage, and advisor. For the first year he followed me like a tail-wagger and with my meager knowledge I counseled him. His primary problem was: he ate too much. I weaned him from the habit of pouring syrup, which we called zip, on almost everything he ate. I constantly nagged him about eating candy, urged him to cut fat from meat and smear less butter on bread. My tutelage paid off. By the time he went home for the summer he had lost fifteen pounds and gained several inches in height. His mother wrote a letter to Colonel Rice thanking him for the great change in her son.

The next year he lost his nickname and we started calling him Bert. He became the school bugler. During his junior year he played back-up center on the football team and I would learn that during his senior year he became first-string. Not only did he advance physically but in esteem. Under his photograph in his graduating class yearbook were the words, "Best liked."

BETWEEN MY JUNIOR and senior years at Castle Heights I spent the summer in a boarding house in Atlanta. One of the boarders was a plump woman about thirty years old, who, while not comely, had a pleasant personality and a fine bosom. By this time I had developed a great interest in bosoms. One evening Hortense and I got to clowning around in the living room, dancing to the Victrola, doing the two-step and the bunny-hug. In the course of our antics, I had an erection. Hortense held me close, moving her hips, the while wearing the most innocent expression. I was mesmerized by the feel and odor of her and got the impression I would be welcome in her bed.

The doors to our rooms faced each other across the upstairs hall. She went up first and I followed. I realized I should wait until everyone had retired before venturing across the hall but was so excited I had difficulty restraining myself. Having hastily shed clothing I stood with an ear to my door to ascertain whether or not the hall was clear. I debated putting on pajamas or going in a bathrobe and decided to don both. From directly under my room came sounds of the landlady moving about.

At last I opened the door and peered down the faintly lit hall. The coast was clear. Heart beating wildly, I tiptoed to Hortense's door and very gently turned the knob. It was unlocked. "It's me," I whispered, my voice changing.

"Shhhh! . . . "

I groped through the semi-darkness to her bed, uncertain how to proceed. She threw back the covers, whispering, "Take off your clothes, for God's sake!" I obeyed feverishly and got into bed. She enclasped me against her soft, warm, cushiony body and I was transported into suspension. At once she took command, kissing and fondling me. I glommed onto the nipple of a big breast. "Take it easy," she whispered, but my excitement was such that, when she finally admitted me, I had an orgasm at once.

There came the sound of slippered footsteps in the hall. Hortense clutched me in a frantic, frozen embrace. We heard a muffled knock on a door. "John?" The landlady was at my door. "Are you there?"

Neither Hortense nor I moved. Presently Hortense whispered, "Get in the closet!" and released me. I got out of bed and tiptoed to the closet door. The knob made a squeaking sound, but that was nothing to the clatter that followed. In the closet Hortense had stored a set of dishes and in my frenzied clumsiness I dislodged a box of them. Plates, cups and saucers cascaded onto the floor. I stood rigid, shriveled with guilt.

The landlady came to Hortense's door. "Hortense, are you all right?"

"Yes, Missus Taylor."

"What was that racket?"

"I didn't hear anything."

"Sounded like dishes."

"I don't know what it could have been."

"I thought John had gone to bed but he's not in his room."

"He must have gone out."

After a long pause: "Well, goodnight." The landlady went down the stairs. Hortense let me know that there would be no resumption of our connubial act, and I slunk back to my room.

Grandmother's teaching took hold. A lady's reputation was at stake. The landlady doubtless suspected that I had been with Hortense and I had to establish an excuse for not answering when she knocked on my door. The thing to do, I decided, was get dressed and leave the house without being observed. If I went by way of the stairs I might be seen, but the limb of a tree outside was within a few feet of my window. Whether it would support me or not was questionable, but I felt it was a risk I had to take. Fortunately it did not break and I let myself down in slow motion, trying not to make any noise and grateful for the covering wail of a tomcat. Moving gingerly around the house to the sidewalk, I fled down West Peachtree Street to North Avenue and stood on the corner for a while to catch my breath and let my emotions subside. To register my entrance when I got back to the boarding house, I closed the front door and walked down the hall heavy-footedly. After pretending to make a telephone call I went upstairs to bed and lay there hoping I had done the gentlemanly thing.

Despite this attempt to protect Hortense, that was the end of the romance. Apparently for her, one sexual experience with an excitable boy had been enough.

CHAPTER FIVE

T O OBTAIN SOCIAL STATUS in the South, it was necessary that one go to college and Mother strained her thin purse to send me. I wanted to go to Harvard, because I had been told that my paternal forefathers had helped found it, or to Princeton because F. Scott Fitzgerald had attended. But the travel expenses were more than Mother could afford, so I matriculated at Alabama Polytechnical Institute in Auburn. It is now known as Auburn University. The year I was there—1922-23—the student body numbered about nine hundred, all boys.

Socially it was important to join a fraternity and I pledged to Kappa Sigma. Eager to make a good impression, I went out for the freshman football team. At Castle Heights I had played second-string quarterback, but at Auburn, because of my lack of heft, I spent most of the time warming the bench. I tried to become a member of the glee club but was turned down because my voice was changing. I was a good swimmer but there was no swimming team because there was no pool.

The only literary recognition I got that year—the senior class used one of my poems in its yearbook.

Twice a year the school held fandangos when girls from all over came to spend the weekends. During one of these I met an attractive and wayward girl named Mildred Murray who introduced me to necking and corn whiskey. She lived in Montgomery, about sixty miles away, and I began going to see her Saturdays. The train fare was a dollar and a half, more than I could afford, so I hoboed, riding between the coal and baggage cars. One of the things that attracted me to Mildred was: she was a friend of Zelda Sayre, who had married Scott Fitzgerald. Through her I met members of the Sayre family and spent delightful times at their house (Zelda and Scott were never there) hoping some of the Fitzgeralds' fame would rub off on me.

Midway through the second semester my romance with Mildred was severed by my fraternity mentor, a senior and fullback on the football team. He gave me a twenty-swat, bare-assed whaling with a blister-raising paddle and warned me: "Spending your weekends in Montgomery, you're neglecting your studies. Keep it up and you'll flunk out."

I quit going.

At the end of my freshman year I received a letter from Mother saying she had done all she could to get me started up life's ladder, that now it was up to me to make my way. She included a check for one hundred dollars.

"I'm sorry to push you out of the nest so soon," she wrote, "but I have no place for you here. I have divorced Robert Lewis and am on my own. I think it best that you start seeing the world. You might go to Kansas City, where Elinor is living, or to Hartford, where the Wilmerdings are now. You'll need to get a job. Good luck. Write to me often and let me know how you are getting along. Love. . . . "

I could not have been more stunned. My umbilical cord had been cut. Suddenly I was alone. I badly needed to be with someone sympathetic. My sister Elinor had recently married William Webb, a cosmetic salesman. She was the nearest relative. I went to her.

She and Bill were ensconced in a one-room let-down-bed apartment. I found a room in a nearby boarding house and, through a business acquaintance, Bill got me a job at the Irving-Pitt Company, a producer of loose-leaf notebooks. My task was to stack and unpack lumber, steel, paper, leather, cardboard and boxes of glue in the factory's basement.

"If you want to be a writer," Bill said, "there's plenty of paper there for you to practice on."

That summer the Missouri Valley championship swimming races were held at the Kansas City Country Club and I applied to compete. After a tryout I was entered in the fifty- and hundred-meter races and won first place in both, becoming that year's Missouri Valley champion. Later Johnny Weismuller came to town on a barnstorming tour and I competed against him. All I remember of those races is his big feet churning in my face.

In Birmingham I had become addicted to vaudeville. Every Saturday afternoon I would go to the Alcazar Theater and, for fifteen cents, get a balcony seat. The other ten cents of my weekly allowance would go for peanut brittle. After performances I would go home, tell the jokes I had heard and try to emulate the acrobats, jugglers, magicians and ventriloquists. I learned to walk a slack rope, to juggle five balls, to throw a hand axe into a stump and to walk on stilts. In Kansas City, not having to work Saturday afternoons, I resumed going to vaudeville shows. Watching Will Rogers perform, it occurred to me that I might do a similar act, telling jokes while juggling instead of twirling a rope as he did. I began compiling all of the one-liners I heard or could remember, practiced juggling and even composed a song, "Goodnight, Sweetheart."

Late in November, having saved train-fare, I set out for New York, going the cheapest way, overnight by coach. When I arrived in the early morning at Pennsylvania Station all I had left was fifteen cents. I used a nickel to telephone the New York University Kappa Sigma house. Talking fast, like a vacuum-cleaner salesman, I said, "I'm a brother from the Beta Eta chapter at Alabama Poly. Just got in town. I'm broke and wondering if you could put me up for a couple of days?"

The answer was, "Sure. Come on."

It had been snowing. I took a subway to 163rd Street in the Bronx and made the long walk through snow and slush to the house and was graciously received. The bed to which I was assigned, merely a frame and a spring, was in the attic. My hosts found a rug for a mattress and gave me a blanket. To keep warm in bed I had to wear my overcoat.

I told them I had come to New York to try and get into vaudeville and, to my surprise, because I doubted it myself, they accepted that aspiration as reasonable. With a senior named Otto accompanying me on a piano, I performed my act for them. Otto, whose jowly face in repose resembled a basset hound's, turned out to be a tutelary saint. He coached me, added jokes, and even loaned me carfare and lunch money. At his suggestion, I made the rounds of "Tin Pan Alley" song publishers and chose two new songs—"Yes, We Have No Bananas" and "Barney Google," both of which subsequently became hits, though not, God knows, on my account.

After a week rehearsing, I repaired to the Times Square office of B.F. Keith, the nation's largest bookers of vaudeville acts. A number of applicants were in the waiting room, some with animals. I sat down next to a blousy woman in a gypsy costume. Her smile lessened my tension. "What's your act?" she asked.

"I juggle and tell jokes."

"What kinda jokes?"

"Oh, all kinds, mostly Negro."

"Tell me one."

Pleased with the chance to practice, I chose one of my best. "A Negro man was beating his mule. A preacher came along and said, 'Don't beat that beast. Treat him kindly. Talk to him. That way he'll do what you want him to do.' The Negro took off his hat, went up to the mule, looked him in the eye and said, 'Hello there, mule. I'ze from New Orleans. Where's you from?' "

The gypsy laughed and said, "That's not funny. Takes too long to tell. Jokes gotta be quick."

"What kind of an act do you do?" I asked.

"I'm lookin' for a partner. How would you like to come work for me?"

I thought of the con-woman who sold needles. I said, "What would I do?"

"I'll teach you."

"I'm sorry," I said, as the squawk-box squeaked her name: "Madame Luiggi!"

She rose, patted me on a thigh and said, "Grow a mustache. It'll make you look older."

Eventually my name was called and I went into the booker's office. He was an exceptionally thin man with black hair and thick eyebrows who, throughout the interview, wadded up bits of paper, and with a rubber band shot them at a distant wastebasket. Exuding all of the vivacity, charm and salesmanship I could muster, I told him I was a juggler who told jokes and sang songs. I tossed out a few one-liners, but he did not so much as smile at any of them. After I had sung the first verse of "Barney Google" his face squinched and he said, "That's enough." I thought I had struck out, but he scheduled an audition for me two mornings later in the Palace Theater.

When I stepped onto the famous vaudeville stage and began my routine I was atremble. My heart was beating paroxysmally and I felt numb and bloodless. Only a few of the footlights were aglow and there was no spotlight. My only audience was the pianist in the pit and three booking agents in the third row whom I could barely see. What I did see was not encouraging. Their faces were and remained expressionless.

Talking fast, I began: "Just got in from Philadelphia," and started juggling. "That's the place where people in bed are either wed or dead. . . . A lady got off the train and I asked if she had had a nice trip. She said, 'Yes, but this wasn't it. . . . ' A rich man was with her. You know what a rich man is? He's a fellow who always bargains for something cheaper and is slow to pay his bills. . . . I knew a rich man who went to church three times—the first time they threw water on him, the second time they threw rice and the third time they threw dirt. . . . "

There was no applause, nor any response when I sang, not even when I did my acrobatic jig.

When I got to the last stanza of "Saint James Infirmary," my closing number:

> . . . and on my tombstone written,
> in letters bold and black,
> "Here lies my sweet, sweet lovin' Daddy,
> May the good Lord bring him back."

There was not a sound. I bowed, hoping for some kind of applause, but none came. When I left the stage the manager, busy getting the next act ready, said, "Don't call us. We'll call you." I waited a week in the Kappa Sigma house for the call but it never came.

I wrote Mother about my vaudeville failure and for my seventeenth birthday she sent me ten dollars, enough to pay Otto what I owed him. She suggested I go see John Meehan, the estranged husband of her close friend and head of the United States Secret Service New York office which was on lower Broadway. He received me kindly. One of the Secret Service's concerns was smuggling and he had influence in the shipping industry. I told him my plight and he said, "How would you like a job on a ship?"

"I'd like it fine," I said.

"Young men should travel. It's educational." He picked up a telephone and arranged an interview for me at the United States Lines office in Hoboken. Thither I went and was hired forthwith as bellboy for the upcoming voyage to Europe of the SS *President Monroe*. The stipend: one dollar a day. The stipulation: I had to obtain a bellboy uniform. The chief steward directed me to a shop in Hoboken where boys pawned their uniforms between voyages. The fact that the jacket I rented was too large, the trousers too short and the cap too small—they were the costume of office and would suffice. The pawnbroker agreed that I could pay the rental fee—five dollars for a round-trip—when I returned; however he wanted collateral, so I left him my fraternity pin—a gold star and crescent studded with seed pearls. It was the only thing of value that I owned and I parted with it reluctantly.

WE SAILED on a blustery day in March with about one hundred passengers. The ship had one class accommodations. My hours of service began at 5 A.M., when I swabbed the main companionway. I was at the call box to serve passengers at six. An Englishman: "Please bring tea. It helps move me bowels." Others wanted breakfast in bed or complained about one thing or another—the water wasn't hot, the plumbing out of whack or they wanted seasick pills or clean towels or soap. During lunch and dinner I was in charge of desserts and cheeses. Between three and five I napped, and thereafter was on call until midnight.

The sea was rough the third morning and, while swabbing, I became nauseated and barely made it to the rail before heaving breakfast. I managed to finish swabbing and, feeling like walking death, went to the Chief Steward's cabin. My knock on the door awakened him. "What the hell do you want?" he growled.

"I'm sick."

"Oh, for Christ's sake, take a pill, suck in your gut, get back to your post."

The ship took ten days to reach Tilbury, on the Thames south of London. Departing passengers gave me tips amounting to nearly twenty dollars, beside which the purser paid me wages of ten dollars. Before returning to New York, the ship was to be docked for three days, and I took the occasion to go to London.

Everything was strange to me: the train, the money, the people and the way they dressed and spoke, the left-way traffic, the blatant advertising posters, the red omnibuses, the architecture; but meandering London's ancient streets I felt the spiritual roots of my forefathers. I rode on the upper decks of buses, got a thrilling glimpse of the Royal Palace and attended a vaudeville show matinee at the Palladium.

After a dinner of fish and chips in the Lyon's House in Piccadilly, I stood outside wondering where I would spend the night when an attractive girl, strolling with a woman I took to be her mother, smiled at me. Uncertain, I smiled back. She said something to the older woman, left her and approached me. The older woman went on.

"Hello," the girl said, as if she knew me.

Thinking she had mistaken me for someone else, I said, "Hello."

"You must be an American."

"What makes you think so?"

"Oh, I don't know. Maybe your hat. What're you doing in London?"

"Just looking."

"Where you stayin'?"

"I work on a ship. It's at Tilbury."

"How would you like a frig?"

"A what?"

"A bang. Come along." She put an arm through mine and led me to the Underground. We got off at Charing Cross Station and walked arm in arm for several blocks between precisely-alike houses, I was feeling as a lamb must feel when it is being led to slaughter. She asked me about the United States and was particularly interested in Indians. Finally she mounted the stoop of a house and rang the bell. The door was opened by a woman who stood in shadow and Becky led me directly upstairs to a small bedroom. Forthwith she began disrobing. I made no move to do so. She paused, skirt in hand, and said, "Come on, Lovey; let's get at it."

I hung my jacket on the back of the only chair and began unknotting my necktie. To unbutton my trousers, I turned my back to her. By now she was nude and came to help me remove them, saying, "You're a shy one. Haven't you been with a girl before?"

"Sure. Of course." I thought of Hortense.

"Well, I'm gonna show you a good time," she said, and pulled me to the bed.

During the night, between 'bangs,' Becky expressed a pathetic hope that one day she would go to America. "I've never been able to save up the fare," she said. "If I got there, what would I do?" I thought she might do what she presently was doing but did not say so. "The only way I'll ever get there," she went on, "is to marry an American. How about it? Would you marry me?"

Stunned by the absurdity of the proposal, but not wanting to hurt her feelings, I said, "I sail tomorrow."

"When you come back then?"

"Maybe."

In the morning a woman brought us tea and crumpets and Becky told me to give her four pounds. I took the money from my jacket and paid her. It was within a pound of all the money I had and I suspected that during the night my resources had been ascertained. When the woman had withdrawn I asked Becky how much I owed her.

"You don't owe me nothin'. That charge was for bed and break-fast."

"I'd like to give you something," I said. "I only have a couple of crowns left and I've got to get back to the ship."

She hugged me. "You've given me a good time. An' I wanna see you when you come back." She accompanied me to Tilbury, paying her own fare. Kissing me goodbye, she said, "Don't forget me."

I never will.

CHAPTER SIX

WHEN THE *President Monroe* returned to Hoboken I headed for Hartford, Connecticut, where Aunt Sarah and Uncle Billy Wilmerding were living and where I could get free board and shelter. Looking for a job there I read a help-wanted advertisement by the Scat Handsoap Company for a salesman. Attired in my only suit, a Palm Beach model which had set me back fifteen dollars, I hied to the company's sales office, there to find a half dozen men seated in the reception room waiting to be interviewed. I had read Horatio Alger, Jr., stories, which stressed the importance of ingenuity and pluck, and without speaking to the receptionist went directly to the door marked *Charles Adams, Sales Manager* and entered. The preceding job-seeker was preparing to depart and the sales manager, believing I was the next in line, greeted me politely and asked me to sit down. He explained that the company wanted a man to go through New York State calling on jobbers and hiring salesmen in principal cities. The remuneration was twenty-five dollars a week and expenses.

"Scat handsoap," Mr. Adams said, "is used by people whose hands become embedded with dirt and grease. There is nothing like it on the market, so it is easy to sell. How old are you?"

I was seventeen but said I was twenty-three and, afraid he might not believe me, went on to say that the reason I was unemployed was because I had just returned from Europe. "I know I can do a good job," I said. "The way to succeed is to find a need and fill it. If there's one thing people need it's clean hands."

I must have told Mr. Adams what he wanted to hear because he telephoned me that afternoon and said the job was mine. "There's just one thing I forgot to ask you," he said. "Can you drive a car?"

When I was thirteen Mother had taught me to drive a Dodge. Shortly thereafter, driving alone, I had been involved in an accident and had not driven an automobile since. "Sure," I said. "What kind of a car is it?"

"A Ford."

I hesitated, knowing that Fords had different gears than Dodges. After a moment, I said, "Fords're easy."

The president, sales manager and I went over the route I was to follow. Kingston was to be the first stop, then up the Hudson to Albany and along the Mohawk to Schenectady, Utica, Syracuse, Ithaca, Binghampton and Newburgh, before returning to Hartford. As soon as I arrived in a town I was to place an advertisement for a salesman in the leading newspaper. The next day was to be spent interviewing applicants, hiring one and showing him how to sell Scat. Then I was to move on to the next town. I was to be gone a month. Besides an advance of a week's salary, Mr. Adams gave me twenty-five dollars expense money and said that when that was gone he'd send more. The sales manager was eager for me to get started. "Time's a-wastin'," he said, and led the way out into the yard.

There stood the black Ford coupe. It was several years old. The rumble was loaded with cartons of handsoap. When it came time for me to get into the car I was so concerned about revealing my ignorance of it that I hardly acknowledged the president's handshake.

Mr. Adams manned the crank. Looking at the three pedals, I surmised one had to be the brake, one the clutch and the third the reverse. But which was which? Mr. Adams advanced the gas lever on the steering post and then went back to the crank, braced himself with one hand on the radiator and spun the crank with the other. The engine did not start. He spun it several more times without effect. "Needs more spark," he said, and I adjusted the spark lever. Now the engine started with a backfiring bang.

The moment of truth was at hand. I shook the sales manager's hand and pushed down on the middle pedal, hoping it was the proper one. It wasn't. The car lurched backward toward a brick wall. There were shouts of warning. I quickly took my foot off that pedal and stomped on another, whereupon the car leaped forward like a bucking horse. I was so unnerved I forgot to watch where I was going and, as the car passed into the street, it scraped one of the wooden gateposts. I made no attempt to stop but went chugging down the road, headed, I hoped, for New York.

The Ford, which I named Esmeralda, and I crossed the Hudson River at Poughkeepsie and reached Kingston about mid-afternoon. I paid for a help-wanted ad in the local newspaper and went to call on the first of two jobbers, a man with a heavily creased face and half-lidded eyes who greeted me grumpily. Using my most sterling spiel, I suggested that, on account of my company's new promotional policy, he might want to put in a few more cases of Scat. Whereupon the jobber exploded "Handsoap!—for God's sake, young feller! Don't talk to me about handsoap! I'm in Scat handsoap up to my ears! I've got cases I've had for five years! I don't want any more damned handsoap!" He lifted his eyelids and looked up at me. "What I should do is sell you some."

The second jobber I called on was equally adamant. "It moves like glue," he said.

That day I didn't sell a can. The next day I spent waiting in the hotel for replies to the want-ads. Nobody came. No one telephoned.

Albany wasn't much better, although, after demonstrating that Scat would remove printer's ink, I sold a case of it to the newspaper which ran the ad. The one reply to the ad was by telephone. The man wanted to know how much the job paid. When I said it was on a commission basis, he hung up.

In Utica a stout man in his late thirties, who obviously had spent the better part of his life on a farm, answered the ad. On him I applied all of the enthusiasm I could muster and even went so far as to buy his lunch. He agreed to give the job a try and, by what seemed a miracle, the two of us actually went out and got rid of a half dozen cases. The farmer accepted the job and for the first time I reported encouragingly to the home office.

Before I got to Syracuse, Esmeralda's battery went dead and had to be replaced, so I telegraphed the company for funds. Then on the road to Rochester a tire blew and I had to purchase a new one. In Buffalo I was arrested for speeding, going eighteen miles an hour in a fifteen-mile zone, and the unsympathetic judge fined me eighteen dollars. This sum came out of my salary.

Meanwhile my sales of handsoap were not sufficient to offset expenses. I was not surprised when, after having been on the road for almost three weeks, I received a telegram directing me to return to Hartford.

I headed Esmeralda home.

In the course of her peregrinative life she had developed several cantankerous characteristics. If pushed too hard she would boil over; paced too slow, she would shake like a hoochi-koochi. Even at the speed she preferred—thirty-three miles an hour—she was a hard rider and a genius for finding chuckholes. Somewhere west of Binghampton she hit the grand-daddy of them all and the shock not only sent pain up my spine, it broke one of the two braces which supported the engine. The engine conked out and began dragging.

It was about midday and several miles to the nearest town. There was little traffic, merely an occasional horse and wagon. With a forlorn sigh, I set out, walking eastward. After a mile I came to a classic roadside blacksmith shop under a proverbial oak. The blacksmith was a sawed-off, flimsy fellow, who, with surprising kindness, promptly dropped what he was doing, gathered some tools, hitched a horse to a buggy, and we rode to Esmeralda.

With a fence post we managed to lift the engine back into place and somehow the smithy clamped it. He then got into the driver's seat and told me to crank her up. "Let's see if she'll run." The first time I spun the crank Esmeralda gave such a vicious kick it almost tore my arm off, and the next couple of times she backfired in protest; but then, suddenly, she had a change of heart and began to percolate. It was mid-afternoon by the time my benefactor had made a new brace and welded it onto the frame. I paid him what he asked, three dollars, almost all I had, and resumed my journey.

Darkness overtook us before we reached the bridge at Peekskill and when we drove over the Hudson River the headlamps were flickering. Shortly thereafter they went out entirely and I had to drive by the light of a three-quarter moon. Then the radiator began boiling and I had to add water. Esmeralda would go but a few miles before she would boil again. Householders I asked for water in the early evening were accommodating, but after nine o'clock they got increasingly hostile. I would drive up to a house and a voice would call accusingly from a window: "Who's there?" After explaining my predicament, I'd be told to help myself. "Well's out back." And every time I got out of the car dogs would sniff me so menacingly my hair follicles froze.

Esmeralda steamed into the Wilmerding's driveway about one o'clock in the morning. Not wanting to awaken anyone at that hour, I curled up on the seat and went to sleep.

Aunt Sarah gave me breakfast, after which I, ashamed of my failure and fearful of the upcoming scene, trepidatiously drove to the Scat plant. The sales manager greeted me coldly. I apologized for my poor performance and said that there did not seem to be enough demand for handsoap to support a salesman.

"It was an experiment," Mr. Adams snapped. "I don't think you were the one to do it. I think you lied about your age. You're not twenty-three."

Shamefacedly I said, "I'm sorry. I did my best."

"We don't like liars around here. You're through."

I collected what monies were due me and the next day left for Atlanta to see Mother, renew my confidence and get a fresh start.

CHAPTER SEVEN

I was standing in front of Nunnally's on Peachtree Street in Atlanta with a couple of other drugstore cowboys, Ed Mimms and George Morris. All of us were footloose and fancy free, meaning out of work, whiling away time, shooting the breeze and watching Georgia peaches pass. After I had recounted my voyage to Europe, George said, "The place I want to go is Hollywood."

"Why don't we all go?" Ed said, glancing at his Model T parked at the curb. "I've got the wheels."

Like a cog, the idea meshed. One minute we were purposeless idlers, the next we had resolution and direction. The fact that it was winter and Ed's touring car had no side-curtains to deflect the wind and shed rain were matters of vast indifference. Within a week, having enlisted another musketeer, Hunt Armstrong, we drove out of Marietta before dawn. The day was February 4, 1923. Within three weeks I would be eighteen.

Driving an automobile across country that year was fraught with unmarked railroad crossings, cattle guards, chuckholes and culvertless roads. There was a paucity of directional signs, besides which maps were all but non-existent and gasoline stations, lodgings and restaurants were few and far between.

We spent the first night in the Kappa Sigma house at the University of Alabama in Tuscaloosa, having traversed some two hundred hard miles. It was raining the next morning when we set out and by the time we got to Mississippi the gumbo road was of such an ornery consistency that within five miles we twice had to be extricated by mules. Farmers, with little else to do in the wintertime, had discovered that, with the coming of the automobile, a mud hole and a pair of mules were a profitable combination. The fee for extricating a hapless motorist usually was five dollars. After two pullouts by these pseudo-Samaritans we took to muscling the Ford onto terra firma by ourselves.

Somewhere between Meridian and Jackson a black man emerged on a white mule from a clump of trees and, as we approached, took off his battered felt hat and held up an empty fruit jar. Ed Mimms, who was driving, said, "Looks like a bootlegger," and braked the car.

"Where 'bouts you gentlemens gwine?" the black man asked. When Ed said, "California," he pretended to be dumbfounded. "California!—well dad-blass, kiss my ass!—that's a fur piece. You is gwine need some good corn licker to take wid you." He held up the jar. "I kin git you sho-nuff drinkin' whiskey."

"How much is it?"

"Dollar a quart. Three a gallon."

We agreed to buy a gallon. The black man said he would not be able to get it without the money, so we gave him three dollars. He climbed on the mule and took off through the trees.

After waiting for the better pat of an hour we began to suspect we had been conned; and at the end of an hour, we set off in pursuit, heading into the trees and bumping across a meadow.

We had gone about half a mile when we saw coming towards us the bootlegger on his sway-back steed, a half-gallon fruit jar hanging from a rope on the mule's either shoulder. Ed stopped the car. The Negro rode up, slid off the hybrid and stood unsteadily, obviously intoxicated. "I know y'awl thinks I has been a while," he said apologetically, removing the jugs from the mule's neck, "but I is had to wait for a new batch."

Using the jar's caps as cups, we sampled the hootch while the black man watched us wistfully. George poured him a drink and he downed it thirstily. We even gave the mule a slurp. By the time we pulled away, the bootlegger was sitting on the ground glassy-eyed, his back against a tree, singing, "You'ze off ter Califorry wid a banjo on yo' knee," and waving abstractedly. George swore he heard the mule hiccup.

At Vicksburg we drove onto a ferryboat to cross the Mississippi River and were told by the captain that, once we were in Louisiana, not to drive directly west to Shreveport but to detour northward through Arkansas and thus circumvent the Bayou Macon and its tributaries. But when we learned that the detour would take us more than a hundred miles out of our way and that the swampy area covered only thirty miles we decided to risk taking the shorter route.

For a while it looked as if we had made a good decision. From the Mississippi the road ran along the ridge of a levee and we made good time, but gradually the character of the road changed. There were places where it had been washed out and we had to fill in the ditches before we could proceed. Toward nightfall the road ran into a forested bog so densely hung with moss that little light of the dying day filtered through. On either side of the soggy road, roots of the smothering trees were great, many-fingered fists clutching the mud under stagnant water. Screeches of birds and animals pierced the congealing darkness. When we had to get out to push the car we were up to our ankles in mud. Sometimes, using saplings under the rear axle, we were able to thrust it forward but a few feet at a time. Adding to our frustration and discomfort it began to rain. We were soaking wet when we got back into the car where we expected to spend the night. Almost unbelievably as if by conjure, there presently came through the deluge a mud-spattered, salt-and-pepper horse bearing a red-haired, freckle-faced youth riding bareback and carrying a shotgun. From his belt hung a number of birds.

"Evenin'," he said, reining his horse, water dripping from his nose.

"Good evening," we exclaimed in unison. "Where in God's earth did you come from?"

The boy looked behind him. "Yonder."

"Where you headed?"

"Home." He pointed through the trees.

"Is there any place hereabouts we can find shelter?"

"Next town's twelve mile," the boy said. "You wanna come home with me you'll be welcome. It'll git you out'n the rain."

We clambered out of the car and sloshed after the horse. A flickering lamp was our first sight of the house, a jerry-built shack on a swell of ground beneath a canopy of gigantic cypresses. It was less than a mile from where the Ford was mired. Later we were told that the nearest neighbor lived "ten mile away as the crow flies."

Long-lost relatives could not have received a more generous welcome than that accorded us. A host of children crowded around while their father shook hands and their mother said, "You're just in time for supper. I'll put a few more birds on to cook." She hung our soaked jackets to dry, poked up the stove and poured us cups of tea. A big-busted woman whose belly bulged with yet another child, she filled basins so that we could wash our mud-caked hands. The house had three rooms: a kitchen-eating-and-sitting room, a sleeping chamber for the parents and a larger one with wall-to-wall beds for the children. Over our polite protestations, the hosts assigned their sleeping room to us.

The patriarch was tall and exceedingly thin. He had a narrow, pinched face and a long hooked nose. Such hair as he had was tinged with red and, back-lighted, gave the effect of a halo. During dinner of roasted birds, turnip greens and cornbread, he released his pent-up rhetoric. He said he and his wife had lived in the swamp since the year they were married.

"We came up here to get away from the hustle and hullabaloo of New Orleans." Flinging his hands for emphasis, he went on: "That damn town is goin' to hell in a hand-basket. There's too many people. Used to be a nice place. Today everything is steal all you can. I wouldn't give you a plugged nickel for any part of it. With its taxes, its insurance, its doctors and opera singers, its preachers an' prostitutes, with its nigger music an' store-bought bread." He paused to pick up in his fingers another piece of bird, took a big bite and went on talking as he chewed: "No sir-ree-Bobskeedee, I wouldn't give you a nickel for all of it. All a man needs in this world is somethin' to eat, a little whiskey and solitude. You wouldn't think, us livin' back here the way we do I'm descended from the French nobility. My great-great-great grand-father was Charles de Lessups. He came to New Orleans during the

Revolutionary War with Lafayette. At one time he owned half the state of Louisiana. This swamp's all that's left. I got ten thousand acres, almost all under water. I don't need no more." He cackled. "All I need's a boat. If, like me, you don't have no insurance and don't pay taxes, you got no use for money."

After a pause to reach for another piece of cornbread, he went on: "These birds you're eatin' are more numerous around here than mosquitoes. Me and Jody," he indicated his eldest son, the red head, "went huntin' last week and with one shot I killed so many we couldn't count 'em all. Between us we picked up a hundred and seventeen." He wiped the gravy from his chin with the back of a hand. "There're so many deer hereabouts the children kill 'em with sling-shots. The biggest alligator in the world lives in the swamp; he's twenty-three feet long and can swallow a hog whole. We call him Elijah, after my wife's big-mouthed uncle. The swamp's full of crawdads and crayfish, some as big as catfish, and there're bullfrogs that can jump thirty feet . . . "

He went on regaling us in this way throughout the meal. He bedamned politicians, the League of Nations and Woodrow Wilson, and was for sending all of the Negroes in America back to Africa. I never was sure whether he was serious or joking.

We four guests slept crosswise on the big bed, though not very well. For breakfast our hostess cooked a cake smothered in pink icing. In departing we offered four dollars—one for each of us—in payment for board and lodging, but our host refused to accept the money. "You boys need it more'n I do," he said. "The world'd be better off without the stuff. Never knew a rich man who was worth a damn. Most of 'em 're miserly son's-o'-bitches." When we offered him a quart of corn whiskey though he quickly accepted it. He and his children went out and got the Ford unmired and us on our way.

From Shreveport, Louisiana to El Paso, Texas, by way of Dallas-Fort Worth, is approximately eight hundred and fifty miles, and it took Ed Mimm's Ford, running day and night, something less than forty-eight hours to traverse it.

Dawn was breaking when we rolled up to one of El Paso's second-class hotels. We bathed an went to bed; but soon, full of youthful enthusiasm and inquisitiveness, we were up and on our way across the Rio Grande to Juarez. There we went from one gambling casino to another. In a short time I lost most of my wherewithal. Ed Mimms and Hunt Armstrong also were unlucky. Only George Morris won. With dice, he made twenty-one passes without once doubling his bet; when he crapped out he quit twenty dollars ahead. Somewhere in New Mexico we had to spend most of what we had left of our resources for a new drive-shaft. We crossed the Mojave Desert from Yuma to San Diego on a plank road in a sand storm and finally reached Los Angeles. The journey had taken us twelve days. Among us we had less than five dollars.

CHAPTER EIGHT

ALTHOUGH WE FOUR adventurers were without funds, we were not without resources. We had learned that one can cover a multitude of deficiencies with graciousness and good manners. Using salesmanship born of desperation, we persuaded a landlord to let us occupy a furnished apartment, a grocer to sell us a substantial food supply and the proprietor of a garment cleaning establishment to clean and launder our clothing, then set out to find work in the movie studios. The extras were paid seven dollars and a half a day and there was a chance of instant fame, no experience necessary.

At that time there was no Central Casting Bureau. Those who wanted to work in the movies applied at the casting offices of the studios. Paramount was on Vine Street, First National and William Fox were on Sunset Boulevard, Film Booking Office was on Santa Monica Boulevard, and Metro-Goldwyn-Mayer and Universal were respectively in Culver City and San Fernando Valley. Mary Pickford, Douglas Fairbanks, Charles Chaplin and Samuel Goldwyn had recently established their own studio, United Artists, on Santa Monica Boulevard, not far from where Harold Lloyd had his.

Day after day, exuding charm to make friends, we went the rounds of these fantasy factories. Eventually we got a nibble at Harold Lloyd's. After applying several times we were told that twenty male extras were to be hired the next morning. We were on hand bright and early. So were a couple of hundred other hopefuls. By the time we got to the casting window, hiring for the day had been concluded.

After two unsuccessful weeks making the rounds, Ed, George and Hunt, all of whom had received money from their parents, began talking of going back home. George was homesick, Ed had lost interest in acting, and Hunt wanted to see his girl. I made it clear that I would not go with them. We had come a long way and for me going back so soon would be another admission of failure.

The only friend any of us had when we arrived in Los Angeles was Richard Marchman, whom Ed and George had known in Marietta. He was employed as a private investigator for the Hooper-Holmes Bureau, a psuedo-detective agency. When a person applied for a sizable loan or a substantial life insurance policy, a Hooper-Holmes investigator would be sent to authenticate him. How was he physically? How did he and his wife get along? Was he a gambler? What did his neighbors think of him? The written report would go to the client for a fee. An investigator was expected to make from twelve to fifteen reports a day.

I importuned Richard to introduce me to the manager of his office in the hope he might employ me. The idea of becoming a detective appealed to me. It was romantic and might be adventurous, besides which the reports would be a good way to practice writing.

Richard was the star investigator in the Hooper-Holmes branch and the manager must have assumed I had his sterling character because he offered me a job. There was one stipulation: that I get an automobile. The job would pay twenty dollars a week plus five dollars car allowance. Thinking I could use Ed's Ford, I hurried home with the good news.

Running up the stairs, I burst into the apartment building shouting, "Hey, fellows . . . !"

There wasn't a sound. The place was empty. No garments were draped over the chairs. Hunt's alarm clock was missing. I found a note on the kitchen table:

So long, Jack. We're shoving off for home. Sorry you're not coming with us. We paid the landlord and the grocer. Good luck. We'll be looking for you to make good in the movies . . .

I was crushed. I not only wouldn't be able to use Ed's car, I had lost my buddies. What to do? In the course of looking for a job I had learned that the Ford dealer in Culver City was a fraternity brother. I had even thought of asking him for a job selling cars. He was my only hope. I rode a trolley to the end of the Washington Boulevard line and walked the several miles to Culver City. Fortunately the dealer was in his place of business. I gave him the secret handshake and poured out my tale of woe. He listened sympathetically and within an hour I was the possessor of a much-used Ford coupe containing ten gallons of gasoline. I was to pay twenty dollars a month for ten months. There were no interest or license charges and as yet sales tax had not raised its ugly head.

As an investigator for the Hooper-Holmes Bureau I was assigned to the Glendale-Eagle Rock area. It is a big territory and to glean information about twelve to fifteen subjects a day kept me hustling. I was instructed not to go directly to the subject but to question neighbors. When the neighbors could not answer my questions, I would inquire at the subject's business and church. Most of the information I got was supposition and did not give true pictures of the persons. More often than not I had to write the reports at night and, having no typewriter, used a pen.

I worked hard and would have continued in the job had it not been for my atrocious spelling. It seemed to be pathological. Even today I spell phonetically, the way words sound when uttered with a southern accent. Because of my many misspellings, the manager of the bureau had to edit and oftentimes rewrite my reports before he could submit them to clients. It took lots of his time and much of his patience. Finally one day he called me into his office.

"When I hired you," he began, "you told me you wanted to become a writer. I think you're on the wrong track. You can't spell for sour apples. I'm gonna have to let you go. If I were you I'd set my ambition on something besides writing."

By now I was ensconced in a boarding house on Wilshire Boulevard near Hoover. In another time it had been an elegant home. Built of stone it had a porte-cochère and several stained-glass windows. Now it was considerably run-down and was smothered in ivy and Cecil Brunner roses to hide its shabbiness. There, for nine dollars a week, I got a room, breakfast and dinner.

I had chosen to live in that area because it was near the Ambassador Hotel which had a swimming pool. I had become a member of the hotel's swimming team and spent most of my leisure time there. The team was coached by Roger Cornell, a seam-faced character who had been so exposed to the sun that his skin was parchment and his spare, once-auburn hair was colorless. Our team swam against those of the Los Angeles Athletic Club, the Hollywood Athletic Club and the Santa Monica Swimming Club. These were among the few places that had swimming pools in the Los Angeles area. As a member I was permitted to use the pool gratuitously and to patronize the renowned Coconut Grove without paying a cover charge.

Soon after Hooper-Holmes fired me I got a job as an extra in a nightclub sequence at Paramount. It was also Constance Bennett's first picture and the director chose me to dance with her. The job lasted for three days. Thereafter I got several jobs at Paramount and thus my movie career began.

The Coconut Grove was a glittering gathering place for the young social set and Saturday evenings I would dress up and go there to stag dance, the only expense being seventy-five cents for a lemonade plus a twenty-five cent tip. Break-dancing was the custom and I was able to pick and choose partners. I soon got to know a number of beautiful people, among them Joan Crawford, then a stock actress at Metro-Goldwyn-Mayer; Jane Peters, who became celebrated as Carole Lombard; and Chotsie Noonan, who was Sally O'Neill, also became a noted actress.

Fox Studio advertised for swimmers and divers to appear in a film to be made of Dante's *Inferno*. Applicants were assembled at the Ambassador pool. I and other members of the swimming team were there and so were several hundred girls, forty of whom were selected to portray mermaids. Another member of the Ambassador team, Gordon Cravath, and I were chosen to perform as Neptune's swimmers and divers.

The film was to be shot on Santa Cruz Island, off Santa Barbara, and thither we went. The director was Henry Otto, a short, thick, white-haired German, and the female lead was a frail, then unknown girl, Billie Dove. A few days after the company had been working on the island the assistant director, Horace Hough, asked Gordon and me if we could dive together from a cliff at the south end of the cove. From where we were on the beach, the cliff did not appear prohibitively high, and when Horace said that each of us would be paid a week's wages, sixty dollars, the cliff shrank considerably. Unbeknownst to Gordon and me, two stunt men, Harvey Parry and Duke Green, had been asked to do the dive and with lariats had measured the cliff's height to determine remuneration. They calculated it to be one hundred and thirty-seven feet. To do the stunt, each had asked to be paid one dollar a foot for the first twenty-five feet, five dollars a foot to fifty feet, and ten dollars a foot thereafter. Under these terms each would have received a thousand dollars take or give a dollar or two. Gordon and I, ignorant of all this, thought sixty dollars apiece was generous compensation. After all, the dive would only take a few seconds.

To climb up the cliff it was necessary for us to be rowed across an inlet. When I was getting out of the skiff a rock above became dislodged and, as if thrown by the hand of fate as a warning to give up what I was about to do, struck me on the head. Stunned, I toppled into the water. Fished out and rowed back to the beach, the doctor took three stitches in my scalp. Meanwhile four cameras had been positioned to photograph the dives and everything was at a standstill. Henry Otto was eager to get on with the filming. After two shots of brandy my nausea subsided and, although groggy, I set out again, made it across the estuary and climbed barefoot to the summit where Gordon was waiting. Looking down, I was dumbfounded by the distance to the water. Those on the beach looked like pygmies.

"How do you feel?" Gordon asked.

"Shaky."

"Think we oughta do it?"

"We don't have much choice."

There *was* an option. We could descend the way we came. Unfortunately I had bragged to one of the girls that the dive was a skimption, a nothing. I couldn't crawl back down and face the ignominy. "I didn't realize there was that projection," I said, indicating a shelf more than half way down.

"That doesn't worry me as much as the depth of the water," Gordon said. "It's only about fourteen feet."

"We don't have time to worry about that," I said, and managed a sick smile. "If we don't make it, it'll be a nice way to go." I gave him a hand to help him stand up and we positioned ourselves side by side in our fish-scale shorts, our eyes on the director's megaphone. When he dropped it we were to go.

The wait was agonizing. I recalled the fifty-foot dive I had done when I was eleven.

I did not hesitate when the megaphone dropped. Taking a deep breath, I sprang out in a swan dive, head back, back bowed, arms outstretched. From a corner of an eye I saw Gordon follow, doing an untucked one-and-a-half.

The descent was whizzingly swift. My arms crumpled as I entered the water and it seemed my head was on the way out before my feet got in.

I was astonished that I was still alive. My back ached and blood streamed down my face as I swam out of the scene. This time my scalp needed eighteen stitches.

It was imperative that I do the dive. At that time in my life I badly needed self-confidence and a proud heart. It was my first movie stunt. I did many more and became a member of the coterie of stunt men known as the Twenty-Eighty-Three Club, so called because when one of us got hurt, the State of California paid unemployment insurance compensation of $20.83 a week until he was able to work again.

When I returned to Hollywood from Santa Cruz Island I had business cards printed identifying me as "World Champion High Diver" and delivered them to casting offices. I had always wanted to be champion of something or other, so awarded myself the spurious title.

Stunting was crucial to motion pictures at that time. Being soundless, they relied on action for dramatic and comic effect. Stunts were much used in two-reel comedies, then in vogue. In them the action would begin with the first scene and build throughout the film until, invariably in the final reel, the hero and/or heroine would have to do something spectacular to escape from a horrendous predicament. Leading actors and actresses were not allowed to perform dangerous feats, even had they been so inclined; if one was hurt it would delay the production.

Most of the stunt work I did my first year in pictures was in these two-reelers. That was, to use a Hollywood phrase, the golden age of such films. In all of the country's movie theaters, feature pictures were preceded by two-reelers, usually comedies. These had an inflexible formula. The leading character, always a bumbler, would inadvertently do something disastrous. There would follow a chase featuring a series of gags. In the end the bumbler would get the best of his pursuers. By far the most important part of these entertainments was the chase, and it was in the chase that stunt men were frequently used. We skidded cars off wet pavement, drove them through fences, out of breakaway buildings and over cliffs. We dove through windows, did pratfalls, high gruesomes and hundred-and-eights from a variety of elevations. I rode a buffalo, an ostrich and a hippopotamus, and I even boxed a kangaroo and fought a "man-eating" shark.

The first stunt I did after returning from Santa Cruz Island was for a two-reel comedy. I was stretched out face down between two cars, my feet on the running board of one, my hands on the other. The cars were to pass on either side of a power pole and leave me wrapped around it. One of the cars was driven by a little known comedian named Harold Goodwin, whom William Fox was attempting to build into a comedy star, the other by a bit player named Oliver Hardy.

The stunt itself wasn't very difficult, but it was important that the cars be kept equidistant. We were moving only about ten miles an hour, but to give the effect of speed the cameras were grinding slowly. Unfortunately, before we got to the power pole, one of the drivers allowed his car to drift and I landed face down on the pavement. Skinned up but not badly hurt, we successfully did it again. One was most likely to get hurt doing simple stunts like that. You couldn't plan or prepare them; you just had to do them and hope for success.

It wasn't long after this that Hardy, who was considered one of the best at the "slow burn," an expression of frustrated anger, teamed with an English vaudeville comedian named Stan Laurel and they went on to film immortality.

The only time I was injured badly enough to draw unemployment compensation was performing a comparatively easy stunt, one for which I was paid twenty-five dollars. The picture was *The Man On The Box* which starred Sydney Chaplin. Attired in a policeman's uniform, I was standing on the roof of a moving hansom cab in which Chaplin was riding when the horse became frightened and bolted, jerking the cab from under me. Tossed on my back, I broke a wrist.

Life on a comedy set was a series of zany, hare-brained gags—the sillier, the funnier. John Ford, who had been a stunt man and was then directing two-reelers for Fox, liked to have stunt men on his set because the inane and sometimes imaginative didoes we did often suggested gags he would use. All of those who worked for him were the butts of his practical jokes and we tried to repay him in kind. Once during a lull in filming, three of us stunt men were clowning around, chasing one another up ladders and onto the rafters of the huge stage. While other members of the company bemusedly watched our antics, we pretended to lose our footing, barely saving ourselves in the nick of time. Unbeknownst to those below we were laying the groundwork for a shocker. During lunch a couple of us sneaked back into the rafters, taking with us a dummy. By now the members of the company, while aware of us, were paying us little heed. Suddenly there was a chilling scream and down came the carefully-aimed dummy to land near Ford. For a moment everyone was horrified. Then abundant laughter rewarded us.

I was the victim of a freak accident on that same picture. For the camera I backed into the set, keeping an eye on something offstage, while the villain came in another door and shot at me with a shotgun. Somehow into the propman's box of blank ammunition a live twenty-gauge shell had found its way. Although I was wearing a dungaree jacket, a shirt and an undershirt, a doctor spent the better part of an hour picking lead pellets out of my back.

The jobs were sporadic, of short duration, and the pay was poor, usually less than twenty-five dollars. In feature films I doubled for women as well as men—Gloria Swanson, Zazu Pitts, Leatrice Joy, John Barrymore, Charlie Chaplin and Buck Jones. I got one job doubling for both Stan Laurel and Oliver Hardy which lasted a week. Laurel and I were about the same size, but to double for Hardy I had to stuff myself with pillows. The film was shot in a cemetery at night. Meanwhile I had another job, working days for Paramount in the production of *Peter Pan* starring Betty Bronson and Mary Brian, which was being shot on a ship off San Pedro. I was hard-pressed to get from the Hal Roach Studio in Culver City to San Pedro and vice versa.

During the nights I did belly-floppers into open graves and during the days I fought in and fell out of the rigging of the *Jolly Roger*. The only sleep I got were catnaps between camera setups. At the end of the week I was zombied, but for the first time in my life I was able to open a one-hundred-dollar bank account. I intended to use it to get out of Hollywood. I had sought work as a reporter on several Los Angeles newspapers and had applied to the scenario departments for any kind of a job at Fox, Paramount and Warner Brothers, to no avail.

I worked frequently at Fox, doing stunts and as an extra. The studio's principal activity was making Tom Mix and Buck Jones "horse operas," pictures in which there were always stunts—falling off horses, pratfalls, fights, breakaways, tumbles down stairs or falls off balconies. My first, most hazardous job after the Santa Cruz Island dive was in a Buck Jones film. The script called for Buck, chased by a posse of black-hat bad guys, to ride onto a bridge over a railroad track. A train is coming. He dismounts, climbs over the bridge railing and escapes by dropping onto the train. George Marshall, the director, chose me to do the drop.

"How fast will the train be going?" I asked.

" 'Bout twenty miles an hour. We've got to have the effect of speed. The stunt's got to look dangerous."

"How much will it pay?"

"What do you think it's worth? How about fifty dollars?"

I had learned from other members of the Twenty-Eighty-Three Club not to accept a first offer. I said, "How about a hundred?"

"Whoa! We're not making *The Ten Commandments*, for God's sake! How about seventy-five?"

"It's my neck," I said. "If it's not worth a hundred, it's not worth a dime."

"Okay. You'll get a hundred."

The bridge was a wooden structure in the San Fernando Valley. It had been selected for its antiquity. The train was an old engine and five coaches. I went onto the bridge and optically measured the distance I would drop. I figured about seven or eight feet. I did not like the roofs of the coaches; they were rounded and there was nothing to hang on to. If I slid off, how should I fall?

Marshall ordered a trial run and Buck came riding hell bent over the rise, turned to look back at his pursuers and headed for the bridge. The posse was close behind. Buck reached the bridge, did a pony-express dismount and vaulted over the railing.

The scene worked out fine, so they did it again with the cameras rolling. After that take, the engineer backed the train and I, attired in chaps, shirt and hat like Buck's and wearing tennis shoes painted brown to look like boots, hung from the bridge. Engulfed in the smoke of the engine as it passed under me, I waited until I heard the sound of the posse's horses' hooves before letting go. Landing on the coach I fell forward on my hands, but there was nothing to clutch and I began sliding. When it became evident that I couldn't hang on, I went feet first and pushed off to clear the gravel roadbed. In landing, I lost consciousness. I heard people shouting, but they sounded faint and far away. Then, as if plugs had been yanked from my ears, I heard George Marshall's voice: "Are you all right, kid? Can you answer me?" He was shaking me. His face was close. I noticed he needed a shave. I began sucking air into my lungs. The thing to do, I said to myself, is smile. Reassure everyone. I tried to speak but words would not come. The prop man brought a bucket of water and offered me a dipperful. I slurped some of it.

Buck said, "That was a nasty fall. Are you hurt?"

"Can you move your legs?" Marshall asked.

I struggled to sit up and he and Buck helped me. I moved one leg and then the other. Both seemed to work.

"Can you wiggle your fingers?"

I wiggled them. My hands were bleeding. The prop man washed and bandaged them. Presently he and Marshall helped me to my feet. For a few moments I stood unsteadily, then, to show that I was all right, I did a little jig and everybody was relieved. Some laughed. Suddenly the troup's attitude changed from concern to apathy. Some turned away, as if to say, "Fools will be fools," Soon the camera on the bridge was rolling again, photographing Buck sitting cross-legged on the roof of a moving coach thumbing his nose at the posse. To the audience he would be the hero.

After working in films for about a year I was hired to double regularly for comedian Earl Foxe. He was a stage actor who had been brought to Hollywood to star in a series of comedies based on Richard

Harding Davis' *Van Bibber* stories. The fictional Van was a dashing, adventuresome, athletic fellow who got out of scrapes by outrunning and outwitting his adversaries. Although Foxe looked the part, being inordinately handsome in the Arrow Collar genre, he was ungainly; and because of his ineptness I was used for many of the medium and long shots. One of these two-reelers was shot on location in the area around Truckee, California, a railroad town near Donner Lake. We went there to make an ice-skating picture, but by the time we arrived the lake had thawed. However, there was a good deal of snow in the area, so George Marshall, the director, and Monte Brice, the gag-man, re-wrote the scenario and made it a skiing story. I had learned to skate on a pond in Colorado but had never been on a pair of skis; nevertheless after a couple of days' practice, I became sufficiently proficient for the filming.

The picture's climatic scene called for Earl to do a ski-jump and pick up a dummy disguised as the villain. In doing this I once again had the air squashed out of me.

At Truckee I learned of the Donner Party, that group of pioneers who, in 1846, crossed the country in covered wagons. Here in the mountains, a day or two from the sunshine of the promised land they had been caught in a blizzard. Half of them died from cold and starvation. The others suffered to the outer edges of endurance. Fascinated by this tragedy I tucked it in mind as a subject for a novel. When I got back to Hollywood I began researching it at the library.

How mysterious and fragile are destiny's doings. What happened over a hundred years ago would seem to have no bearing on what happens today, and yet the Donner Party incident changed the course of my life.

CHAPTER NINE

ARCHITECTURALLY, the cottage Jack Welch and I lived in could be called gingerbread quaint. Its exterior looked as if it had been copied by a child from a book of fairy tales. The windows were leaded, the eaves curved inward, and there was a cement cat on the roof next to the false chimney. As I limped up to it at eventide, back from Truckee, I heard the phonograph playing "Can't You Wait 'til the Cows Come Home?" and the opening lines of Gray's "Elegy" came to mind: "The curfew tolls the knell of parting day, the lowing herd winds slowly o'er the lea . . . "

Jack was entertaining Harold Goodwin and his date, a stunningly beautiful girl I had never met named Josephine Butterly. Her auburn hair framed a flowerlike face, the green eyes of which had a frankness that was refreshing, and her figure was a fine example of nature's art. At the sight of her, much of my weariness fell away. Taking her hand I had no way of knowing that within a week we would be married.

I had walked into a situation which was fated to ensnare me. I did not learn until after Josephine and I were married that for two reasons she was eager to wed as soon as possible: one was to spite a horn player in Abe Lyman's band who had jilted her to marry a wealthy widow, and the other was because her mother was pressing her to marry an older man whom she could not abide. As the fates worked out the plot, Harold passed out during the course of the evening and it fell to me to drive Josephine home.

It was a beautiful night, radiant with stars and a lopsided moon. We drove with the top down and the fresh air was soft and exhilarating. The several gin drinks I had consumed put me in an expansive mood, and with Josephine cuddled in an arm the world seemed an especially fine place to be. I'm sure I exaggerated in talking about myself and I probably revealed my longing to find a home. Jo was sympathetic and before she bade me goodnight I had made an appointment to take her to the Coconut Grove the following evening. She wanted to show me off to the horn player.

While we were dancing at the Grove she asked me to marry her. Although I had told her and almost everyone else I was twenty-three, I was nineteen. I had no more business marrying her than I had going to the moon. True, I was eager to have a home and a woman to love me, but I had no funds, no prospects and was living from hand to mouth. It was utterly reckless of me to say that I would, but I did.

The next day we went to the Hall of Records and got a license.

To me it always had been an absurd world and it seemed to get more illogical. Paying the woman two dollars and writing our names gave Jo and me the legal right to cohabit. But that wasn't the end of it. Now we needed to get a preacher to make it right with God. I looked at Josephine—could I afford her? I felt the money in my pocket, sixty-five dollars. My entire estate.

On the sidewalk I turned her to face me. "You understand, don't you, that you're betting on a horse that's never won a race?" Her green eyes blinked. "Are you sure you want to go through with this?"

The question startled her. "Why, that's silly. Of course I'm sure. Aren't you?"

"Sure," I replied. "I just want you to be. I don't know what we're going to use for money."

"For richer, for poorer." She went to a pay phone and called her Aunt Margaret to make arrangements for the wedding.

The day we were to be married, I parachuted from the first airplane I had ever been in. The prop man dug a dusty World War I surplus parachute out of the loaded trunk and we unfolded it for inspection.

"Well," he said jokingly, helping me into the straps, "at least it hasn't got any holes in it."

I was not certain how the contraption worked, but, not wanting to show ignorance, I didn't ask any questions. I had heard about the ring which opened the 'chute and that one counted to ten before pulling it. I tried the trigger mechanism a couple of times to see that it was in working order, put on a helmet and goggles and went over to get instructions.

The two wings of the two-seater plane from which I was to jump were joined and strengthened by struts and guy wires. It looked awfully flimsy. The pilot showed me where to step to squeeze into the forward cockpit. At his signal a man spun the propeller to start the engine. We taxied for takeoff. It occurred to me that one clings to life with great tenacity, yet if given the chance few would choose to relive it.

A handkerchief-parachute dropped from the camera plane was to be the signal for me to climb out of the cockpit onto the lower wing. I was to make my way to its tip and stand there for twenty seconds or more before dropping off.

We were about five thousand feet when the handkerchief fluttered open. I looked over the side. Below, Wilshire Boulevard wriggled through dusty fields to Santa Monica and the Pacific. The earth's surface seemed impossibly far away. I began doing what was expected of me: struggling out of the cockpit into the eighty-mile wind. With one leg over the side and a foot on a wing, I white-knuckled a strut and risked a furtive glance at the pilot. He nodded his goggled head. He was smiling. I read his lips: "Good luck." The camera plane was about a hundred and fifty feet away, slightly above us. I could see the camera and the people inside. I reached out for the next strut and drew myself to it. There was a third nearer the wingtip and, after pausing to summon the necessary resolution, I got to it.

I thought of Josephine. I had known her but five days and already we were to be married. It didn't make sense. But for me, marrying a girl I hardly knew was in character. I was rescuing a lady in distress.

How beautiful the world looked and how precious every second seemed. I saw hands in the camera plane motioning me to tumble. "What's your hurry?" I asked, the words sucked up by the wind. "Well, here goes." Closing my eyes, I opened my fists and consigned myself to uncertainty.

I skipped a few numerals on my way to ten before pulling the ring. The fact that nothing happened did not surprise me. All along I had suspected the parachute would not function. I tumbled as in a dream . . .

The silk opened slowly, like a flag unfurling, like a sail catching a gentle breeze. Now suddenly with a jerk, I was stabilized and for a moment it seemed I was soaring. But no, the earth was rising toward me. I landed feet first, rolled into a somersault, and ended sitting entangled among the silk and shrouds.

BECAUSE JOSEPHINE did not want her mother to know of the marriage until it was a *fait accompli,* she arranged for the ceremony to be performed in her Aunt Margaret's cottage. Aunt Margaret, a spinster schoolteacher whom I had never met, greeted me at the door, impulsively kissed me on a cheek, took the bouquet of lilies-of-the-valley, and said that Jo was dressing.

Aunt Margaret had arranged for the minister of her Episcopal church to perform the ceremony and he duly arrived in a light gray suit and a black shirt with white ecclesiastical collar. Even now I can see his pious, pink face and his plastered gray hair parted in the middle. He read from a beautifully bound, gilt-edged prayer book held in a very clean, polished-nails hand. I stood erect, trying to appear substantial and mature. The minister enunciated well, but there was in his resonant voice a certain soporific quality that lulled me. As he read the preamble to the marriage ceremony I kept trying to avoid looking in the mirror over the mantelpiece; to do so at such a time seemed not only vain, but sacrilegious. I followed the meaning of the words for a while, but then lost the thread and had a difficult time keeping my eyes from closing. I remember making the necessary responses and Aunt Margaret sniffling into a handkerchief. Perhaps she was crying because she presciently could see that the marriage was doomed. I marveled at what was happening. The lady beside me and I hardly knew each other, and yet here we were linking our lives together "until death do us part." She wasn't getting any prize. There was no future in stunt work. On the other hand, it would be nice to found a home with someone who loved me and it might work out just fine.

The minister's voice stopping aroused me from my meditation. He accepted the ring from Jack Welch, blessed it, and gave it to me. My hand was shaking slightly as I slipped it on Jo's finger. The immortal words were uttered and I took my wife in my arms and held her in a tight embrace, my heart full of hope. Jack paid the minister ten dollars, which I had given him. The latter kissed the bride and wished us happiness and asked us to be sure and come to church. In effect: "Sow thy seed, and bring me your progeny." As Josephine and I went out to get into the car, Aunt Margaret and the other guests pelted us with rice to emphasize fecundity. At Josephine's insistence we drove directly to her mother's house to break the news.

Jo used the key to enter the front door and went directly to her mother who was crocheting on a divan amongst brightly colored pillows. Jo kissed the older woman on a cheek, but this perfunctory gesture was hardly acknowledged, so fixed was Mrs. Butterly's attention on me. Her eyes were protuberant, and as she was looking up I could see her large nostrils: an umlaut above her slight mustache. She regarded me questioningly, fearfully, suspiciously.

"Mother," Jo said, turning to me, "meet your son-in-law."

The older woman recoiled as if she had been slapped. For a long moment she did not speak. When Jo asked, "Isn't he handsome?" the question aroused her as if from somnambulism. She flung her hands to her face.

"Oh, my God!" she wailed. "Oh, my God!" Then abruptly she looked up at her daughter. "You're teasing me?"

"We were married just now at Aunt Margaret's."

More wails, more calls upon the Deity, then: "Why didn't you tell me? Your very own mother? Why didn't you tell me?"

"You know why?—Because you'd have tried to stop me."

Mrs. Butterly turned to me, "And who, pray tell, may you be?"

I told her my name but it sounded inadequate. Whenever I am emotionally moved I am more likely to laugh than to weep. At that moment there was in me a strong impulse to laugh.

"What do you do?" Mrs. Butterly asked.

"I work in the movies."

"Don't tell me you're an actor?"

"I do stunt work."

"You what?"

"He doubles for the stars," Jo said.

I offered the older woman my arms and somewhat to my surprise she came into them. The gesture seemed to mollify her, but she put her forehead against my chest and sobbed. "You should have considered me. After all I *am* her mother." Mrs. Butterly turned to her daughter. "What will Bert say?"

"Why should I care what Bert says?"

"Who's Bert?" I asked.

"He's the man Mother wanted me to marry," Jo said. Then: "I've got to get packed," and she went toward a bedroom.

Her mother followed, imploring, "Are you going away?"

"You don't think we're going to spend our honeymoon here, do you?"

THE SCENES are so sharp in my memory it is as if I were re-living them. The drive through the night to La Jolla. The hotel room. I exhaustedly performing my husbandly duty. The drive back to Hollywood almost as strangers. The one-bedroom apartment on Franklin Avenue. Jo feigning illness. I sleeping on the divan in the living room. Us running out of money. Within a few days she is back to live with her mother and I move back in with Jack Welch.

In due time a process server appeared and handed me a document by which Josephine had petitioned the State of California for an annulment. It alleged among other things that the marriage was never consummated, but the unkindest cut was that I had misrepresented myself as a man of means.

Jack Welch was older than I, about thirty, an Australian who had come to California as an officer on a United Fruit Company banana boat and had found work in the movies that featured ships. We had met during the filming of *Peter Pan*, drawn together by our interest in literature. He was an avid reader and something of a poet. Both of us were trying to become famous. He finally made it.

Richard Halliburton, who was writing best-selling books about his athletic exploits around the world, decided to cross the Pacific from China to San Francisco in a junk. He hired Jack to be the navigator. They and a crew of several others set out from Taiwan in high spirits, the junk loaded with food and liquor. A few days later a typhoon engulfed them. The only answer to Jack's wireless SOS came from the United States Liner *President Coolidge,* which reported it was seven hundred miles away but would change course to assist them . . .

Jack's last message has become a classic:

Up to armpits in water. Seven hundred miles too damn far. Having great time. Wish you were here instead of me.

SORELY WOUNDED by my marriage, I cried inside. For a while I avoided companions and kept to myself, trying to regain my balance and self-respect. Fortunately a job came along at this time which replenished my coffer and helped cure my depression. I drove a car over an opening drawbridge.

The drawbridge, a big steel structure which opened in its center, was over an estuary of Los Angeles Harbor. The stunt was difficult because it was an imponderable. There was no way of knowing what would happen to the car as it left the bridge. Would it sail out? Would it nose down and turn over? I couldn't even be certain that the car could climb the bridge while it was opening. If it conked out what would happen? Would it slide backward? If it slid there would be one hell of a bump at the bottom. One thing was certain: the car would have to start up the bridge at top speed to clear it. And once it left the bridge, to avoid its falling on me, I would have to leave it. At that point, I figured, I would be about sixty feet above the water and from then on the only thing I would have to worry about was the flotsam. A piece of two-by-four or a floating bottle could maim or even kill me.

The car I was to use was a ready-for-the-junkheap Jordan roadster. For easy egress I had the lower half of the steering wheel cut off and the door on the driver's side removed. I also had the tires over-inflated. I reasoned that the car, being heavier in front, would nose down as soon as it cleared the bridge and that it probably would hit the water upside down.

Several cameras were involved because, there being no way to rehearse the stunt, it would have to be a one-take shot. As the moment for action approached I started the car's engine; it misfired, stuttered and backfired, and it would not idle at all. A mechanic eventually got it running fairly smoothly, although its bearings sounded as if they were going to fly through the oil-pan.

When I announced I was ready, the assistant director gave an all-clear signal and the bridge-tender started the lift mechanism. All I could get was about a quarter of a mile running start. Sitting lightly on the seat, much of my weight on my left leg, I eased the accelerator to the floor. The Playboy and I were doing our utmost. The roots of my hair were chilled by the exhilaration I always feel when in danger. My eye was on the speedometer needle which, as we hit the bridge, registered sixty-two. "Come on, Sweetheart," I urged it coaxingly. The bridge continued to open as we mounted it, and as its angle increased so did our speed decline. Approaching the edge we were doing a choking ten miles an hour. "Come on, Baby!" By now the bridge was at a thirty-five degree angle and still rising. I pressed against the steering wheel trying to help. The front wheels got over, but the undercarriage settled on the bridge edge and I felt the rear wheels spinning uselessly. For a moment we balanced there and it was uncertain which way the car would go; then the heavier front-end tilted forward and it began to turn over. It was at that point I abandoned it to its fate, diving from the sloping runningboard and flinging myself as far outward as I could. The Jordan Playboy and I entered the water almost simultaneously and about fifteen feet apart.

CHAPTER TEN

O NE AFTERNOON A couple of friends had cause to go to the
Otis Art Institute and I went with them. There I met Elizabeth Bumiller. I was intrigued by the paintbrush tucked in her golden
hair, by her azure eyes, retrousse nose and cupid-bow mouth and I liked
the size, shape and stance of the figure under the paint-smeared smock.
She was holding an unlighted cigarette between beautifully manicured
nails. For some zany reason she had blackened her long blond eyelashes.
I found hypnotically pleasing the frankness with which she looked at
me in acknowledging the introduction. At that time I was sorely in
need of female companionship. I was hungry for the affection, approval and encouragement only a woman can bestow. Elizabeth, called
Betty, invited my friends and me and two of her female art students to
have cocktails in her nearby apartment. I began at once to woo her.
When I had money we went to The Coconut Grove or The Plantation
and when I was short of funds she entertained me in her apartment.

Betty's mother, Mrs. Bumiller, owned the small apartment building
and occupied the penthouse. She was a gentlewoman widow and still

beautiful at middle age. Betty was the youngest of four daughters. Of the others, one was married to a German novelist, Hanns Heinz Ewers, and lived in Düsseldorf; one was married to an attorney in New York City, and one was married and living in Los Angeles. The family was listed in the Social Register.

Mrs. Bumiller took a fancy to me, possibly because of my Southern-gentleman manners, and frequently invited Betty and me to dine with her. One evening, while we were guests, Betty dropped the news that her mother was going to Germany to visit her sister, adding, "She's asked me to go with her."

I said, "Gee, that's wonderful!" not thinking it was wonderful at all, but trying to cover my disappointment. "You're going, of course."

Seated at the piano, she turned to the keys, and said, "I'm torn. I think I'd rather stay here with you."

"I'm a poor substitute for a trip to Europe."

She began playing *The White Monkey* and said, "Not to me."

Mrs. Bumiller came in from the kitchen carrying a tray of old fashioneds. I toasted her, wishing her a bon voyage and asked, "How long're you going to be gone?"

"Oh, I don't know," she said. "Six months, maybe a year. It's a long journey to go for a short visit. I've asked Betty to go with me, but she says she'd rather stay here with you."

"I'm flattered," I said.

"I don't want to leave her alone."

"I'll take care of her."

"That's what worries me. I don't want you living together." She took a sip of her cocktail and said, "Why don't you get married?"

I said, "There's nothing I'd like better. The trouble is: I can't afford a wife. I have no job. I've been trying to find one, but I'm getting nowhere."

"Two can live as cheaply as one when they love each other."

I looked questioningly at Betty. "Are you game? Are you willing to marry a pauper?"

She nodded. "Of course."

The next day we went to the Marriage License Bureau in the Hall of Records. It had a musty odor of old paper and embedded dust. The frowsy, gray-haired woman who waited on us couldn't have been more matter-of-fact if she had been wrapping fish. She filled in the license form and, tightening her lips, scribbled her name thereon. "That'll be two dollars."

"World's greatest bargain," I said, forking over the fee.

Betty and I signed our names. I looked at her, pretty as a stolen peach, and handed her the license, saying, "Let's frame it and hang it on the wall."

Though I felt insecure, I was elated. I adored Betty and sorely needed a wife who would love and have faith in me. There was the problem of supporting her; I had always had a hard time supporting myself. It was a gamble, but as Don Quixote said, "Faint heart ne'er won fair lady." We were ecstatically happy. It seemed there was nowhere to go but up.

TWO MAY BE able to live as cheaply as one, but our marriage failed for lack of money. Her mother gave us five hundred dollars as a wedding present and we stretched it, but eventually I had to scrape the bottom of my savings-to-get-out-of-Hollywood account. There was a hiatus in movie production; stunt jobs were far between and even extra work was scarce. Betty became pregnant. There were doctor bills. I borrowed from friends and tried to get any kind of a movie job such as electrician, a carpenter or grip. Betty earned twenty dollars posing for a photographer and this caused our first serious quarrel. I had been brought up to consider it degrading to a man for his wife to work and her doing so pointed up my failure to provide.

"I don't like you posing for photographers," I said angrily. "Next thing, they'll want you to pose in the nude."

"They pay well for that," she said.

When not looking for work I wrote a scenario about a young man who inherited an insane asylum from his uncle. I took it to story editors at Fox, Paramount and Columbia and would have taken fifty dollars for it, but all rejected it. I don't believe anybody ever read more than the first page.

Burdened with debts and self-doubt and with a child on the way, I became desperately discouraged. Betty was equally despondent. When she was almost three months pregnant we had a brief but serious quarrel. I was at the typewriter trying to compose a short story for possible sale to a magazine. She came out of the kitchen obviously distraught. "I wish you'd leave that typewriter and get some money. I've got to see the doctor, but I can't go back to him without paying him something."

Without a word, I got up and left.

As chance would have it, I got a job that afternoon to do pratfalls in a comedy to be made at Lake Arrowhead. The company was to leave the next morning and be away for several days. I hurried home with the joyful news. Betty was not there. I telephoned her sister. There was no answer. Betty did not come home that night. Before leaving the next morning I left her a note.

At Lake Arrowhead I did balcony breakaways, hundred-and-eights and mattress dives and earned two hundred dollars. When I returned home the apartment was bare save for its furnishings. Betty had taken her things and moved out. I telephoned her sister.

"Where on God's earth have you been?" she screamed. "We've been trying all over to find you!"

"Where's Betty?"

"She's in the hospital."

"What's the matter?"

"She's had an abortion."

I got off the hospital elevator at the third floor, hurried to number 317 and pushed open the door. Seeing me, Betty's face flushed. She said, "Hi," without warmth.

I approached her, saying "Darling!—Are you all right?"

She picked up a mirror, ran a comb through her hair and spoke perfunctorily: "The doctor says I'll live."

"Didn't you get my message?" I began opening the box of roses. "I got a job and made some money for a change. When I came home you were gone."

"I had an abortion."

"Why?"

"It was then or never."

"You should have told me. I had a right to know."

"You didn't want the baby."

"What gave you that idea?"

"I'm not blind."

A nurse came in and Betty asked her to bring a vase. I looked out the window. A lineman was climbing a powerpole. My mouth was dry and I felt nauseous. When the nurse retired, I asked, "When are you coming home?"

"I'm not."

I was shocked. I said, "You can't mean that!—I love you."

"I think you did—at one time. In your way you did."

"I still do."

"It's too late. You've changed."

"How?"

"You're not as you were. Anyway, it's all over. I'm going to New York."

"Oh, Betty, darling, please—! I'll be a better husband. I'll get a job. I promise."

She pulled up the sheet to cover her face and began weeping. Her words, "I'm not coming back, Jack," were muffled.

I touched her, "Please—!"

She shrank and, between sobs, said, "I've been through hell and I'm not going through it again."

I looked at her golden hair. The rift was my fault, another failure. "I'm sorry," I said abysmally. "Give me another chance. I'll make it up to you."

"It's too late."

Self-righteousness and pride prevented my begging any more. I said, "You're breaking my heart," the words coming from a choked throat. I lifted her left hand and kissed it. The wedding band was still there.

Without uncovering her face, she said, "Goodbye, Jack."

I was stunned, unable to speak. I turned away and went out the door.

HAVING GOTTEN A call from the casting director at Paramount, I parked under one of the dusty pepper trees on Vine Street. The hungry actors lounging outside the studio watched me enviously as the gateman let me in. The casting director greeted me graciously. He could be effusively courteous when he wanted something and rude when one wanted something from him.

"How you feelin'?" he asked.

"Fine, thanks."

"We want you to do a jump into the Feather River. You'll be doublin' for Zazu Pitts. She has broken up with her husband and is trying to commit suicide."

"From how high?"

"Oh, about forty feet."

I surmised it was higher. Casting directors always minimized dangers. "What else do I have to do?"

"Float the rapids. For you that's duck soup."

"I hear that's the most dangerous river in California. Didn't a stunt man drown up there?"

"Not in this picture. We've budgeted the stunt at a hundred dollars. You want to do it?"

"How about two fifty?"

"Two fifty!" He sat back and put a hand to his head. "Are you crazy? We can't spend that kind of money. I could get Mary Pickford to do it for two fifty."

It was funny. I had to smile. I said, "It's the river that bothers me. It's cold and treacherous."

"Tell you what I'll do," the casting director said, leaning forward. "We'll make it a hundred and fifty."

"Sorry," I said, "it's not enough. I'd be up there several days." I started for the door. It was a ploy I had learned.

"How about two hundred?"

I needed the money. I turned back to him. "If the cliff's over forty feet, I'll get five bucks a foot. Okay?"

"Okay," the casting director said and pulled out a contract.

The Feather River flows out of Lake Almanor high in northern California's Sierra Nevada. It has some of the most beautiful and turbulent rapids in the state and is much used by movie makers. On film it is spectacular; in reality it is dangerous. The assistant director and I measured the cliff from which I was to jump. It rose from the water fifty-seven feet. I would enter the water in a very small, rock-bound eddy. We found that at its deepest it was only seven feet.

In places the river was a waterfall. It came from around a bend and turned again about three hundred feet downstream. On the other side trees overhung the bank, their leaved lower limbs lying fringe-like in the water.

For the jump cameras were set up below the cliff, on the opposite bank and downstream. The property man brought me a brown wig, a heavy woolen dress with puffed, leg-o-mutton sleeves, and a wide-brimmed hat.

"Take care of the wig," he said. "It's the only one we've got."

To give my head some extra padding, I stuffed a hand-towel into it before strapping it down. The dry dress would be much heavier wet. Several men with ropes were stationed on either bank to fish me out, but because of the rushing water, rocks and trees, I did not have much faith in them.

The last thing the director said to me was: "After you get into the rapids and have gone about a hundred yards, get out as soon as you can."

The clapboard registered the scene number and he waved a red handkerchief as the signal for the cameras to roll. I bent down and pretended to kiss the baby in the basket, then straightened up and stood a long moment contemplating the river. I jumped with my arms at my sides to keep the skirt from billowing over my head. The fluttering cloth counterpointed the roar of the river. To break my descent, I entered the snow-melted water arms akimbo, but because of the buoyancy of the dress I barely touched the rocky bottom. At once I was sucked into the cascading stream. So powerful was the current and so heavy and cumbersome the Mother Hubbard all I could do was stay afloat and dodge the rocks. Where the rushing water went, I went. As I slithered over stones and bounced off boulders my hips, arms, legs, shoulders, buttocks, and belly all got their lumps. The water was so cold I felt no pain, but breathing deeply was difficult. I swallowed a lot of water. I couldn't swim. Every time I avoided a boulder the stream would swing me around and I would be swept headfirst. It quickly became apparent that if I were to survive I would have to get rid of the dress. My hands were needed to ward off the battering, so shedding it was not easy; whenever I could I ripped away at the cloth. Twice I got a glimpse of a man running beyond the trees trying to get a rope to me and once a rope fell nearby but I could not reach it. Incredibly, a stanza of *Saint James Infirmary* went through my mind:

Now I'll tell you how I wanna be buried:
straight-laced shoes, box-back suit an' Stetson hat.
Put a twenty dollar gold piece on my watchchain
so the boys'll know that I'm standin' pat . . .

I had bobbed half a mile or more before I managed to shed the dress. I still wore the flounced sleeves. My only other garment was swimming trunks. Eventually the main stream veered toward a bank and I was able to catch hold of an overhanging bough. Under my weight and the force of the current, it broke off. I snatched at another and another before I caught one which held. My numb hands locked onto it. I needed a few moments to catch my breath. Eventually I managed to work my way to the bank and crawl through the thick growth. I lay there panting and thought how paradoxical it is that man, who lives in continual fear of hunger, disease, ignorance, poverty and death, struggles to stretch out the time allotted him.

WITH THE MONEY I made fighting a shark in a swimming pool and killing it with a knife and from the Feather River stunt, I was able to buy a second-hand Stutz. It was priced $182 and I paid $25 down. It had belonged, the salesman told me, to Jack Pickford, Mary's playboy-actor-brother. It was a four-door, lemon-yellow beauty, long and snazzy with a canvas top, leather seats, brass-framed windshield, spare wheels set in front-fender wells and a leather trunk in the rear. The gearshift and handbrake levers were outside the driver's seat. The engine had a fine basso roar which was hard to ignore. I always drove it with the top down because I thought it distinguished me. In those days it was important in Hollywood to become a personality. One had to promote oneself.

I moved into a small hotel on Sunset Boulevard, across the street from Warner Brothers Studios. Behind the hotel lived a friend who worked as a dress extra, which means he owned a tuxedo and tails and, when hired to wear either, was paid twice the extra's $7.50 wage. His name was Clark Gable. Together he and I would go looking for work, calling on the various studios. We usually went in my Stutz rather than his old Dodge because we deemed it gave us more pizzazz. When the Stutz was *hors de combat,* we'd use his car. Clark was four years older than I, but we were about the same size. During our peregrinations we exchanged backgrounds and talked about what we were going to do with our lives. To me acting seemed a dilettantish way for a man to earn a living and I said as much, but Clark was serious about it. "It's what I want to do," he said. "It's a hell of a lot better than falling on your ass, as you're doing."

He had been brought up on a farm in Ohio and had quit school to work in a tire factory in Akron. There, under fate's machinations, he became interested in theatrics and began helping backstage in the local opera house. In time he was called on to play bit parts. Eventually his father quit farming and took him to Oklahoma to work in the oil fields. By then the acting bug had infected him, so after a few months in Oklahoma he latched onto a touring troup and set out on a thespian career.

That first step didn't take him far. The company became stranded in Oregon, where, he told me, he worked as a lumberjack until he was able to join another show. The leading lady and owner of the show was Josephine Dillon. She was considerably older than he, but romance bloomed and they were married. An old hand in show business, she coached him in the acting art. Eventually they made their way to Hollywood where he sought work in the movies and she opened an acting school.

"I don't want to stay in stunt work," I said. "I want to be a writer."

"I don't know what my potentials are," Clark said, "but I sure as hell don't want to go back to the oil fields."

"I think the place for you is in the theater," I said. "Not the movies. Movies are too phony. There's no way you're ever going to become a movie star. Your ears stick out too far. And if you do get leading roles you'll have to change your name. Clark's too namby-pamby for a marquee. You'll have to make it Ace or Duke or King, something gutsy or noble."

"How about Bozo?" he suggested, and we both laughed.

CHAPTER ELEVEN

T HAT YEAR—1926—I left Hollywood. The unlikely key to my escape was Pepi Lederer, a large, rather ungainly girl and a niece of Marion Davies, the actress and infamous common-law wife of William Randolph Hearst. Pepi invited me to escort her to a charity ball which Miss Davies was sponsoring. I went to the Davies home on one of the high-walled, shrub-enshrouded streets behind the Beverly Hills Hotel, and was greeted by a butler in tails. He took my hat and said Miss Lederer would be down presently. He then went to the head of a few-step stairway and sonorously announced me to those in the living room. As I descended, Miss Davies came to welcome me. She introduced me to her guests: Lita Grey Chaplin, and her husband, Charlie; Bebe Daniels and her beau, track star Charles Paddock; actress Lila Lee and her husband, James Kirkwood.

Perceiving my shyness, Kirkwood led me to the bar and poured me a scotch-and-soda. Glass in hand, I made my way to a divan. Miss Daniels and Paddock were rehashing a party they had attended the night before and I was surprised by the banality of their recounting.

I had thought that illustrious people spoke illustriously. Presently a door opened and in came Hearst, a large, corpulent and imposing man to whom Miss Davies flew with esteem and affection. He greeted the guests casually and Miss Davies introduced me. He offered a limp hand and sat down beside me. The immensity of his reputation intensified my feeling of unimportance. It occurred to me as a rare opportunity to ask him for a job on one of his newspapers, but decided the time and place were inappropriate. For an agonizingly long time neither of us spoke. Then I said something platitudinous and he said, "I surmise, by your accent, that you're from the south," then went on to say, as if dictating an editorial, that the greatest problem the nation faced was how to absorb the Negro into the Caucasian culture. I was somewhat relieved that, while he was speaking, Pepi came in.

Miss Davies had promoted the ball to raise money for the family of a film worker who had been killed in a studio accident. She, Pepi, and I rode to the affair in a chauffeur-driven limousine. Among the persons to whom Pepi introduced me were Louella Parsons and her daughter, Harriet. Mrs. Parsons wrote a widely read newspaper column about the movies and movie personalities, and because of its publicity value she had become a power in the film industry. Harriet and I quickly became friends, drawn by a mutual admiration for Beaudelaire. For the next few weeks we gallivanted together, swam in Charlie Chaplin's pool, played tennis at Pickfair and attended film parties.

I broke a wristbone doing a breakaway fall in John Ford's *The Fighting Heart*. That evening, while dining with Parsons, Louella said, "I think you ought to give up doing stunts. That's no way for a good-looking young man with a pleasing personality to make a living. I believe I could get you a screen test at Em-Gee-Em."

The suggestion knocked me off balance. "Gee, Louella, that would be marvelous but—but I don't have much faith in my acting ability."

"I think you'd do fine. If I can get you into Metro's stable of upcoming young stars you might become another John Gilbert."

"Sounds wonderful," I said. "But what I want to be is a writer. I'd much prefer your helping me get a job on a newspaper. You've got lots of influence there, too."

Louella said: "I guess I could do that, but it won't pay as well. At Metro you'd start at seventy-five dollars a week with a seven-year contract and your salary could go up every year. As a cub reporter you'll get twenty-five."

"For me it would be a step in the right direction. And I can live on peanuts."

"Well, I'll see what I can do. To go into newspaper work you should go to New York. The opportunities there are much greater than here. Mr. Hearst has three papers in New York. I should be able to get you a job on one of them."

Shortly thereafter she and Harriet left for New York, Harriet en route to Wellesley to start her freshman year. Louella said they would be in New York for two weeks and suggested I come while they were there. I scurried around, sold the Stutz and bought a train ticket. One of the last things I did in my haste was to seek out Clarke and bid him good-bye. When I told him that Louella had offered to get me a contract at M-G-M he exploded: "You mean you turned it down? Why, you half-assed idiot! That's got to be the stupidest thing I ever heard. Falling on your head you must have lost your marbles."

"I had a choice, and chose what I want to do. Meanwhile you'll be here, lost in mob scenes, while I'll be getting somewhere." We laughed, embraced Mexican style and wished each other good luck.

It happened that shortly after I left he got a small part in a touring theatrical company and also left Hollywood. Eventually he made it to New York where he got the leading role in *Machinal*, which boosted him up the thespian ladder and honed him for stardom in the movies. I did not see him again until after he had become the celluloid King. After going over our early struggles in Hollywood, I apologized for not having foreseen his talent. He said, "I remember you told me your mother was a professional astrologer. Obviously you didn't inherit her fortune-telling genes."

LOUELLA gave me a letter to the managing editor of the *New York American*:

> This will introduce my friend, whose aim is to be a writer. I would consider it a favor if you would take him under your wing and give him a job. He has a number of attributes and, in my opinion, has literary talent. I think, with your help, he will do well . . .

I was hired by the Hearst newspaper as a cub reporter. I quickly came to learn that pictures were an important ingredient in this medium. Often they were difficult to obtain and buying and stealing them were common practices. A few days after I joined *The American* I was sent to Queens to obtain photographs of a woman who had been murdered in Manhattan. When I arrived at the apartment building where she had lived, a few other reporters were in the basement talking to the janitor. I found the victim's name on a mailbox, ascertained her apartment was on the second floor and went up and tried the door. It was double-locked. My turning the knob alerted a canary inside and it began chirping. I went to the janitor and told him that the bird would die if it didn't get food and water. Of the two keys necessary to effect an entrance, he had only one, so I suggested going through a window. There was a roof over the front entrance from which one could get to the window. Stressing the plight of the canary, I said that, with his permission, I would try to get in. He supplied a screwdriver and a ladder and I climbed up. The window was unlocked and I had no trouble opening it. By the time the janitor and other reporters, all of whom had been on the sidewalk watching me, had climbed the stairs, I had rifled the dead woman's desk and pocketed the snapshots therein. In my haste, I forgot all about the canary. The next edition of *The American* was the only paper in New York that printed the pictures of the deceased and her family.

Thereafter, whenever there were pictures to be procured, I was sent to get them. Such assignments did nothing for me literarily, but they earned me the approbation of my bosses.

Mostly my assignments as a cub for the next few months were interviewing celebrities and reporting their scandalous activities and marital troubles. Now and then I would cover a suicide or a speakeasy raid and I wrote a number of feature stories such as an old woman who was evicted because she kept a house full of cats. Those early pieces were either rewritten or so changed at the copy desk that I could hardly find one phrase of my composition. However, from the corrections I learned to write short, declarative sentences, to stick to facts and to be careful about my abominable spelling.

After a long while my words as I had arranged them began to appear in print, now a sentence, then a paragraph and eventually, after about nine months, an article of my authorship actually appeared much as I had written it and with my by-line. It was about the death of Arnold Rothstein. The circumstances of the notorious gambler's murder were unknown, but from my investigation I reconstructed the scene in the form of a play. The story appeared spread across all eight columns of page two. I was becoming a writer.

Rousted out of bed before dawn one Sunday by the night city editor, I was informed that the body of a young woman had been found in a field near a highway south of White Plains. She had been doused with gasoline and set afire. Her face had been burned beyond recognition. Police were stumped for identification. Sundays usually are dull news days, and this had the makings of a front-page story.

When I reached the White Plains police station I learned the only clue to the woman's identity was a fragment of the house-dress she had been wearing when she was murdered, that part which had been under her buttocks. The garment had been made of printed material—flowers and fruit—and I thought, if I could snitch a piece of it, the paper could run a picture of the pattern and it might be recognized. With this in mind I presented myself at the coroner's office as a relative who might identify the corpse. A policeman led me to the morgue. The piece of cloth lay on the sheet which covered the body. With my back to the policeman I ripped off a fragment and stuffed it into my shirt pocket. A reproduction of it appeared on the front page of *The American*'s bull-dog edition which came out about five o'clock that afternoon and that evening a woman telephoned the paper, said she had made a dress of such a print for her daughter and gave her daughter's address. Thither I hastened.

The landlady informed me that the person I sought, a Mrs. Peacox, had gone out Friday night with her estranged husband and had not returned. We found his address among the missing woman's effects. It was in the Bronx. I took a taxi. The house was dark but after several knocks Peacox opened the door. I identified myself and he let me in. Weepingly he blurted out the whole ghastly tale, how he and his wife had quarreled because she refused to come back and live with him, how he had shot her, stuffed her body into the trunk of his car and driven into the country to disperse of it. He kept wailing that he wanted to die. Throughout the trial he was referred to as Dementia Peacox. He was sentenced to life imprisonment.

Another cub on the paper was Henry Stansbury, whose father was head of the London bureau of Hearst's *Universal News Service*. Hank and I quickly became friends and moved into a small apartment on West Ninth Street. The apartment contained only one bed, which made it awkward when one of us had a liaison. At such times the other occupant would go for a walk. One night Hank unexpectedly brought home a small, dark-haired, brown-eyed girl he had met in Barney Gallant's speakeasy. I promptly left the place and spent more than an hour on a park bench in Washington Square. When I returned the lady was still there and both were asleep, so I got into bed with them. Her name was Martha, but we did not think it suited her and renamed her Juliana. She stayed with us for six weeks. She had come to New York from Sioux City with the intention of making her way as an artist. For Hank and me, this *maison à trois* was a fine arrangement and Juliana seemed quite happy with it. She kept the apartment neat, marketed, cooked our meals, did our laundry and, sleeping between us, gave equally of her favors. Hank and I considered the alliance idyllic. Even now I am not sure but that we may have stumbled onto a higher plane of social existence. The relationship came to an end one morning. Juliana cooked our breakfasts and, as Hank and I were leaving for work, announced that she was to be married that afternoon to one of our friends, a United Press reporter.

As a cub reporter I saw so much of death that I should have come to understand it. I covered the tragedy of the *Morro Castle,* a ship which caught fire off the coast of New Jersey one winter night on its way to warmer climes. Unable to get lifeboats launched, crew and passengers leaped into the freezing water. Stiff bodies were washed ashore with arms outstretched in a swimming stroke. Dozens of them were taken to the morgue of Belleview Hospital, a place I had gotten to know well. Its refrigerators were always full of corpses culled from the streets and warrens of New York City—victims of accidents, the murdered and those who had died by their own hands. The attendant was a dwarfish fellow with fringe white hair who might have been old Beelzebub himself. He would greet arriving cadavers as if they were invited guests. "Why, howdy-do, Miss Ellen. I'm glad you could come." He took iniquitous delight in showing off his charges to visitors. I remember he had an irreverent way of fingernail flipping the nipples of females. His favorite anecdote was about a woman who came to identify a black cadaver with abnormally large genitals. "No," she said saidly, "that ain't my Malcolm, but some lady has shore done lost herself a good friend."

After we had been on the *American* about a year, Hank and I decided to go to Europe. It was the sophisticated thing to do. "Everyone," from debutantes to be "received" by Queen Mary to rich widows on the prowl for titled husbands, were going. We had read Ernest Hemingway's *The Sun Also Rises* and it seemed to us that wandering through Europe living on wine and women was the way to go. Also in our minds was a hope that Hank's father would give us a job.

To resign from the *American* and go abroad was rash of me. I had little money, only enough to get to Paris and survive for a few weeks. The freighter passage to Antwerp was ninety dollars. To get back I'd have to bum or work my way. However, impulsiveness is a wide streak in my character. The trip promised to be providential. I had sold a short story entitled, "I Didn't Love My Husband When I Married Him" to *True Stories* and had been paid fifty dollars. That was my first fiction sale and it bolstered my confidence. I bamboozled myself into thinking I could write a story a week and live on truffles and champagne. Mother gave me a little money—twenty-five dollars—and I put the bee on one of my father's sisters who lived in New Jersey. She and her husband, a banker, were childless and I thought they might want to contribute to my cultural education. But when I told her I was going to use the money to go to Paris she refused, saying, "That's no place for a young man. I don't approve you going there."

During the weeks before Hank and I were to resign our jobs and sail on a Belgian freighter, I was assigned to cover the Great Air Race. Raymond B. Orteig, a Franco-American hotel man, had offered a prize of $25,000 for the first non-stop flight from New York to Paris. Admiral Richard E. Byrd and his crew with one plane, and Bert Acosta and Clarence Chamberlain with another were at Roosevelt Field on Long Island awaiting favorable weather before taking off on the perilous adventure. Their preparations and activities were front page news and it was my job to report them.

The day before Hank and I took off for Europe a plane flew onto Roosevelt Field piloted by a tall, skinny young man who announced that he intended to fly to Paris alone. His name was Charles Augustus Lindbergh. The consensus was that he had lost his marbles.

CHAPTER TWELVE

HANK AND I WERE the only passengers aboard the coal-laden freighter. After a few days at sea the captain received a wireless message that Lindbergh had taken off and was flying the Great Circle route. He was asked to keep a watch for the single-engine plane and help the aviator if he got into trouble. For a couple of days thereafter all of us spent a lot of time scanning the always cloudy sky.

Hank and I reached Paris a few days after the "Lone Eagle" had landed at Le Bourget Airport. By then Lindbergh madness was at its height. Overnight he had become a legend. He had risked his life against great odds to win a fortune and had become the most famous person in the world. There was insatiable demand for information about him. No detail was too insignificant. Thanks to Hank's father, Hank and I were assigned to cover the hero. My job was to follow him and note down every word he uttered, no matter how banal. He was staying at the United States Embassy as guest of Ambassador Myron T. Herrick. I followed the hero and the ambassador wherever they went and recorded Lindbergh's every utterance. I reported everything he ate, how he liked his eggs, if he used cream in his coffee or lemon in tea, and whether or not he liked steak rare or well-done.

To almost everyone on earth Lindbergh was a demigod, but not to me. I considered him an incredibly lucky, rather stuffy young man. I had done a number of dangerous stunts, for none of which had I been extolled; indeed, for doing some of them I had been considered nitwitted. Here was a rather unsparkling fellow who had won $25,000 and was going into the history books along with Noah and Columbus. To me the awards seemed extravagantly overdone.

When Lindbergh returned to New York our jobs with Universal ended and, unable to find other work in Paris, Hank and I went to Le Touquet-Paris Plage, a resort on the English Channel, to work on our novels. There, due to distractions we did not get much writing done, but we did a spectacular job of sowing our seed.

The pension we lived in, Le Beau Soleil, was situated on a beach and run by Mademoiselle Georgette, a plump, henna-haired French woman about forty years of age who, when our money ran out, let Hank and me work out our board on her bed. We alternated the job, neither of us being capable of contenting her alone. Sexually speaking, she was marvelously imaginative and innovative. We would perform gymnastics akin to the high-gruesome, the hundred-and-eight and the barrel-roll, then, with Hank or me hanging on, we would bounce as on a trampoline. In all of my fantasies, I had never envisioned such a variety of sexual aberrations. It was more a contest than a collaboration.

Georgette was not the only divertissement in her establishment. The hotel was aswarm with younger and prettier French women, wives and mistresses on *toutes seules* holiday, sent by their husbands or lovers to give themselves a little rest. There were more of these receptive women than Hank or I could accommodate, but we gave them the old college try. It was a losing battle, and how we managed to survive the summer is one of those feats like going over Niagara Falls in a barrel and living to tell the tale.

Despite the ladies, we trudged the dunes, studied French and occasionally practiced the art of writing. The only flaw in this exhaustive paradise was a need of *argent*. We were down to our last franc when *Collier's Weekly,* to which I had submitted an article about stunting in the movies, sent me a check for three hundred dollars. This permitted me to pay off our creditors. Hank's father sent him the fare to go home and I went to Paris and got a job on the *Herald*.

I moved into a tiny apartment on the Rue du Lambre just behind the Café du Dôme. It was on the fifth floor and there was no elevator. Advertised as *confort moderne*, there was little heat, and the bath, which served six of us and for some reason was referred to as "Turkish," was down the hall. The Dôme was, and still is, the most famous bistro on the Left Bank. It was the well for artists and would-bes of all breeds and nationalities. It became my sitting room, dining room and bar and it was there that I met a number of well-known and upcoming celebrities, among them Ford Madox Ford, Jacques Lipshitz, Gertrude Stein and her *fide achates*, Alice Toklas; Alexander Calder, Pablo Picasso and James Joyce.

That, the fabulous 'Twenties,' was an era of literary high jinks and wonderful nonsense and the Paris edition of the *New York Herald-Tribune* was its chronicler. The paper was edited and written by an assortment of bizarre characters—expatriots, wanderers, iconoclasts and romantics—among them Elliot Paul, whose hobby was frequenting bordellos. On his days off he would go into one and not come out until he had to go back to work. He called it "research," and out of his experience came his highly successful *The Last Time I Saw Paris*. From him I learned to peel away the preconceptions and evaluate without prejudice. Inspired by him I applied myself more seriously to writing the novel I had started in Paris-Plage.

I went to work for the *Herald* when it was in a dingy building on the Place de la Louvre, in the midst of Les Halles, the great central market Zola called "the belly of Paris." From midnight to morn hundreds of people were in the streets pushing carts of fruits, vegetables, meat, fish and fowl brought in from the countryside and the sea for the million meals of the coming day. Another memorable character on the paper besides Elliot Paul was Sparrow Robertson. Small, like a jockey, he was seventy-two years old and wrote a column, "Sporting Gossip," that was precisely that, a record of his daily and nightly wanderings, the persons he met and their chit-chat. It was the most popular feature in the paper. Consequently Sparrow was a kind of mini-celebrity. He had been born in Edinburgh about 1860 and emigrated at an early age with his parents to New York where he had little schooling but worked at a number of jobs. About 1900 he opened a sporting goods store near City Hall which became a rendezvous for athletes and sportswriters. When Prohibition came into effect he sold the business and moved to Paris.

He was a heavy drinker and alcohol seemed to bring out the best in him. Oddly enough he came to France with a contingent of the YMCA. How he was able to get a job writing for the *Herald* is a story which even in the twenties was lost in the mists of time. But it was a lucky day for him and for the paper. Elliot Paul said, "The thought that he might not have been hired because he couldn't type or spell is sobering enough to close all the bars in Christendom."

His column was like a diary. He would tap it out on a battered typewriter, take it, misspelled, badly punctuated and often illegible, to a copy editor and expect that unfortunate to decipher and correct it. Because the job was so time-consuming, the editor often panned it off on newcomers. Soon after I started work Sparrow's copy landed on my desk. "Don't change anything," I was told. "Just make it readable."

I had to concentrate for several minutes before I was able to understand the lead sentence, not only because much of it was exed out but because Sparrow disregarded syntax. Here is a sample of his writing:

The end of a perfect Thanksgiving Day. Early in the afternoon of Thursday I dropped into Jeff Dickson's office and he prevailed upon me to remain and hear the returns of the Royal Wedding in London. I did, and during the come-over some refreshments were offered and not refused. After, it was a case of making a call at Henry's Bar in the rue Volney, where an excellent free lunch, drinks included, was served. It was a swell layout and it was deeply appreciated by the mass which attended.

Then it was a visit to Otto's Bar, where we found the champion cocktail shaker in fine form. After an hour or two passed with Otto, it was time to make a visit to Harry's aquarium, and what a bunch we did meet there! While in old boy Harry's place I met a pal, one well known in the American, English and Canadian colonies of Paris. He said, "Sparrow, come to my home tonight and we will eat cold turkey, drink White Horse and smoke nine-inch-long Havana cigars." It sounded good to me so I told our old pal that I was on.

It appears that our old pal should have been at his home at two o'clock to carve Mr. Turkey for his missus and a few guests, but he fell in (probably was accused of) with some evil companions. He was evidently wise to the fact that he had done something wrong when he invited me to have some cold turkey with him and I was being made his alibi after his being about nine hours late for his family Thanksgiving dinner.

We left Harry's and hopped into a taxi bound for Johnny's Bar in the rue Pierre Charron. "We need a little priming up before meeting my missus," said our old pal, "and I want to present you to Mamma feeling quite jolly. What time is it now?" he asked, as we were going up in the lift to his apartment.

"Eleven fifteen," said I.

"I am just ten hours late for our turkey dinner," said our pal. "But better late than never."

Mamma opened the door of the apartment. It was one swell looking place.

"Mamma, meet Sparrow Robertson. I have brought him home to eat some cold turkey, drink some White Horse and smoke a few of my Havana cigars!" It sounded good to me, but when I took a look at Mamma's eyes, I thought a get-away was the best for me, and she helped me leave when she said, "There will be no cold turkey, and Mr. Sparrow, you had better come around some other night as there will probably be a fight in this establishment tonight."

I beat it down six flights of stairs, and believe me the laugh I got out of what our pal was in for did me just as much good as a dish of cold turkey washed down with White Horse and nine-inch Havana smokes would have done. It sure did make an end of a perfect day for me, but maybe not for our old pal!

This prose fascinated many people. Eugene O'Neill lived near Tours during the Twenties and he told a drama critic who came to interview him that he went to the village first thing every morning to get the *Herald*, saying he could not start the day until he had read Sparrow's column.

My mother, the astrologer, believed that people lived their lives according to the time when they were born. Those born early in the morning became early risers; those born after midday were inclined to live their lives at night. That might be true. In any case, Sparrow was a night person. His day started in the late afternoon, usually at Harry's New York Bar on the rue Danou, and ended at dawn or later in the *Bal Taborin* or some other *boîtes de nuit* in Montmartre or the Place Pigalle. Enroute he made a number of stops here and there for gossip and a drink or two.

He usually traveled his beat alone, but sometimes he would take pals part way. It's a safe bet that none of them ever went the distance.

After I had been on the paper a few months, he asked me to join him. Eager to learn about the celebrated nightlife on the Right Bank, on one of my days off I met him about six o'clock in Harry's New York Bar. I got there first. When Sparrow entered he was greeted so effusively it was some time before he saw me.

"Glad you're able to make it, old pal," he said. "What'll you have to drink?"

Harry McElhone was behind the bar. He was English, blond, chubby and ingratiating. He greeted Sparrow warmly, and Sparrow introduced me. We shook hands and he indicated a man standing nearby. "Meet Pete Emerald," he said. "He's just in from New York."

"Howdy, pal," Sparrow said, and shook Emerald's hand. "How's my old home town."

Emerald looked as if he might be an actor, a prizefight manager or professional gambler. He was slender, about my height, six feet, and his eyes were gray and cold under heavy dark brows. The skin around his eyes was dark. He looked dissipated. He was well dressed: gray, pinstripe suit; blue shirt and darker blue tie; black, snap-brim fedora. He shook our hands, said, "Howdy," but did not smile.

It turned out that Pete and Sparrow had mutual friends in the sports world and Sparrow immediately adopted him as a pal. When we left Harry's, Pete joined us. Our next stop was at Henry's on the rue Volney, the oldest American bar in Paris. Harry's had been lively, even raucous; Henry's was sedate. Most of the patrons were dignified businessmen some of whom gathered regularly to have a few drinks and play dominoes. Everyone greeted Sparrow warmly. We stayed long enough for one drink and Sparrow to make some notes, then went on to the Hotel Chatham bar where the racing crowd hung out. Sparrow received his usual fervent greeting, we had a drink, he made more notes and we proceeded to the Silver Ring, a bar recently opened by Jeff Dickson. Jeff was a Mississippi boy who had come to Paris some years before as an assistant cameraman for Pathé Movie News. When he lost that job, he began staging boxing bouts. Boxing was primarily an American sport, but the French took to it quickly, and Jeff became very successful. When I met him he was operating the *Palais de Sport* and the *Salle Wagram,* an auditorium larger than Madison Square Garden. He had become a local celebrity and the *New Yorker* had printed a profile of him written by George Rehm, sports editor of the *Herald.*

In most of the places Pete and I paid for our drinks, but Sparrow got his for free. If a waiter brought him an *addition,* he would tell him to take it to the boss.

By the time we left the Silver Ring, I had three sheets to the wind and was sailing. Pete appeared to be holding his own and Sparrow, looking sober as the proverbial judge, said he thought it was time to *manger,* so we got into a taxi and went to Luigi's, an Italian-American restaurant between the Opera and the Madeleine; it was frequented principally by Americans and Englishmen, thanks largely to the publicity generated by Sparrow. We were served a sumptuous dinner and consumed two bottles of wine, all at the expense of the house. Luigi ran an all-night cabaret on the floor above the restaurant. It was there, Sparrow told us, he had come upon the Prince of Wales. "I walked up to His Royal Highness, shook his hand and said, 'Howdy-do, old pal?' and rendered for him my favorite song, 'Mister Dooley's Geese,' which pleased him very much."

Our next two stops, Otto's and Johnny's, were both on the rue Pierre Charron, off the Champs Elysées. At Otto's, I switched to beer. It was after midnight when we got back to Harry's. The place was packed. Sparrow's arrival was greeted with intemperate shouts of gaiety and glee. He went about, greeting pals, gathering gossip and accepting kudos and drinks, while Pete and I squeezed into tight places at the end of the bar. I was glad to have a respite from imbibing. While we sipped coffee waiting for our guide to free himself from his admirers, I questioned Pete about himself. He said he was married and lived in upstate New York.

We went on to two cabarets, *Bricktop's* and *Florence's*, both run by black women. *Bricktop's* was a favorite of Sparrow's because when he ran out of gas—as he sometimes did about there—she gave him a place to take a nap. The night I was with him he did not need a rest, but I did. I had gone about as far as my strength and endurance would carry me. Daylight would find Sparrow at one of the other *boîtes de nuit*, but I left him at Florence's at about four o'clock. I don't know what happened to Pete and I don't remember getting home.

How Sparrow managed to make this pilgrimage five nights a week and stay alive is one of the great human mysteries like the Siamese twins. Maybe he got a lot of nourishment from the food he nibbled during his peregrinations and from the scotch and wine he drank. Small as he was, he drank more without getting sozzled than anyone I ever knew. The juice of Scotland seemed to recharge his batteries. Then, too, he had the ability to take short naps at will. Sometimes after his nightly sojourns he would go back to the *Herald* and take a long nap in his cubicle of an office before writing his column. We all marveled at his durability.

I had a hunch Pete Emerald was traveling under a false name. I saw a small item in *The New York Herald Tribune*, which always got to Paris a week late, that Jack (Legs) Diamond, the notorious gangster, was in Europe and it suddenly dawned on me that he might be Diamond. I mentioned this to Eric Hawkins, the managing editor, and he assigned me to find out. I cabled the New York office and asked for a file on Diamond. I received this reply:

Thirty-three years old, married, lives in Acra, Green County, New York. Born in Brooklyn where he was arrested for burglary when he was sixteen. Served a brief time in the workhouse, one of the two times he has been jailed. The other was for deserting the army in 1917: he spent six months in the federal prison at Fort Leavenworth, Kansas. He became body-guard of Jake Orgen (Little Augie) east side gang leader, and was with him when Little Augie was killed. Diamond was also shot. He and Frankie Marlow were indicted for the murder. Police were able to arrest Marlow, but they couldn't find Diamond. Eventually he showed up with a lawyer at police headquarters, saying, "I understand you want to see me." He was locked up in the Tombs on the Little Augie charge, but both he and Marlow were exonerated. No witnesses.

Later drug smuggling charges were brought against him and again he was jailed. Arnold Rothstein, for whom Diamond and his brother Eddie worked, put up $15,000 bail-bond for Legs and he jumped it. The bond was forfeited. When Rothstein was shot and killed both Legs and his brother were arrested for the murder but released because the prosecution was unable to produce any witnesses.

Shortly after that, in March 1930, Legs was indicted for the murder of W. Cassidy and S. Walker in the Hotsy Totsy Night Club, of which Legs was part owner. Bail was denied him. He remained in jail for two days, was released because the State's case collapsed. No witnesses.

Jack Diamond was arrested for the twenty-third time this year charged with the murder of G.F. Miller in Newark. Again the prosecution let him go for lack of evidence. It was shortly after that that he sailed for Europe on the SS *Belgenland.*

I went to the Hotel Continental and waited in the lobby for about an hour, but Pete didn't show up. I left a note for him and went to Harry's New York Bar, thinking he might be there. He wasn't. But on the way back to the *Herald,* I ran into him on the rue Royal. He was on the way to the American Legion Post and asked me to come along.

The Post was housed in Pershing Hall, a new building which had been paid for by subscription. It was a hang-out for veterans of the war. Pete and I went into the barroom. The bartender, a middle-aged man with a bulbous nose and a wrinkled forehead, asked us if we belonged to the Legion.

"I was with the Hundred and Forty-seventh Field Artillery," Pete said.

I showed my press card.

Pete blowing on his hands, ordered a hot rum. I didn't want anything to drink. It was middle of the afternoon and I had to go back to the office. I ordered coffee. We took our drinks to a table in the corner.

Pete asked me about Parisian brothels and I told him about a new one, The Sphinx, which had opened recently near where I lived. He said he would like to see it. I said I'd take him, then dipped into my courage and said, "May I ask you a personal question?"

Immediately he was on the defensive. "What do you wanna know?"

"Are you Jack Diamond?"

He put his glass down so fast that some of his drink sloshed over the rim. "For Christ's sake!" he whispered, "Where'd you get that idea?"

"It's in the papers that Diamond is in Europe. Diamond—Emerald. I just wondered."

For a few seconds he stared into my eyes. Then he leaned toward me and in a low voice said, "Okay, okay. I'll square with you but don't put it in the paper. I'm John Diamond."

"I won't expose you," I said. "Why are you here?"

"I came to Europe because every piss-ant in New York was trying to rub me out. Just a couple nights before I left I was on my way home, an' some goons drove up an' riddled my car with bullets. It's a miracle I'm alive." He got up, downed his drink, obviously disturbed. "Let's get the hell out of here."

On the street he said, "Now you know who I am, how 'bout showin' me around?"

After work that night I joined Pete at the Continental and we took a taxi to The Sphynx, a large building on the avenue Edgar Quintet. There were seven floors of lavishly furnished rooms, including a movie salon, a small theater, two bars and a huge reception hall. The motif was Egyptian. In Arabic on the façade was a motto which read, in translation: *Top Closer Cooperation in Everyday Life Between the Sexes.* A uniformed guard stood on either side of the doorway. A girl wearing a transparent blouse, a maid's apron and cap took our hats and coats. We entered a large hall where a four-piece orchestra was playing. Behind the band, lights produced a waterfall effect. Women lounged in chairs against the wall; all wore white silk pantaloons and pinafores.

Two of the girls got up and came over to us. They spoke in French, saying they were enchanted. Their names were Mimi and Claudette. Mimi took Pete's arm and I took Claudette's. We went across the dance floor to a table near the orchestra. Pete and I ordered whiskies, and the girls asked for cerises, a non-alcoholic drink. Pete said, "Like lucky Adolph, I've always wanted to go to bed with two women. Ask 'em how much it would cost."

Claudette said a thousand francs.

The band began to play *Parlez-moi d'Amour* and the girls suggested we dance. I refused, but Pete and Mimi got up and sashayed about the floor. After our second expensive drink, Pete, Mimi and Claudette went upstairs and I went home on foot.

CHAPTER THIRTEEN

CHARLES GATES DAWES came to Paris from London and I was assigned to interview him. A Chicago banker, he had served as vice president under Calvin Coolidge and was at that time U.S. Ambassador to the Court of St. James. I met him at the Gare St. Lazare. He had just come from London.

The public image of a banker was a humorless, conservative fellow who smoked a big cigar, smiled thinly when you made a deposit and glowered when you wanted a loan. Dawes was certainly not like that. He was gracious, charming and debonair. When I began to interview him he interrupted and apologized, saying he was late for an appointment with Jo Davidson, who had been commissioned by the U.S. government to sculpt a bust of him for the Senate Gallery. "Why don't you come to Davidson's studio?" he said. "We can have a chat there while I'm posing." I was delighted.

A maid ushered me into the studio, where the ambassador was sitting in a straight-backed chair on a platform. Davidson, a muscular, dynamic man, was hacking away at a block of marble. When I came in

Dawes was talking about a visit he had recently made to an archaeological dig of pre-Ice Age people in the south of France. He interrupted himself to introduce me to Davidson, and to Lincoln Steffens, the muckraker and humorist, who also happened to be there. He then continued his story, saying he had concluded from the evidence he had seen that today's homo sapiens should not consider themselves important. "That goes for pontiffs, princes and politicians," he said, and chuckled. "We are all mere plankton on the waves of time."

I asked him for permission to quote that remark.

"Oh, no," he said, with a wry smile. "I'm afraid it would offend some of my colleagues in Washington. But it's true: mankind would be better off and life would be a lot more enjoyable if people—especially so-called big shots and muckety-mucks—took themselves less seriously."

I said I thought this comment from a person of stature should be recorded. Steffens agreed with me.

Dawes went on posing for a couple of hours and then invited all of us to lunch with him at the Ritz. Midway through his martini he consented to let me quote him. After lunch I hurried to the office and wrote the story. It carried my by-line and was picked up by the wire services and reprinted around the world.

That wasn't the only fortuitous thing that happened to me because of my acquaintance with Charles Gates Dawes. It was through him that I met Patricia Warington. While in Paris, he gave a cocktail party in his suite at the Ritz and invited me. She was there. Her father was an associate of Dawes and she had come to Paris with her mother to study music and steep herself in culture. I set out at once to charm her, only to learn she was engaged to be married. Her fiancé, Count Charles de Rouselle, was in the south of France, so I invited her to be my partner in a bridge game with Elliot Paul and his new wife. She accepted.

The bridge party took place the night before I was to leave for Nancy with Ambassador Edge who was to receive an honorary degree at the university there. It was after midnight when I took her home. Both Patricia and I were pretty tight, which may be why she permitted me to kiss her goodnight. I had to get to the Gare de l'Est early. I overslept and didn't have time even for a cup of coffee to assuage my hangover. I went to the station by subway, lugging a suitcase containing my tuxedo for the ceremonial party, a typewriter and an overcoat. I got to the station about two minutes to nine and ran through the gate without a ticket. The train was already moving; I shoved my typewriter and case onto the platform of the last car, gripped a handrail and swung myself aboard. Recovering my breath, I picked up my possessions, walked down the corridor to a compartment and stashed my luggage on the rack. Folding my overcoat over it, I bade the two other passengers *"Bon Jour"* and went through several cars, including the diner, to the ambassador's private car.

Press attaché Robert Pell, exclaimed, "Ah ha! There you are! We were wondering what happened to you." The ambassador and his retinue were wearing striped trousers and frock coats. Even the *Tribune* reporter, Kosputh, was tastefully attired in a dark blue suit and tie. I was very much out of place in my brown tweeds and red necktie. All of the seats were taken; I had to perch on the arm of Kosputh's chair.

Ambassador Edge got up, came over and shook my hand. "We thought you'd missed the train," he said. "That would have been a calamity."

"My alarm didn't go off," I said lamely.

It was beginning to rain; big drops spattered the windows, blurring the scene. The red-roofed houses in the villages looked fresh and clean, but the cattle standing in the fields appeared woebegone. At noon we all went into the diner for lunch. Pell, Kosputh, the Naval attaché and I sat at a table together.

Pell ordered the wine, a Strasbourg white. It was very good and my hangover vanished. The food was typical French railroad: hors d'oeuvres, pork chop, lettuce salad, cheese and fruit. During the meal the train stopped at Bar-le-Duc, and by the time we finished we were nearing Nancy.

I got up from the table saying, "I'll get my things," and made my way toward the rear of the train. To my astonishment there was no car behind the diner. I asked the steward what had happened to the rear cars. He said they had been switched off at Bar-le-Duc. My typewriter, suitcase and overcoat were gone. I felt helpless and frantic, like one who has come home to find his house on fire.

The platform at Nancy was covered with red carpet; lined up was a reception committee of dignitaries in long-tailed coats and stove-pipe hats. Behind them stood a troop of brass-helmeted soldiers in dress regalia. As the train glided to a stop a band struck up "The Star Spangled Banner."

The moment the porter opened the ambassador's car door I, in my anguish, leaped down the steps before anyone else and strode up and down the front of the reception committee shouting, *"Où est le chef de gare? Où est le chef de gare?"* The city and university officials stared at me aghast. The appearance of the ambassador was anti-climatic. I told the station master what had happened. He promised to do what he could to rescue my belongings. The ambassador and his party were ceremoniously received by the relieved dignitaries and taken to waiting automobiles. I did not go with them.

Since I could not attend the ceremonial party in my tweeds. I had to eat dinner alone in a small café. My only saving grace was: the next day news was scarce and my story was played on the front page.

I returned to Paris. Days went by and I heard nothing of my lost effects. Then one morning I got a call from Pell at the Embassy; my suitcase, typewriter and overcoat had been returned, "from somewhere in Russia"!

PETE INVITED Sparrow and me to the races at Longchamps. Sparrow told us that he knew more about betting on horses than anyone alive and Pete wanted him to prove it. "The only way to bet on horses," Sparrow said, "is to get to the trainers and jockeys; otherwise, it's a losin' proposition. All of them are my pals."

Before each race he conferred with his horsy friends, getting the dope. Pete and I bet the way he did. Pete extravagantly; Sparrow and I moderately. We bet every race but won only a couple. Each time we lost, Sparrow blamed the condition of the track, the misjudgment of the trainer or the dishonesty of the jockey.

After the races, Sparrow and I went with Pete to the Continental Hotel, he having offered to take us to dinner. When we went to the desk for him to get his key, the concierge said, "Mister Emerald, there are two gentlemen here to see you."

Pete stiffened.

"From the *Sûreté.*"

"What the hell is that?"

"The police," I said.

The concierge signaled to two men in plain clothes and they came over. The taller showed his credentials and in English asked, "Are you Mister Emerald?"

"Yes."

"We'd like to speak to you privately."

"These are my friends," Pete said, indicating Sparrow and me. Sparrow and I showed our press cards and Sparrow, addressing the policemen, said, "What's the matter, pals?"

The tall inspector drew forth an official document and handed it to Pete. Unable to read it, Pete handed it to me. I read it, looked at him and said, "You've got twenty-four hours to get out of France."

"Why?"

The inspector said, "You are wanted in New York. May I see your passport?"

Pete dropped his passport on the table. It was issued to John Diamond, aged thirty-three and bore Pete's picture.

"You're John Diamond?"

"If that's what it says."

"Come with us."

Pete looked at Sparrow and me. "I guess this is goodbye," he said.

The next day a policeman escorted him to Cherbourg and put him aboard a freighter bound for Philadelphia.

Some months later I read that while he was driving a car on a road not far from his farm near Acra, New York, he was shot and killed.

CHAPTER FOURTEEN

GOVERNOR FRANKLIN DELANO ROOSEVELT OF New York
came to Paris on vacation, and I was assigned to interview
him. I met him when he arrived at the Gare St. Lazare. With him was
his son James who helped him off the train into a wheelchair. Governor
Roosevelt greeted me graciously and answered my questions as I
strolled along beside him. He said he had fled to Paris to get away from
politics.

"How about the rumor you plan to run for president?"

He smiled and patted his legs. "I can't run," he said.

"That's not true," James said. "If they want him to run, he'll run."

"Pay no attention to him," Roosevelt said. "He's my son."

"It's a good quote," I said.

"Then quote him, not me."

I wrote the story and put in on Spencer Bull's desk. He was the new
city editor—a short, stocky man with a shock of white hair. He had
been a newsman in Paris for several years and had been hired the day
before by Laurence Hills, the director of the *Herald.* Bull's reputation

had been permanently affected by a story he had produced when he was a rewrite man for the Paris edition of the *Chicago Tribune*. He was given a routine story that had come in from the British Embassy about the dedication by the Prince of Wales of an orphanage for children of British soldiers who had served in France. Bull was told to liven the story up a little. He did. He created a scene in which the Prince, inspecting the orphanage, stopped to ask a little boy how he liked his new home. "What the hell do you care, you rich son-of-a-bitch?" the child said. And Bull, in the throes of inspiration, added, *Whereupon the Prince hauled off and gave the tyke a belt with his swagger stick.* Somehow this story was printed in the *Tribune*. The result was to be expected: Bull was fired.

"Here's one of the best political stories of the year," I said, jokingly.

Bull read it and looked up at me. "The American people will never put a cripple in the White House."

When I left the office a cold wind was blowing torrential rain. In front of the hotel across the rue de Berri a uniformed porter, huddled under a small, lop-sided umbrella, was frantically trying to summon a taxi by blowing a whistle. I turned up the collar of my coat and headed for the Champs Elysées. There I took shelter under a café awning and eventually a taxi stopped at the curb to discharge a passenger, and I dove headlong into its shelter.

We crossed the Seine over the beautiful Pont Alexander III. Patricia Warington and her mother lived in an expensive apartment house in the fashionable district near the Chambre des Députés. Mrs. Warington opened the door. A small woman, her white hair rolled in a chignon, she smelled of lilacs. She said that Patricia, whom I was to take to dine, was dressing. The living room was impressive. It contained a grand piano and paintings by El Greco and Holbein. French windows led onto a terrace and even through the rain one could see the lights of Des Invalides and Sacré Coeur.

After we had exchanged pleasantries, I said, "I'm very disappointed that Patricia is going to marry that Frenchman. I'm going to try and talk her out of it."

"He's a member of one of France's oldest families. I'm afraid she's made up her mind."

"It's the classic story: rich American girl marries poor nobleman with title."

"His family owns property in Avignon."

"He's much older than she, isn't he?"

"Yes—in his forties."

Patricia came in beautifully dressed saying, "Sorry I'm late." Her mother excused herself and left the room. Patricia poured scotch and we clicked glasses. I said, "Here's to your upcoming error."

"Error!" she laughed musically. "Don't be silly."

"Why don't you marry someone in your age group, one of your own kind?"

"I have a better idea," she said. Her eyes glinted, "I'll marry Charles and take a lover."

I said, "Great idea! When do we start?"

I GOT TO THE Mairie early for the wedding, and was waiting outside when the principals arrived in a taxi. The Count alighted first. In attempting to help Mrs. Warington, she lost her footing and fell against the Marquis de Chambrun, whose silk hat fell into the gutter. Count Charles was of medium height, had rather short legs, a large midriff and a somewhat puffy, pink face. His coattails nearly touched the ground. When he removed his hat his toupée was obvious.

I followed them up the stairs and into a small auditorium where rows of chairs faced a dais on which was a high desk draped with a French flag. After we were seated, the mayor appeared. He wore a heavy silver chain around his neck, bowed slightly, said, *"Bonjour, Messieurs, 'Dames,"* and sat down behind the desk.

We all responded *"Bonjour, Monsieur,"* in ragged chorus.

The Mayor then spent some moments studying papers, and we sat motionlessly waiting. Presently the Mayor asked the bride and groom to rise, which they did. They were then subjected to a long speech concerning the joys of marriage, the dangers and delights of passion and the importance of fidelity. The ceremony was brief and after the couple were pronounced man and wife an attendant went through the assembled carrying a collection box and chanting, *Pour les pauvres! Pour les pauvres!* Because it was customary to pay the Mayor in advance, I assumed the collection was truly for the poor. The Mayor descended, shook hands with the groom, kissed the bride on both cheeks, wished them luck and retired.

We went directly to the Warington apartment for the reception. The Count's servants, Ambrose and Nana, were there. Nana proved to be quite deaf. She was English and spoke little French and Ambrose was French and spoke little English. Piled in the hall were suitcases, valises and boxes in various states of decrepitude. Patricia told me that most of them did not belong to the Count but to his servants. They were all moving in. Apparently the Count's possessions consisted of his title and his servants.

As I left the party I congratulated the Count and, taking Patricia aside, whispered, "When do we start?"

She laughed, put a finger to her lips and whispered, *"A bientôt."*

It was tomfoolery, silly-talk. The whole idea was ridiculous.

CHAPTER FIFTEEN

THE ENTERTAINING OF VISITING firemen was—and probably still is—one of the minor annoyances for Americans living in Paris. Hardly a week passed during the tourist season that someone didn't come to see me with a letter of introduction from relatives, friends, or casual acquaintances. Sometimes the letter writer was little known to me. "Going to Paris? Look up old John. He'll show you the town."

Speed Denlinger, a friend of mine on the *New York World-Telegram,* sent me one such visitor. Her name was Rhea Gore Huston. Rhea had been working for the *New York Graphic,* a yellow sheet, and had come to Paris to get another newspaper job. I took her to my favorite restaurant on the rue Jacob for châteaubriands and a bottle of Côte de Rhône rouge. While we ate, she talked incessantly about her son John and his father, an actor named Walter Huston, of whom I had never heard. She told me how she and Walter had met in 1904 in St. Louis where she was a theatrical reporter and he was performing in *The Sign of the Cross.*

"I watched the show and when I went backstage to interview the star," she said, "I ran into this handsome young man. I didn't remember having seen him on the stage and asked if he was in the show. He said he was; he played the old Christian, the fellow with the whiskers who carries the staff. I couldn't believe it. I said, 'You mean that old man was you? I'd never have known it.'

"We went to an ice cream parlor. I told him I wanted to write plays and he was very encouraging. After that, while the show was in town we saw each other almost every day. We went to the World's Fair, we roller-skated, bicycled, visited penny arcades and had our fortunes told. The gypsy told me I was going to marry a rich man and have five children, and become famous. Well, I married Walter who wasn't rich, and we had only one child, John. I never became famous—but Walter did."

"Are you still married to him?"

"No. We were divorced long ago."

She was not really interested in talking about Walter; she much preferred talking about John. A book he had written, based on the folk song *Frankie and Johnny*, had recently been published with illustrations by Miguel Covarrubias, an upcoming Mexican artist. She considered this one of the important literary events of all time. She told me that writing was only one of John's talents, that he would make a strong mark in the world.

I had never heard a doting parent brag so shamelessly and was bored to distraction. I certainly did not believe that anyone—with the possible exception of myself—could be as lavishly talented as Rhea Huston insisted her son was. I could not even break into her encomium to tell her about the book I had recently finished. When I finally mentioned it she did not respond. She just went on talking about John. I gave her the names of some people who might be able to help her get a job. But she was not successful and, after a relatively brief time, she went back to New York. I never saw her again, but I did meet John Huston. He and I eventually became close friends. We were having dinner together the night his mother died.

I wrote to my mother about Rhea Huston and asked her if she spent a lot of time extolling my virtues. I was relieved when she replied that, when she spoke of me she tended to be complimentary, but brief.

Another visiting fireman that spring was Maxwell Bodenheim, the author of *Replenishing Jessica* and *Georgie May*, among other novels. I had known Max in Greenwich Village. We had both lived in the same apartment house on Barrow Street. He had been born in Mississippi. He looked me up as soon as he arrived in Paris. He was in financial difficulties. He had come to Europe with a girl and she had deserted him in Antwerp, taking most of his money.

"Do you know where she went?" I asked.

"I believe Capri. With a woman she met on the ship. I was going to marry her."

"Lucky you found out in time."

"It's demeaning to have a dame walk out on you, especially after you've paid her way over here."

"I thought you were an expert on female psychology."

His bloodshot eyes gazed sadly at me. "There is no such a one, not even Kraft-Ebbing."

Max moved in with me until he could get some money and that night we went to the Trianon Restaurant because Max was eager to meet James Joyce and the Joyces sometimes dined there. Joyce wasn't there that night, but Ludwig Lewisohn was, and I introduced them. Max was pleased to meet another Jewish writer. During dinner Max told Ludwig and me about *Naked on Roller Skates,* a novel he had just finished. He talked about Sacco and Vanzetti. Their trial and the appeals had gone on for years and Max, along with many others, believed the two men had been executed for political reasons.

As we were leaving the restaurant, Max went ahead while I paid the check. An American who had been sitting at a nearby table took me aside and asked, "Who is that fellow you're with?"

I told him.

"Well," he said, "whatever he's trying to sell, don't buy it."

As soon as we reached the street Max said, "What did that guy want?"

"He wanted to know who you are," I said tactfully. "I told him you're a famous writer."

"I didn't like his looks."

Max reminds me of a couple of other similar types I knew in Paris. One was Harold Sterns. Harold was an intellectual who talked well, sometimes brilliantly, but lacked self-confidence and never really accomplished much. He had been the shining light of the *New Republic* but apparently New York became too confining for a person of his talents and he came to Paris. He worked for awhile on the *Herald,* but he was not an easy person to get on with and was fired. Then he became obsessed with horse racing and made daily racing selections for the *Tribune* under the name of Peter Pickem. That job didn't last long either and after that he spent most of his time cadging food and drink from whomever he could, before making his way back to New York.

Another poseur was Mike Romanoff, who had been born in Brooklyn and claimed to be a Russian prince. He had only one talent, charm, but he had plenty of that. He could turn it on whenever he needed it. He became something of a minor celebrity in Paris because of his ability to eat and drink without spending any money. Newcomers found him entertaining and bought him drinks. People who invited him to parties quickly learned what old-timers had long known: he was adhesive, difficult to remove. He had no permanent address and slept wherever he happened to be. I don't know where he kept his few belongings—I do know that he always carried a toothbrush and comb. He turned up at my place shortly after I met him, saying that he wanted to take a bath. He did, and stayed with me for more than a week. When he found another host, he left, remarking that what he had really appreciated about his stay with me was being able to get his laundry done.

Montparnasse swarmed with Americans who lived on stipends sent from home. They were supposed to be working on artistic or literary projects, but the vast majority of them spent most of their time sitting at sidewalk cafes, drinking Pernods, talking endlessly, and watching the world go by. There were notable exceptions, of course. One was Alexander Calder, who lived in my neighborhood. He was a plump young man, seven years older than I, who had studied engineering in college but had come to Paris to paint, having been influenced by the work of Joan Miró.

The first things one noticed in his place were several wire and metal chip concoctions hanging from the ceiling. They were in motion, and he considered them avant sculpture. He was very proud of them. I thought he was pretty childish and this opinion was reinforced by the entertainment he provided his guests: a miniature circus. No one in his right mind, I thought, could expect this kind of nonsense to be accepted as art. To me Calder needed psychiatric help. These concoctions were of course the first of Calder's "mobiles," the name suggested by Marcel Duchamp. It never entered my head that anyone would ever take them seriously.

COUNTESS PATRICIA and her husband spent their honeymoon on the Riviera. Weeks went by. Then one listless afternoon she called me at the office. I was overwhelmed with surprise and delight. The next day was my day off and we met at *La Cloiserie des Lilas* just down the avenue Montparnasse from my lodgings.

When I arrived she was sitting behind a table in the bar and looked more beautiful than ever. I greeted her, "My darling *Comptessa!*" and kissed her hand. "This is a pleasant surprise!" I ordered Pernods and asked "How goes the matrimony?"

She uttered a brief laugh, shrugged and said, "Oh, so so. I'm getting used to it."

"I warned you," I said.

"Charles is all right. He's kind of old fashioned. He's never worked in his life and is with me twenty-four hours a day. His servants are something of a nuisance. They don't take care of me; I take care of them."

"Do you have to pay them?"

"Oh, yes. Charles has very little money."

"I don't get it," I said. "Beautiful young lady, intelligent and rich, gives herself up to an old fogey just because he has a spurious title."

"It's not spurious; it's for real."

"How is he in bed?"

"Oh, about average, I guess."

"What about us? When are you going to keep your promise?"

"How about this afternoon?"

We went to my quarters. Later, when I offered to take her home she said, "Better not. Charles is extremely jealous."

Thereafter she came to my place several times, telling her husband that she was taking painting lessons at the Ecole des Beaux Arts. One afternoon we were having tea in my apartment, both fortunately fully dressed, when there was a knock on the door. I was dumbfounded to face Charles. Behind him stood a swarthy fellow with an abundant bristly mustache.

"Well, hello Charles!" I said. "Please come in. You're just in time for tea."

Charles pushed past me without speaking. His companion followed him, shut the door and stood against it with his arms folded.

"Is this your art school?" Charles said to Patricia.

Her face was very white, but she answered calmly. "Actually I've just come from there."

"I happen to know that you did nothing of the sort." He indicated his companion. "This person is a detective; he has been following you."

"Really, Charles!" she said. Probably it was all she could think of to say, and I was speechless.

"What are you doing here?"

"Having tea, as you see."

He scooped up her coat from the settee. "You're going home right now."

"Why are you so upset?" Patricia asked and got up.

"I don't like being lied to."

She snatched her coat from him. "You're being very rude. There's nothing more innocent than a tea party."

Charles turned his attention to me. Now his face was red and his round chin was quivering. "As for you," he said, shaking a forefinger, "you will hear from me."

I said, "I'll look forward to it," in a weak attempt to mollify him.

The next day when I got home from work the concierge handed me a note. It was from Charles on his embossed stationery.

You have insulted and humiliated me. I challenge you to a duel with foils. Be at the Porte d'Anteuil Saturday at 6 A.M. I will bring the foils.

My first reaction was that it sounded like a joke. Charles couldn't be serious. He was forty-odd years old and overweight, while I was a pretty good athlete. I had learned fencing as a stunt man in Hollywood. It was a dangerous sport; one of us could be hurt. I decided I would ignore the challenge, but when I told Elliot Paul about it, he advised me to go. "It's an ancient custom in France," he said. "Today it's against the law, but the police don't really give a damn. What this guy wants is to humiliate you."

"Humiliate, hell!" I said. "He wants to kill me."

"Oh, no. That would be ungentlemanly. All he wants to do is carve his initials on your belly." He smiled. "I'd offer to serve as your second, but I can't get up at that ungodly hour. The only one who is up then is Sparrow. Ask him. He'll do it to get an item for his column."

Sparrow agreed and about five-thirty on Saturday morning I engaged a taxicab by a Russian named Igbagnatchev and we picked him up at the *Herald* office. He had not been to bed that night but was in fine fettle. On the way to the Porte d'Auteuil we stopped at a bistro for coffee to warm us up. The zinc bar was crowded with men on their way to work. We sweetened our coffee with brandy like everybody else. Sparrow had to go to the toilet before we got going again. There was very little traffic. A squat, green streetcar was almost empty.

At the Port d'Auteuil we spotted a large, shiny, black limousine. "Pull up beside it," I said to the Russian. I got out of the cab and looked into the back seat. Charles, wearing a top hat and overcoat and a white silk muffler around his neck, was sitting with the Marquis de Chambrun.

"Good morning," I said, with forced cheerfulness.

"You're late," Charles said. "Follow me."

I got back into the taxi and we followed the limousine down a road leading into the woods. We stopped in a secluded area surrounded by tall pines. Everybody got out of the cars. The scene was unreal, like a movie set. "I think it's too foggy to fence," Sparrow said.

I went up to Charles, who was removing his overcoat. "I beg your pardon," I said politely, "but I would like to know the rules of this game. How do we begin and when do we stop?"

"We stop when you are unable to continue," Charles said. He handed his overcoat to the Marquis and began to remove his jacket. He looked at me with contempt. "When the first blood is drawn, that will be the winning sign."

Sparrow came up to us. "Come on, pals," he said. "I'm freezing. Let's get on with it."

The Marquis offered the foils. Trying to lighten the atmosphere, I said to Charles, "Sparrow Robinson is my second. He won't permit me to proceed unless he is guaranteed the newspaper rights."

"You won't want the publicity," Charles said taking the foils from the Marquis. Holding the tip-ends with his left hand, he presented their handles to me over his right arm. I hurried out of my jacket, tossed it to Sparrow, and chose one. Its handle, in the shape of a figure eight, was backed with a piece of leather. Charles walked away and turned to stand facing me, balancing the point of his weapon on the toe of his right shoe. I did likewise.

"Ready, gentlemen?" the Marquis asked. "On guard!" We raised our foils. "Go!"

Charles feinted once, and I parried. He lunged forward with surprising agility thrusting at my chest; I parried with high prime. He withdrew quickly and riposted. My salvation obviously depended on defense, so I kept parrying, trying to keep him off balance. He moved with extreme dexterity. The whish of metal in the silent grove was a chilling sound. I made a long thrust; he backed and riposted so quickly that he barely missed my face. Soon I noticed he was perspiring, though he showed no signs of slowing down; indeed, he increased his pace, thrusting and riposting, and I had to use every ounce of my wit and agility to keep ahead of him.

"You've done this before," I said, still trying to mollify him.

The chauffeurs were arguing about which of us would win. The Russian had the louder voice. The clash of the foils continued. Thrust, parry, riposte, recoil. To my relief I could see that Charles was tiring. His thrusts were not as swift and frequent. He was breathing through his mouth. "You can stop whenever you like," I said hopefully, which caused him to begin another flurry.

After we had been fencing for about fifteen minutes it became obvious that we were merely going through the motions.

"Hey, why don't you gentlemen stop this foolishness?" Sparrow said, and Igbagnatchev said something in Russian.

Suddenly Charles stepped back and lowered his foil.

I lowered mine also. "Is that it?" I asked.

The Marquis said, "It is over. My friend's honor is satisfied."

"Permit me to apologize for offending you," I said to Charles.

He grunted and wiped his face with a white handkerchief. "Where did you learn to fence?" he asked.

"In Hollywood," I said. "John Barrymore taught me." It was the truth.

His bulging eyes studied my face for a moment. "You surprise me," he said.

We began to put on our jackets. "Let's go get a drink," Sparrow said, and that is what we all did. Suddenly the atmosphere was friendly.

Sparrow's account of the contest did not identify the contestants:

One of my pals was challenged to a duel by a titled gentleman whom he had inexplicably offended. I went along as his second. The foiling was done among the fallen leaves of the Bois de Boulogne the other morning before the cocks began to crow. It was a contest to behold and went on until both adversaries got petered. Neither of the gentlemen won or was injured and in the end they kissed and made up. We all went to a fashionable saloon and had a champagne peace party. It was great fun.

Of course, the gossips found out who the principals were and I got flack from my confrères. The whole episode was ludicrous and it ended my brief affair with Patricia. She and the Count went to live in *Juan les Pins*. The last time I heard from her she told me she had fallen in love with a dentist.

As for me, another lady soon came into my life.

CHAPTER SIXTEEN

I MET LACY KASTNER, European head of United Artists, when Charles Chaplin came to Paris to promote his film *City Lights*. I interviewed Chaplin and wrote some nice things about him and his picture. Thereafter Lacy and his wife Pricilla often invited me to their house in Neuilly, particularly when, for a dinner party, they needed another man. Through them I met a number of notables, most of whom were in the film world. One was Nan Sunderland. She was tall, about five feet nine, had auburn hair and her nose and cheeks were sprinkled with freckles. She was several years older than I. After we had shaken hands I said, "Pricilla tells me you're an actress. What kind?"

"Of the theater," she said, smiling.

"What are you doing in Paris?"

"On my last lap of a trip around the world."

"Alone?"

"Perforce. I'm engaged to be married, but the gentleman involved is getting a divorce and doesn't want me around until it's settled. He and his wife were in vaudeville together and, now that he's become successful in two movies, she doesn't want to let him go. If she knew I was waiting in the wings she'd demand more money."

"What's the gentleman's name?"

"Walter Huston."

"That's a coincidence," I said. "I'd never heard of him until recently, when his ex-wife brought me a letter of introduction. Her name is Rhea Gore Huston."

"That's his first one. She's the mother of their son, John. It's his second wife he's divorcing. Bayonne Whipple. They had a very successful vaudeville act."

"Rhea bored me to death talking about their son John. Do you know him?"

"Yes. We've met."

"Is he a genius?"

"I wouldn't say so. He's different, can be charming."

It was a pleasant evening. As always at the Kastner's, the food was delicious, the conversation was uppertalk and the wines superb. When the other guests had left, Lacy asked me if I would escort Nan back to her hotel.

"It's on the rue Jacob, near San Germain des Près. That's on your way home."

"I'll consider it a privilege," I said.

Lacy whispered, "Don't forget—she's engaged to be married." He summoned a taxi.

Soon after we were under way, Nan, to my utter surprise, turned my face with her hands and kissed me on the lips. "There," she said. "That's for taking me home."

I was nonplused, elated, aroused and emboldened. "One kiss deserves another," I said, and we kissed again, more fervently this time. "How long are you going to be in Paris?" I asked.

"I really don't know. I'll be signaled when the coast is clear."

"Well, you don't want to be by yourself while you're here. You'll need an escort. I hereby apply for the job."

"I'd love it," she said. "I've been by myself for almost four months, ever since I sailed from Los Angeles."

"That's the plight of sailors who've long been at sea."

She laughed nervously and took my hand in both of hers. "We'll just be friends," she said, "have fun together, share expenses. We mustn't forget that I'm going to be married."

"I'll do my best," I said, "but it's not going to be easy."

And it wasn't. Passion kept popping up, testing our moral strengths. Wine weakened us too. Some mornings we were together for an hour or two and we spent all our evenings together. We were here, there and everywhere, the while concentratedly trying to keep our relationship platonic.

But there was a fervent, intoxicating magnetism between us that proved to be such a powerful force it would have been a small miracle if we had not succumbed to blissful conjugation. Our brief affair cast no dishonor on her. She had made no promise to be chaste. We simply enjoyed a rare and delightful opportunity to indulge a fling without hurting anyone. We never discussed the propriety of it. I don't think Nan ever felt any guilt. I certainly didn't. We were healthy, sophisticated adults and keenly aware that we had but a short time to be together.

Nan enhanced my life. She was a delightful companion. While I worked she went to the Alliance Française to learn French; when I was free we touched the bases and high spots. I did not get much serious work done. My stunting book suffered. I had titled it *Men are April When They Woo*, from Shakespeare's *As You Like It*. I realized I was playing second fiddle and that the performance time was short, so I did a lot of wooing. We visited art galleries, went to theaters and one and two star restaurants, sat on cafe terraces and watched the world go by.

Nan was interested in the literary scene. I introduced her to Ford Madox Ford, Ludwig Lewisohn and Elliot Paul. Eugene O'Neill came to town from his place at Cap d'Antibes and she was overjoyed and awed to meet him. I took her to Shakespeare & Company, the becoming-famous bookstore on the rue de l'Odéon. Sylvia Beach, its proprietor, served us tea and told how she had come to publish James Joyce's *Ulysses*.

"Joyce always had difficulty getting his work published," she said. "*The Little Review* in New York began publishing *Ulysses* in segments, but censors ruled it obscene. Joyce was heartbroken and I felt sorry for him. In a wild moment I offered to publish the entire manuscript. I didn't realize what I was getting into. It was almost four hundred thousand words of manuscript—in English of course—and his proof revisions and corrections drove the French printers mad. It took almost a year to produce the book and it was riddled with typographical errors."

She told us the first edition ran to nine hundred pages and was printed on cheap paper. It sold for sixty francs, a high price for a book at that time. However, it sold well. Tourists by the hundreds bought it for what they considered its scatological passages and smuggled it home. It was banned in both England and the United States.

Pricilla and Lacy Kastner invited Nan and me to lunch with them in a restaurant outside of Paris and picked us up in a large chauffeur-driven limousine. With them were Gordon and Mary Ellen Pollock. Gordon, tall and classically handsome with curly white hair and vivid blue eyes, was an outstanding cinematographer and was working on a United Artists film being shot in Europe. His wife was a darling. The chauffeur was diminutive about five feet tall, and thin. He wore a necktie, a jacket, a visored cap and horn-rimmed glasses. The skin of his face was pale and did not seem to have any whiskers. Nan whispered that he looked like a woman.

The restaurant was a remodeled ancient mill. Restoration had turned it into a luxurious haven. We were seated at a table under a huge elm at the fork of two brooks. Before lunch was served, I excused myself and went to the w.c. While there the chauffeur entered. I paid little attention to him, but as I was buttoning my fly I looked up to see him squatting over a hole in the floor which served as a toilet. Because he had not used a urinal, I asked, "Are you all right?"

He looked up at me and smiled. *"Je suis une femme."*

Taken aback, I apologized. *"Pardonnez moi."*

"Ça ne fait rien, monsieur."

I did not know what to say, so I said, *"Bon chance,"* which was silly.

"Bon appétit," she said as I left.

On our way back to town after a sumptuous lunch I whispered to Nan: "You were right. The chauffeur is a female."

The driver overheard me, *"Oui,"* she said and went on to tell us that she dressed like a man because it was dangerous for a woman to drive a taxi, particularly at night. She came from Nice and her child was living there with her grandmother. She had been separated from her husband for five years. She said she worked as many as sixteen hours a day, seven days a week, saving money so that she could go back to Nice and open a bistro.

I saw the Pollocks several times in Paris and later, when I returned to Hollywood, we became close friends.

Nan and I usually met at the Deux Magots after I got through working. One evening when I joined her she handed me a cablegram: *Hallelujah! Coast is clear. Hurry home. Walter.*

She said, "I've arranged to sail tomorrow on the *President Garfield.*"

"This calls for a celebration and a mourning," I said.

We had dinner at Lipp's and went to the Viking so that she could say goodbye to our friend Billie, the bartender. I saw her to her hotel and we kissed goodbye, lovers no longer. The next morning I accompanied her to the depot. While waiting for the train to start, I asked her to call my mother when she got to New York and she kissed me for the last time. I helped her aboard.

"This is not the end of our friendship," she said as the train pulled away. "You're going to sell your book to the movies and come to Hollywood!"

She was a prophet. A few days later I received a letter from Jean Wick. What I read staggered me. McBride had accepted my stunt-man novel and there was an advance-royalty check for $300.

I have secured a contract for you to write a scenario for Columbia Pictures. They want you to do one about a stunt man. Salary two hundred dollars a week. I've told them you'll report for work within a month, so start packing. . . .

I had the urge to weep and laugh at the same time. It was ironical. During the three years I had spent in Hollywood I had tried my utmost to get any kind of a job in a scenario department. No one would have me, not even as a janitor.

The day before my departure I went to say goodbye to James Joyce, who as usual was at work in his cluttered study.

Though he did not like interruptions, he greeted me amiably. "So, you're going to write for the movies. I understand that's quite profitable."

Jesting, I said, "I'm going to adapt *Ulysses* for the screen."

"I hope you do. I'll get some royalty."

"I trust your work is going well."

"Slowly, po'ly," he said, giving the words a Southern pronunciation he had learned from me. He did not like to talk about his work-in-progress, but he was always ready to talk about his method of operation. He believed himself to be the most laborious writer who ever lived and may have been. He spent hours every day researching, reading and making notes from books and periodicals in several languages. "I go slowly," he said, "because writing doesn't come easily for me." The truth is, he went slowly because of his poor eyesight. He had had numerous eye operations and often was fearful that he would never be able to write again. For him that would have been like dying.

I thanked him for his advice and counsel.

"What have you learned?" he asked.

"I've learned to explore and to concentrate on the unusual, to avoid the trite and to work assiduously."

"I hope you have also learned to school yourself against discouragement. As long as you're alive, there is no failure."

I shook his bony hand, wished him well and promised to send him a copy of *Men Are April When They Woo*. He said he liked the title.

I made the rounds, saying goodbye to the Kastners, Ford Madox Ford, Alex Calder, Jacques Lipshitz, Sylvia Beach, and people at the embassy and the consulate, where my close friend, Robert Murphy, was vice-consul. Bob was working his way up the diplomatic pole, having started as a clerk in the United States Post Office. He would become a public figure during World War Two as a negotiator of the Murphy-Weygang accords.

I also bade farewell to my laundress, who lived and did her washing in back of the rue Du Lambre police station. A large, shapeless woman, she always had more work to do than she had energy. I gave her a hundred franc note and she kissed my hand.

The night before I was to leave, my colleagues, Elliot Paul, George Rehm and Tommy Cope, joined me for a farewell fling at our favorite watering holes. We started at Harry's New York Bar. From there we went to the Silver Ring. We hit Otto's and Johnny's before going to Les Halles for onion soup. On the way home I stopped at the Café du Dôme for old time's sake. I was sipping a cup of coffee when a taxi rolled up and two expensively dressed women and a man alighted. They were typical American tourists. I was astonished to recognize one of the ladies as my ex-wife Betty. The recognition came like a thunderclap and she was equally astonished to see me. I had the feeling that her immediate reaction was embarrassment. I needed a shave, my hair could have been improved by clipping and my attire, to say the best for it, was casual. We shook hands and she permitted me a cheek-peck before introducing me to her companions and identifying me as her former husband.

I joined them and, hoping to impress Betty, boasted about working on the *Herald* and having a book of mine accepted for publication. "Would you believe it?" I asked her. "I've gotten a contract to write for the movies and I'm going back to Hollywood."

"That's a switch!" Betty exclaimed, and to her friends: "When we were married and poor as mice he did his best to become a scenarist."

"I leave tomorrow on the *Acquitania*," I said.

It turned out that Betty and her friends were also aboard the *Acquitania*, but in first class. Tourist passengers, of which I was one, were not permitted free access in the first class section, but the second night out, Betty managed to have me join her for dinner. We had cocktails in the lounge before the great fireplace and I learned that she was married to a partner in the John Pierpont Morgan Company and had come to Europe to visit her sister in Düsseldorf. When we went into the dining room the maitre'd' gave us the VIP treatment and we were given a special printed menu:

MRS. E. THURSTON CLARKE *&* GUEST
TUESDAY, APRIL 19, 1932

Grapefruit Cocktail · Consommé Daumont

Homard à la Newberg

Noisettes d'Agneau rôti

Haricots verts sauté

Asperges Hollandaise

Chocolat Soufflé

Fromages · Fruits · Demi tasse

Betty and I rehashed our experiences together and I learned she had a child, a boy two years old, "cute as a button." I thought of the child we might have had but did not speak of it. We talked of her brother-in-law, the German novelist, Hanns Heinz Ewers, and James Joyce.

It was a pleasant evening. The resentment between us disappeared and some of the affection that had bound us came back. I got glimpses of her several times during the cruise but we did not get together again. When we reached New York I looked in vain for her in the customs area to bid her goodbye. Apparently her husband had whisked her away. I am sure she was pleased not to have to introduce me to him.

CHAPTER SEVENTEEN

W HEN I GOT THROUGH CUSTOMS I went at once to see
Mother, who had moved to New York and was now
pursuing a career as a professional astrologer. Under the nom de plume
Deborah Lewis, she wrote monthly articles on international affairs for
American Astrology. As a child I remember her studying occult reli-
gions. She learned to read Hebrew so that she could delve into the
Talmud and Gemara. She was intuitive. She believed in immortality
and had a firm conviction that she once had lived in China.

Because she was five feet two, I had to stoop to hug her. She always
showed me strong affection, but inately she did not like the responsibility of children, which is why, as a child, I had been shunted from one
place to another.

Bringing forth a chilled bottle of champagne, she said, "Been saving
it for this important occasion."

After clicking glasses and her "Welcome home" toast, I asked, "Tell
me, Madame Clairvoyant, how am I going to do in Hollywood?"

"It's one of the manifestations of Divine Intelligence that we be
ignorant of our destinies," she replied. "If you want to know about

your future, look into yourself. However, it doesn't look too good, because of the Depression. But you might have a romance."

"I'd like to get married and settle down. James Joyce says that writers should marry rich women, that we need angels to support us."

"Marrying a rich woman is a hard way for a man to make a living." Mother mentioned Nan Sunderland, who had come to see her on the way to California to marry Walter Huston. "That's the kind of woman you should marry."

"Perhaps my stars will guide me to one like her."

"The stars won't do it. That's your job."

We went to the Lafayette Hotel for lunch and along with lots of talk about family and friends she told me that a man who had read her magazine articles wrote to her from Canada saying it would be valuable for him to know precisely what day that spring the ice would break sufficiently to permit navigation of the upper MacKenzie River. If she could tell him, he wrote, he would reward her handsomely. "In replying," she said, "I gave him a date but warned him not to bet on it. Lo and behold, the other day I received a check for one hundred dollars from the gentleman. 'You hit it right on the nose!' he wrote. 'That astrology is quite a science.' I wrote back, thanking him, and told him that the date I gave him was a guess, based on an almanac's weather forecast, that it didn't have anything to do with astrology."

"How about the hundred bucks?"

"I kep' it," she saying, eyeing me askance.

After lunch we walked over to Fifth Avenue. She boarded a bus and I went to the Fifth Avenue Hotel to see Jean Wick, my literary agent. Jean was a large, fervid, heartful lady who worked hard and generously to promote her clients. She was married to Achmed Abdullah, a novelist and playwright, who had been born in Yalta of Russian and Afghan ancestry and educated at Eton and Oxford. Jean's office was in their apartment and they were both there when I called. After ebullient greetings, the maid brought us tea. Jean told me that there had been a second printing of *Gun Girl*. She did not know how many copies, but guessed two thousand. "You've already received three hundred dollars advance for the first printing," she said, "and nothing more will be forthcoming for some time. Publishers have a peculiar way of keeping books. They give authors an accounting every six months or so, apparently unaware they and their agents have to eat. I'm supposed to get ten percent of what you'll earn in Hollywood, but I'll only get half of that. I have an agent there, name's Al Cohen. He gets the other half." She gave me his address and telephone number. "He'll take you under his wing."

"How're you going?" Achmed asked.

"By ship through the Canal. It costs about the same as a train and takes a little longer; but it should be more fun."

They wished me well.

THE DECK CHAIR I chose on the SS *Pacific* was next to that of a little man wearing a brown suit, a pink shirt and a purple tie. A straw hat was over his face when I sat down and I thought he was asleep; but presently he tilted the hat to take a furtive glance at me.

"Hello," I said. "Did I waken you?"

He lifted the hat, said, "That's okay."

We introduced ourselves. His name was Charles Snyder. He said he was a dentist from Cincinnati. About him was a furtive shyness which tapped my sympathy. When I questioned him he replied with almost pathetic eagerness. I asked if he was traveling alone.

"Yeh. My wife don't like ships. She can't swim."

I laughed and said, "You don't have to swim on ships."

"She's funny that way. She don't like to get off terra firma. She's goin' to California by train and will meet me there. We haven't had a vacation in seven years, not since we went to New Orleans for Mardi Gras. That time I got sick." He brought forth a wallet, extracted snapshots of a woman and two teenaged girls. "My wife and daughters," he said and, pointing to the prettier of the girls, said, "That's Bernice. She's gonna be a dancer. That's Clara. She plays the piano."

They were all smiling. I said, "They've got nice teeth."

"You got any kids?"

"Not that I know of. I'm not married." He did not react to my attempt at humor.

The sun began setting beyond Delaware as he went on talking. When finally he paused I said, "The sun's over the yardarm. Let's go have a drink."

He quickly declined, saying, "I don't drink."

I thought it odd the way he said it. There was no conviction in the words. "Then you'll please excuse me," I said and got up. "I think I'll have a snort or two. See you later."

During the three days getting to Havana I noted that my dentist friend did not read, did not play deck games and did not join in other passenger activity. When we were approaching Havana, thinking to enliven his day, I asked if he would like to share a taxicab and take a sight-seeing tour. He accepted the invitation so gratefully I was embarrassed.

From the dock we made our way through a horde of children beggars to an English-speaking taxi driver who said he would take us on a three-hour tour for ten dollars. I was eager to visit Sloppy Joe's saloon and try its famous rum punch, so we went there first. When I ordered a punch, Charlie surprised me by saying, "That sounds good. I'll have one, too."

The drink was sweet and mild and tasted so good that he drank his as if it were Coca-Cola. I was still sipping mine when he ordered another. By the time we left the saloon I had become aware of a dramatic change in his personality. Whereas thereto he had been deprecative and obsequious, he had suddenly become overbearing and arrogant. He cursed the children who clustered about us, uttered an obscenity at a comely girl and imperiously directed the taxi driver.

During our tour we visited the Bacardi Distillery and sampled its product, stopped at a winery where we had wine with lunch, and on the way back to the ship guzzled beer at a brewery. We got to the dock shortly before the *Pacific* was scheduled to depart. My companion mumbled something about buying a present for his wife and wandered off, leaving me to pay the taxi driver. I tendered him a ten dollar bill and added a dollar tip, but he refused to accept them, saying the fee was ten dollars per passenger. My hackles stiffened. I had learned that trick in Paris. I tossed the ten dollar bill into the taxi, said, "That's all you're going to get," pocketed the dollar and started to leave. Whereupon the driver summoned the policeman standing nearby, doubtless an accessory to the extortion, and he escorted me to the police station. I went eagerly, certain of justice.

A sergeant in a much-worn uniform leaned back in a chair, feet on the desk, and listened while the taxi driver spoke in Spanish. The sergeant then addressed me in English, asking why I did not pay for the service I had received, saying twenty dollars was a fair price and I would have to pay it. I stated my case and said I would not pay a penny more than the amount agreed upon.

The sergeant sat up, his feet on the floor, and leaned forward. "Don't be a fool," he said earnestly. "If you don't pay it I'll have to send you to jail. You'll miss your ship."

"Let her go," I said grandiloquently and went on to boast that I was a newspaperman and that I could write in jail as well as anywhere else. I said I thought a story of how Cuban taxi drivers gyp tourists would make good reading in the United States. As I was speaking the *Pacific*'s whistle sounded.

My strong declaration of inflexibility gave the sergeant pause. He went into a huddle with the taxi driver. They talked in Spanish. I got the impression the sergeant wanted to get rid of me. Suddenly my friend Charlie appeared in the doorway.

"Hey!" he cried drunkenly. "What th' hell's goin' on? Ship's leavin'!"

The sergeant, sensing a solution to the problem, called him over.

I protested but Charlie paid the taxi driver another ten dollars and the policeman escorted us to the ship.

Thereafter until we reached San Diego I don't think Charlie drew a sober breath. He was taken ashore on a stretcher. His anguished wife, who had come to meet him, told me that he had given his word of honor he would not touch a drop.

CHAPTER EIGHTEEN

AL COHEN ESCORTED ME to Columbia Studios. He was young, rather handsome, had shiny black hair, an optimistic spirit and a money-hungry look. "This is the tightest studio in town," he said as we approached it. "Harry Cohn, the head man, is a hard-crusted, penny-pinching son-of-a-bitch. They're hiring you to dream up a scenario about stunting. I tried to sell them the page-proofs of your upcoming book, but they obviously think they can get a story from you without buying the book."

The cubbyhole office I was assigned contained a built-in desk, a battered typewriter, a chair and what was cornily called a casting couch. It was more like a prison cell than a place to compose. It fronted on a small, one-palm patio, the setting for a classic Harry Cohn joke. His imposing office overlooked the patio. Seeing a man pacing there, he asked an associate who he was. "Why, that's so-and-so, the new writer," the flunky said. Whereupon Cohn is reputed to have said, "Well, if we're payin' him, why the hell ain't the bastard in there writin'?"

There was a telephone, so I used it to try and reach Nan, now Mrs. Walter Huston. She was not at home. To test the typewriter, I inserted a sheet of paper and paused to contemplate. It seemed not only ironic but bizarre and almost incredible that I was back in Hollywood with the chance to do what I had always wanted to do.

The phone rang. It was James K. McGuinness, the studio story-editor well known for his stories in the *Saturday Evening Post*. "Welcome to Fantasyland!" he said. "We'll have our first conference tomorrow morning at ten o'clock in my office."

I said I would be there, turned back to the typewriter and began a letter to Mother. "I am writing this from Columbia Studios moments after I checked in. I begin work tomorrow and am elated at the prospect of upgrading the movies. . . ."

A shadow blocked out the daylight which had been coming from the patio doorway. To my surprise it was Steve Runyon, a newsman I had known in New York. I was delighted to see him. "I'm in the publicity department," he said. "Been assigned to do a story about you."

"How long have you been here?"

"Oh, 'bout two years."

"Maybe you can help me find a place to live."

"How about moving in with me? I've got a house just up the way. There's plenty of room."

And that's what I did.

The cottage we shared was small, vine-clad and above Franklin Avenue. The rent was fifty dollars a month, of which we each paid half. Steve was tall, good looking and dressed well. He had good manners, wore his curly black hair close-cropped and was about my age. He had been born in New Jersey and had attended Yale. I did not know when I moved in with him that he was a schizophrenic.

The publicity story he wrote about me was picked up by Louella Parsons who used it in her column:

FORMER STUNT MAN BACK FROM
EUROPE TO WRITE FOR FILMS

Some five years ago John Weld, a tall lad from Atlanta, came to see me. He craved to write or act. Unable to get a job in either line he became one of Hollywood's leading stunt men, doubling for many of our best-known stars. Tiring of risking his neck, he decided to go to New York, so I gave him an introduction to the *New York American*. . . . After a year on the *American* he went to the *Paris Herald* and while there wrote two books. Imagine my surprise when I learned that John has returned to Hollywood and been hired by Columbia to write a screenplay about a stunt man.

THERE IS nothing like favorable publicity to raise one's standing in a community. Thereto, as a stunt man in Hollywood, I had been an ordinary person, something of a madcap with no esteem and little regard. Suddenly I was a person of repute. Friends of my stunting days called and seemed pleased to know me.

Attending the story conference, besides McGuinness, was a director, Charles Vidor, and the producer, a corpulent nepotist of Cohn whose name I don't recall. Introducing me, McGuinness said, "This is our genius, fresh from Paris. Used to be a stunt man."

The producer asked me what kind of stunts I had done. "Oh, just about any kind," I said. "Did some high dives, turned over automobiles, drove a car off an opening drawbridge, fell off horses, jumped out of the first airplane I went up in," I paused.

My audience exchanged glances. McGuinness said, "Did you get hurt?"

"Oh, sure. Broke a few bones."

"I've read the page-proofs of your book *Stunt Man*. There's not much plot."

"I've been conjuring one," I said. "Want to hear it?"

"Sure. Go ahead."

"Our hero tries out for the Olympics as a diver, but doesn't make the team. He becomes a stunt man." I went on autobiographically, told them the story of the high dive I did off Santa Cruz Island and followed my embellishing my courtship and marriage to Betty Bumiller, interspersing it with stunts which caused our separation. "Meanwhile the heroine becomes a successful actress. Hired to do a very dangerous stunt with her, he saves her life. There is a reconciliation."

When I paused, there was silence.

McGuinness looked questioningly at Vidor.

Vidor said, "Where's the villain?"

"The stunts are the villain," I said.

"How about another stunt man, or maybe the director who likes the girl and tries to kill the hero?"

McGuinness said, "You know, we've got this new girl, Carole Lombard, on contract. Cohn wants a story for her. Maybe she could do stunts, too."

There was much discussion. Eventually I was sent back to my cubbyhole to write an outline about a stunt girl.

By twiddling my thumbs a lot, I managed to stretch the adaptation over three weeks. I was not pleased with what I composed but hoped to be retained to do the screenplay. I wasn't. In the parlance of Hollywood, I was terminated. The stunting picture was never made. The money I got from Columbia kept me afloat while Al Cohen scurried to find me another job.

Meanwhile Nan Huston came and took me to MGM to meet her husband who was working there as Reverend Davidson in Somerset Maugham's *Rain*, with Joan Crawford as Sadie Thompson. I was somewhat shy because of my amourette with Nan, but he greeted me so warmly that my latent feeling of inferiority, usually sensitive in the presence of a celebrity, was not aroused. We went to the Huston's house in Beverly Hills for dinner.

There was an affinity between Walter and me and we quickly became friends. He was very male, very kind, very gentle and very generous; and I, never having known a father, glommed onto him as pal, teacher, advisor and sage. As for Nan, she thought favorably of my talent and considered me a literary discovery.

That summer the Hustons began building a permanent home in the San Bernardin Mountains between Arrowhead and Big Bear, about one hundred miles from Hollywood. Several times they took me with them when they went to oversee its construction. One reached the building site over a mile and a half of dirt road. From it the view was magnificent. One could see the Pacific Ocean to the west and ranges of mountains as far as Mexico. At times a blanket of fog would enshroud all but tips of mountains and one got the illusion of Shangri-La! The huge redwood house was set amongst gigantic oaks and pines. There was to be a swimming pool and tennis court. Two other houses were in the area, actor Reginald Denny's and talent-agent Myron Selznick's. One nearby spring supplied water to all three. There was no telephone in any of them. The only means of communication with the outside world was a telephone in the general-store-and-post-office in Runnings Springs, about three miles away.

Fortunately for me, Al Cohen was new in Hollywood and had few clients, so he devoted considerable time trying to sell my services. He took me from studio to studio and introduced me to the Moguls. The day we went to Universal for an interview with its new boss, Carl Laemmle, Jr., Laemmle was looking for a story editor, someone to supervise the scenario department. It was decided I was not qualified, so Cohen went back the next day, got the job for himself and persuaded Laemmle to hire me as a scenarist. I was back in business.

For my first assignment, Al brought a sheaf of adaptations and scenarios, all entitled *The Suicide Club*. They had been written by different writers from three short stories by Robert Louis Stevenson. Charlie Chaplin had been the first producer to nibble at the notion and buy the film rights; after several tries at a screenplay he sold them to Douglas Fairbanks, who in turn sold them to Metro-Goldwyn-Mayer where several more writers, some of them well-known, had strived to compose an acceptable plot from the stories. Finally Universal had bought the whole kit and kaboodle from MGM. Piling the manuscripts on my desk, Al said, "If you can crack this nut, I think I can get you a long-term contract."

I first read Stevenson's stories, beginning with *The Young Man With the Cream Tarts* before studying the stack of scenarios. The first time I went to lunch in the studio restaurant I met John Huston. He had written dialog for two films in which his father had appeared and had been terminated. I told him about meeting his mother in Paris. "She wanted to get a newspaper job there. I did what I could to help her but nothing came of it."

John said, "She worked on the *Graphic* and so did I. It was the world's worst newspaper and I was probably the world's worst reporter."

"Your mother told me you were a genius."

John grinned. "Mothers're biased."

When I told him I had been assigned to adapt Stevenson's suicide stories, he made a wry face. I asked, "Have you worked on them?"

"No, but I'm told many have."

"Seems to me like a crazy idea. The title is *The Suicide Club*. People don't like dying."

"Thing to do," John said, "is make the leading man a charmer, maybe a gambler. Make him likable and sympathetic so the audience can identify with him."

I had no idea I was talking with someone who would become a movie legend in his own time. John and I became life-long friends. Thus, more and more I was drawn into the Huston family.

I made *The Suicide Club* protagonist a winsome young Englishman who is in love with an upper-class girl whose family refuses to let her marry him because he is a commoner. After drowning his sorrows in a pub and on his drunken way home, he is startled when a man's body lands in the street. The protagonist hurries to aid him, but finds that he is dead. In the corpse's wallet he finds a suicide note which reveals he was a member of a suicide club. Our despondent hero joins the club.

I went on to concoct a highly improbably story, but to my amazement Junior Laemmle approved it and I was assigned to co-author the screenplay. The other author was Laird Doyle. Together we composed a satirical scenario which was enthusiastically okayed for production. There was talk around the studio that Laird and I were going to make it big in films.

Because of my success with *The Suicide Club* Laemmle decided I was good and cheap enough to crack another perplexing nut: how to make a motion picture of H.G. Wells's *The Invisible Man*. A number of treatments of the fantastic story had been written, some by writers whose names I recognized: Garrett Fort, John Balderston, Preston Sturgis, Gouverneur Morris. These rejected scripts were dumped on my desk. Some were beyond the bounds of credulity. *King Kong*, a film featuring a gigantic gorilla, had recently been extremely successful at the box-office and, following the Hollywood custom of duplicating films that make money, most of the writers had taken that nightmarish tack. One had the unseen character go out and wreak widespread havoc by destroying an entire metropolis. When I had digested them all, I went looking for a copy of Wells's book. Incredibly none was in

Cohen's office nor Laemmle's files, so I drove to Hollywood and obtained one at the public library. I was struck by the simplicity of the story and decided to dramatize it. It was logical to assume that Wells would approve his own story line, and his approval was mandatory.

Before beginning to write the adaptation I could not overcome the mischievous temptation to play a practical joke. During my stunting days I had learned that, to be successful in the film industry, it was important to create an identity. One way was to become a waggish character by doing unusual, zany and amusing things. I had the stenographic department prepare a traditional blue scenario-cover bearing title and credits:

An Adaptation of
H.G. Wells's
THE INVISIBLE MAN
by John Weld

With this I bound a sheaf of blank pages and sent it to Junior Laemmle. His reaction was not long forthcoming. To my chagrin, he was not amused. In fact, he got mad as hell. It seems I had insulted him, and Al Cohen was hard pressed to keep him from firing me. Ultimately I was allowed to go on with the adaptation. When I had finished, it was sent to Wells in England and to Laemmle's surprise and delight he approved it.

ABOUT THIS TIME Steve transferred his publicity activities at a raise in salary to Metro-Goldwyn-Mayer and, inasmuch as I seemed set at Universal, we decided to move into a more expensive house in the Outpost section of Hollywood. This entailed us hiring a servant. He turned out to be a Liberian. We paid him thirty dollars a month. I don't believe I ever knew whether Osbourne was his first or last name. He told us he had come to the United States as secretary to the Liberian minister but had been released when the minister's income was reduced. He had made his way to Los Angeles and was one of several applicants who responded to our want-ad. Black as obsidian, he had dignity and poise and spoke English with a British accent. It was the accent that sold him to us, we thinking that when we entertained it would tone up the party. Another reason I wanted him was for his secretarial background. I figured that he could not only cook and clean but type my manuscripts as well. This deduction turned out to be faulty. While Osbourne proved to be faithful and charming in his way, he was well nigh useless for practical purposes. His culinary talents were restricted to boiling and frying; he could not make a bed properly; he did not know the first rule of dusting—don't fluff it; he couldn't type for sour apples, and his spelling was worse than mine. But he was so trustworthy and tried so hard to please we could not bring ourselves to fire him.

I wrote Mother:

Steve and I have moved into an upper-class house from the terrace of which we can see the palm-treed city stretched out for twenty miles. It is beautifully furnished, has two bedrooms, each with bath, as well as a servant's room and bath. You can't have a servant's room without a servant, so we've hired one to cook our meals, clean, do the laundry, press our clothes and shine our shoes. Pretty fancy. I've bought on the installment plan a Wills St. Clair convertible. Steve also has a car, a Pierce Arrow. If you get the impression we're living high on the hog and fighting off females, you're half right. Our friends say we've "Gone Hollywood," which means we assume this cloud nine will float on forever; whereas everyone knows that in Hollywood you can be up one week and down the next. Meanwhile, I'm still looking for that predestined lady you promised me. . . .

CHAPTER NINETEEN

I T WAS SOME TIME before I became aware of Steve's schizophrenia. Early in our association I noticed that his spirits fluctuated. Usually he was cheerful, at other times uncommunicative. One Saturday morning, after we had moved into the Outpost house, he did not get up for breakfast and remained in his room throughout the day. His girl, Gail Greenstreet, called, but when I summoned him he would not come to the telephone.

"Tell her I'm not feeling well," he said, without opening the door. Later he joined me in the library. I was having a martini and mixed him one.

"I get depressed at times," he said by way of apology, sitting down in the leather chair and putting his feet on the ottoman. "I have to get the doldrums out of my system." After a pause, during which I got the impression he was undecided whether or not to confide in me, he took a sip of the drink and said, "When I was in high school my father deserted my mother. She was an alcoholic. I came home one afternoon, there was a taxicab outside our house and I found the Negro driver in bed with her. I got mad and wanted to kill him, but he beat the hell out of me. I went to live with my grandfather." He paused. I didn't say anything. He hit the back of his throat with the martini and said, "That might have had something to do with it."

He was serious about Gail. She worked as an extra and bit player and lived in the Studio Club, a haven for movie girls. She seemed to help him through those low periods. Thinking Mother might be able to guide him I sent her the date, time and place of his birth.

She responded:

> I'm sorry to say that I don't like all I see in Stephen's chart. Perhaps I have been influenced by what you've written me, or perhaps for him this is not a propitious time. Right now he seems to be under a negative sign. I see him on a rollercoaster going through a long tunnel. Marriage might help him. Wives can balance husbands . . .

About that time Metro-Goldwyn-Mayer had hired Jean Harlow who had given a good performance in Howard Hughes's *Hell's Angels*. Steve was assigned to publicize *Red Dust*, in which she and Clark Gable were starring. She was coming out of the shock of sudden success and beginning to realize that, for the first time in her otherwise commonplace life, she could have almost anything she wanted. What she wanted most was a mate who could satisfy her natural urges and get her out of the clutches of her mother and stepfather who, she believed, were defrauding her. Thus when the tall, handsome Steve appeared on the set, she took more than a professional interest in him. She invited him to her recently rented mansion for a swim in the pool. Thus did their affair begin. Most of the males in the world would have envied Steve being in the hay with Harlow, but for him it was disturbing. It gnawed him that he was cheating on Gail. Confused because it was part of his job to keep Harlow happy, he became depressed. I saw little of him. He would come in late at night and leave early in the morning. Once he did not come home for a week. Gail called frequently wanting to know where he was, and I lied that he was on location. When finally he returned he kept to his room, coming forth only to nibble disinterestedly at the dinner Osbourne prepared.

I tried to josh him out of his melancholia, suggesting jokingly that his predicament would make a classic movie and offering to buy the rights.

"I can see the title on a marquee now," I said. "*Horns of a Dilemma,* starring Harlow, Greenstreet and you."

He was not amused. Harlow called him several times and he also talked to Gail. So far as I could tell he fed them the same line. To a schizophrenic, the problem he faced was anathema. Which should he choose—the girl he loved or the glamorous movie star?

One day while I was away he packed his belongings and drove off. He did not leave a message. That afternoon, twilight was still hanging on, his Pierce Arrow rolled up the driveway driven by a gas station attendant who explained he had driven Mr. Runyon to the airport and had been directed to deliver the car and a letter to me. Some of Steve's belongings were still in the car. Osbourne left to drive the attendant back to his gas station and I sat down and read the letter:

> I am sending the Pierce to you, dear John, because henceforth I won't be needing it. Also my typewriter and other miscellany. The suits and shoes give to the Salvation Army or any bum you can find. The swimming trunks will fit you. The writing paper may come in handy. I beg you to preserve the volume *Beyond Life,* by James Branch Cabell, toward which I bear a singular attachment. Keep that, I implore you, until your deathbed, when you'll be needing it. I'm leaving town for a while because a lot of things are in my hair and ordinary shampoos won't remove them. When and if I get back none of this stuff will do me any good. Be of good cheer and remember me kindly. I'm asking my boss, Howard Strickling, to turn over what's left of my salary to you. There is something like $24 due for repairs to the car at the garage on La Brea just south of Melrose. Maybe you can void it. In that case, pay off the utility companies and buy yourself some booze. Adios, Steve.

While I was meditating the perplexing letter, Jean Harlow called. I told her Steve was not available. "He's left town," I said.

"That's strange. Where do you think he's gone?"

"I don't know. Probably New York."

"I saw him yesterday. He didn't say he was going."

"Occasionally he has fits of depression. He might be in one of them." That line about *Beyond Life* by Cabell made me think he was going to commit suicide. "Apparently," I said, "he was going to take a plane. Maybe he planned to jump out of it."

"Oh, my God! Why would he do that?"

"God knows."

"Let's call the police!"

"We don't know the airline or the plane. I think the doors of planes are securely locked. His melancholia will pass. If he can't jump, we'll hear from him."

Sobbing, she said, "It's the craziest thing I ever heard of," and hung up.

I called the Police Missing Persons Bureau and reported Steve's disappearance. I then called Gail Greenstreet and told her what had happened.

"That's strange," she said. "Yesterday I received four dozen roses from him. Recently my roommate received roses from Ernst Lubitsch and I thought Steve was trying to match him. I had hoped to see Steve tonight."

"I'm afraid he won't be coming." I read her Steve's letter. "There may be some of his things, letters from you for example, that you want," I said. "Come on over and take a look."

Before she arrived Howard Strickling, who had been alarmed by Harlow, and his assistant, Ralph Wheelwright, appeared with a detective from the Hollywood Police Station. I had met Howard and knew him to be a master publicist. He was as concerned, and good at, keeping scandal out of the news as he was getting promotional publicity into it. His fear was that Steve's disappearance and possible suicide might bring out his relationship with Harlow. That could hurt her.

I told him what had happened and read Steve's letter. The detective was not satisfied. "How is it he left his automobile, typewriter, clothes and even toothbrush here?" he demanded. "If he was going somewhere why didn't he take his suitcase with him?" He was rudely aggressive.

"That's a stupid question," I said. "How do you expect me to answer it?"

"Well, God damnit, you lived with him!" He went into the kitchen to question Osbourne. Gail arrived. I introduced her to Strickling and Wheelwright and brought out the gin and grapefruit juice.

While the cop was going about his detection I talked to the others about Steve and his schizophrenia. None of us mentioned Harlow and I don't believe Gail knew she had a rival. The gin raised our spirits. Strickling became interested in Gail, and learning she was an actress offered to get her a job at MGM. Presently everyone left, the detective to go to the Texaco gas station to interview the attendant, and Strickling, Wheelwright and Gail, as their guest, to dinner.

As fate would have it, within a few weeks Strickling and Gail, having met for the first time that night, were married. Thus in the divine scheme of things Steve, whom they would never see again, was their catalyst.

ABOUT FIVE O'CLOCK in the morning, a few days later, I was awakened by the telephone.

"New York calling," the operator sang cheerfully. "I have a collect call from a Mister Runyon. Will you accept the charge?"

"Madam," I said, enunciating as if I were John Barrymore, "not only will I not accept the charge, but I beg you to deliver a message to Mister Runyon. Please tell him to go straight to hell." Then, thinking better of it and conscious that Steve doubtless was listening, I asked, "How much is the charge?"

"Eight dollars for the first three minutes."

"How about selling me two dollars' worth?"

"It's eight or nothing," she said cheerfully.

"Put him on."

Steve's voice: "Hello, John. Hope I didn't get you up."

"Don't waste your hopes."

"I'm sorry. I'm in New York and broke. Could you wire me a few bucks?"

"Steve," I said, measuring my words and softening them so they would not sound unfriendly, "nobody knows better than you that I am up to my ears in debt. How can I send you any money?"

"I thought you might borrow on my car or sell it."

"Would you please tell me why you went running away? Do you realize what a mess you've left out here? Harlow, Greenstreet, Strickling, the Hollywood police—they're all on my back. They think I've murdered you, that I've buried you in the back yard."

"I'm sorry. I had to get away. Twenty-five bucks would help."

"Where do you want it sent?"

"Western Union Office, Grand Central Station."

I sighed. "I'll see what I can do. Are you coming back?"

"I don't know."

"Harlow is devastated. So is Gail. What do you want me to tell them?"

"I'll write 'em."

The operator cut in: "Your time is up."

I said, "I'll try to get you some dough," and hung up.

I went to a loan company in Hollywood, borrowed fifty dollars on the Pierce Arrow and telegraphed it to him. A week later I received a letter:

> I'm sorry I caused you so much trouble. I was all mixed up when I left. I thought I could cure it but it didn't work out as I planned. I burned a lot of bridges and now I can't get back. Have gotten a job on *Newsweek*. If you see Gail tell her I'm sorry. Thanks for the kale. It saved my life.

Some years later, having done what he apparently was put on this earth to do, Steve cured his schizophrenia by jumping from the thirty-fourth floor of a building at the corner of Fifth Avenue and Fortieth Street.

WHEN I HEARD that Junior Laemmle had received a cablegram from H.G. Wells approving my adaptation of *The Invisible Man* I began to feel that my screenwriting career was assured. I had not learned that those uncontrollable variables, timing and luck, though not one and the same thing, are interlocked. As it turned out, my modest success had come at a bad time. Wells followed his cable with a letter stating that the screenplay was to be written by his friend, R.C. Sherriff, author of *Journey's End,* a highly successful play about World War One, and that Sherriff was to get full screen credit. This meant that my name would not appear on the film as the adaptor. Such injustices were common in the movie industry at that time, and it was to correct these abuses that the Screen Writers' Guild was founded. I became a charter member.

The Wells job was not my only disappointment. Suddenly all of the studios, reacting to the worldwide financial depression, took dramatic measures to economize. A number of films, including *The Suicide Club*, were postponed indefinitely. Many employees, including me, were discharged and the salaries of those not discharged were cut in half. To economize, I turned the Wills St. Clair back to the finance company and eliminated the gardener. I didn't let Osbourne go for several reasons: (1) I would have had to give him severance pay, (2) I did not want to push him out in the cold, (3) he could help do the garden work and (4) I needed his old tin Lizzie for transportation. Osbourne had bought the wheezy Overland for fifteen dollars down and eleven monthly installments of fifteen dollars. Every month, whether or not there was bread in the house and creditors were pounding on the door, I had to scratch that sum up. In time I came to have a sentimental attachment to the old coupé because, by making it possible for us to go where the sustenance was, it literally saved us from famishment.

Although we were poverty-stricken, my social life in no way abated. Hostesses oftentimes required unattached gentlemen for dinner partners, so I frequently received invitations. Inasmuch as Osbourne was my responsibility, I contrived to take him with me. Happily hostesses were glad to have him help by tending bar, serving dinner and washing dishes. For his services he got food and tips and usually managed to tote leftovers. The leftovers kept us going and the tips bought gasoline for the Overland.

One party Osbourne and I went to was given by Theda Bara, the screen vampire. She was married to film director Charles Brabin and her parties were among the most prestigious in the colony. Though middle-aged and no longer working in films, she was still glamorous. She had been born in Cincinnati, daughter of a Jewish tailor, but when she became a movie *femme fatale* in 1915 she was publicized as having been born in the Sahara Desert, the love of a French artist and his Egyptian mistress. That must have been the mother of what became Hollywood hooey.

At her party I met Mayo Methot, also an actress. While together on the patio she told me a candid anecdote about an affair she'd had with George M. Cohan. I was astonished that she would so quickly reveal such an intimate experience. Seems that she had been born in Portland, Oregon, daughter of a sea captain. While in high school she studied singing and sang in concerts. When a touring musical company came to town she joined it and eventually worked her way to New York. There Cohan chose her to be his leading lady in a musical he was producing. The show opened in Philadelphia and, following the first performance, he invited her to his hotel suite for supper. After brandies he suggested they make a night of it.

"I got the impression," Mayo told me, "that if I didn't accept the invitation I'd soon be out of a job. So I stayed."

"Must have been a clause in the contract," I said.

"Well, it kept my name on the marquee."

"That's show biz."

A few days later she telephoned and invited me to dinner and asked me to bring Osbourne. She was married to Percy Morgan, a wealthy young man, also from Portland. My dinner partner was Anna Mae Wong, the Chinese-American actress. I had known her when we worked in *Peter Pan* in 1924; she was a character actress and I was doing stunts from the rigging of the *Jolly Roger*. She had a round, light-tan face, full lips and beautiful teeth and wore her thick, black hair Dutch-bobbed, the bangs almost covering her black eyebrows. During dinner she and I entertained by telling about a near disaster while we were working on the *Jolly Roger* off Santa Cruz Island. The ersatz pirate ship had been built on a barge with plywood. It was loaded with actors, actresses, cameramen, lighting technicians, the director and prop-men and was hawsered to a tugboat. During the late afternoon a storm of gale strength suddenly came up. Rain fell in torrents. The sea seethed and waves crushed the plywood. The hawser snapped. The barge, without power or rudder, was blown toward the island cliffs. Most of those aboard scurried to the only shelter, under the deck, but several of us remained on deck trying to get a rope to or from the tug. The huge waves made it dangerous for the tug to get close enough and our efforts were in vain. Meanwhile the barge was bouncing about. It was hard to stand. Those below began wailing. Some got seasick. The seven-foot pirate prayed on his knees. There was panic. The fear was that we would be dashed to death on the rocks. "I can't swim!" a girl wailed.

A rope was our only hope. Horace Hough, the assistant director who had seen me do the high dive for *Dantes Inferno,* said, "John, you're a stunt man. How about giving it a try?"

Anne Mae told the party, "He said, 'Gimme the rope.' "

We knotted two lariats together, looped one end to a stanchion and, after I had stripped to my undershorts, tied the other around my waist. Guided by the tug's searchlight, I dove into the black, tumultuous sea. For all my bravado, there was a strong doubt in me. Crawling up and down the turbulent waves, I made little progress. I gulped water into my windpipe. Every time I gained a few feet I would be swept back. Little by little, though, I reached the tug and was hauled on board. With the lariat, those aboard the *Jolly Roger* were able to pull a hawser aboard.

"Just in time," Anna Mae concluded. "We were on the brink of disaster."

By telling most of the story, she spared me the embarrassment of boasting. For the anecdote I must have gotten some merit points, because the Morgans invited Osbourne and me again.

At the time I was working on a play about an actress and a writer in New York who fall in love, get married and come to Hollywood.

I persuaded Mayo to collaborate, figuring that she, a professional actress, would be helpful. We usually worked in her house, but now and then she would come to mine. Percy became suspicious that our playwriting was a front for a concupiscent affair, that he was being cuckolded. One afternoon at my place Mayo and I were well into the second act when Percy arrived. The classic scene ensued: accusations, remonstrances and name calling. In the end, he took her, protesting angrily, away.

Coming from the kitchen after they had gone, Osbourne said, "My, ain't that a shame? There goes a fine meal ticket."

He was right. We were never invited to the Morgan's again. I finished the play and sent it, at Mayo's request, to a producer she knew. He returned it with a polite rejection.

Above: A high dive for the movies, 1923.
Below: Castle Heights Military Academy, May 1920.

Above: in Colorado,
June, 1917
Below: With Walter
Huston and a friend
on Huston's ranch
near Delano,
California, 1941.

*Walter Huston as
Othello; Nan
Sutherland (Mrs.
Walter Huston)
as Desdemona.*

Filming in Lebanon, 1964

*Katherine Weld as she was in the movies (above)
and with John on their wedding anniversary, 1965,
in Taxco, Mexico (below).*

Above: With Governor Earl Warren of California and Ford executive Fred Crook, during the opening of the Lincoln-Mercury plant in Los Angeles, 1948. Below: John and Katy Weld with John Huston, shortly before Huston's death.

CHAPTER TWENTY

I MET FLORENCE BARNES through Mary Ellen and Gordon Pollock and was captivated by her wacky, ribald, wanton personality. Her grandfather, Thaddeus S.C. Lowe, had been a balloonist during the Civil War and Pasadena's Mount Lowe is named for him. Infused with his aerial genes, she had become a celebrated aviatrix. She competed in the first Powder Puff Derby and in 1930 beat Amelia Earhart's cross-country air-speed record.

In creating her, the gods had erred. She had a short neck, a stocky body, a baritone voice, face hair, which she shaved, and an unwomanly personality. Characterwise she was an iconoclast, a nonconformist, a rebel. At Pasadena High School she had become notorious because of her bizarre behavior, one aspect of which was smoking cigars. In her late teens she acquiesced to a family arranged marriage to the Reverend Rankin Barnes, minister of Pasadena's Saint James Episcopal Church. As hostess of church-oriented affairs she scandalized the congregation by telling risque stories and interspersing profanity. No one was surprised when the marriage was dissolved. She had acquired the nickname, "Pancho" when, disguised as a man, she crewed on a banana ship to Panama. Her fame increased during World War Two during which, at Edwards Air Force Base, she was the proprietor of the *Happy Bottom Club*. In his autobiography, Chuck Yeager called it "the pilots' clubhouse and playroom." Apocryphally it was said to have been a bordello. At the time I met her, because of her free spirit, originality, wit and fondness for fun, she had become popular in Hollywood. She had a large oceanfront house in Laguna Beach where she gave lavish parties. When I accepted her invitation to spend a weekend there I had no way of knowing that the wheel of fortune was about to stop on my number.

Whenever Osbourne and I went anywhere together I did the driving because he was one of the most erratic drivers on earth. We managed to cover the miles to Pancho's house in Laguna without mechanical mishap or tire trouble, something of a miracle in the Overland, and were greeted by Pancho and a couple I did not know, Gigi and Dillwyn Parrish. At the sight of Gigi something went kerplunk in my psyche. I was startled by her beauty. She embodied the woman of my fantasies. She was Astraea, the last of the immortals and, in acknowledging the introduction, her voice had the purity of a viola.

For me, it was admiration, lust and acquisitiveness at first sight. Suddenly I was face to face with the most desirable woman I had ever seen. She was five feet four, weighed a hundred and ten pounds and had been sculpted by a master. There was nothing theatrical or embellished about her, no make-up save lipstick, no dyed or frizzled hair. Her habiliments—sunsuit, kerchief and espadrilles—were tasteful. Then and there, if I had had a white horse, I would have borne her away.

I was so hypnotized by her that, while shaking her husband's hand, I was hardly aware of him. He was but an inch or two taller than she, quite thin and not at all handsome. His jaws were awry and a few of his teeth overlapped. "I'm glad to meet you," I said, and he replied in kind. I sensed in him a reserve and would learn that he regarded every male as a rival for his wife's affections.

Osbourne, meanwhile was standing, bags in hand, waiting to be directed.

I asked Pancho where he should go and she said, "The cook will show him."

I said to him, lightly playing the role of master, "Get your tail inside and make yourself useful."

The house was furnished with somewhat shabby chintz-covered wickerwork. A stairway led down the cliff to the beach. Other guests that weekend included Gordon and Mary Ellen Pollock; Ramon Navarro, a young Mexican actor who had become a movie star; Ruth Chatterton and her mother Tillie who hovered worriedly over her prima donna daughter; Eric von Stroheim and the Howard Spreckles of the San Francisco sugar family.

During the afternoon I did a few fancy dives into the pool to show off and body surfed in the ocean for the joy of it. The opportunity to converse with Gigi did not come until cocktail time. She went onto the terrace and I, who had been talking with Pancho about airplanes, excused myself and went out to her.

"I've been hoping for a chance to tell you how meeting you has affected me," I said. "Haven't we met before?"

She gave me a wry glance. "I don't believe so."

"That's funny. The first time I went to Paris I had the feeling I'd been there before and the moment I saw you a bell rang. Has this ever happened to you—I mean, have you ever had that feeling about a place or meeting someone?"

She regarded me quizzically. "No," she said. I sensed a chill.

Discouraged, but still hopeful, I went on: "For years I've had in my befuddled mind the image of the ideal woman, and—bingo!—there you are!"

"Thank you." She drained her glass and looked away.

I said, "You should be in pictures."

She turned back to me. "Pancho tells me you're a writer."

I nodded. "There's some doubt about it."

"That explains the blarney."

Sensing the ice was melting, I said, "My lips speak nothing but the truth."

Talk inside had reached alcoholic decibels and a phonograph was playing *Love For Sale*. Gigi watched the sun which had begun to set beyond Catalina Island. It had become a bright orange and its base was flattening. I said, "Reminds me of the Shell Oil sign."

For the first time she smiled. "Have you ever seen the green spot when the sun sinks into the sea?" she asked. I laughed and shook my head, thinking she was spoofing. "It happens," she said. "But it won't now because Catalina blocks it."

Tacking, I said, "You need another drink," and summoned Osbourne. He came in his white jacket and took both our glasses.

She turned away watching a formation of pelicans glide close to the swelling breakers. I tried to interest her by calling attention to seals on the rocks offshore which were barking.

"That's where they live," she said matter-of-factly, thereby stifling that subject.

My charm ploys had run out. When Osbourne had delivered the drinks I clicked her glass, and said, "I get the impression you don't find me captivating."

She took a sip before saying, "To tell you the truth, I am shocked by the imperious way you treat your servant."

I was nonplused. I did not want to reveal my impecuniosity by telling her that Osbourne and I were living together because I was too poor to pay him and that we were well versed in our roles as master and servant. I said, "Where were you brought up?"

"Boston—New Hampshire."

"I was born in Birmingham, Alabama, and I probably know more about Negroes than you do. Osbourne and I get along just fine. We're good friends. We understand each other."

"I thought you were very rude to him when you arrived. You sounded like Simon Legree."

My snort of laughter came from vexation. "Whatever else I may be," I said, "a racist I am not."

"When I was a child in New Hampshire I knew a Negro woman, and she was one of the nicest, kindest persons I've ever known. She was a Shaker."

"Are they the ones who don't believe in procreation?"

"That's right."

"If everyone followed that philosophy it would eliminate mankind."

"Sister Ernestine made cookies and whenever we children called she would give us some. Because of her, I have great respect for black people."

I told her about my friend Brown. "He was about the nicest person I've ever known," I said. "I still use expressions I learned from him— 'Well, shut my mouth!' and 'I'll be a suck-egg mule'."

Eager to know more about her background I asked, "What brought you to California?"

"My husband and I came on motorcycles. It was our honeymoon."

Surprised, I asked, "Where from?"

"We were married in his mother's home in Claymont, Delaware, and got as far as Maxwell, New Mexico, where I had an accident. We came the rest of the way by train."

"When was that?"

"October, 1927."

"I came from Atlanta in a Ford in 1923. Took us twelve days, traveling day and night. How long did it take you?"

"We only traveled in daylight. Took us two weeks. We stopped for a few days in Colorado Springs. Many of the roads were gravel and full of chuckholes. Sometimes the bikes we rode were like bucking horses. The further we went, the greater the gaps between places to eat and sleep." Her laughter was musical.

"You must have been quite young."

"Sixteen." Evidently she sensed I was fascinated by what she was telling me because she went on: "One evening we came to a little town in western Oklahoma. It was raining. Soaked and covered with mud, we went to the only inn. Dillwyn asked the stubble-bearded proprietor, who was chewing on a cigar, if we could get a room. Without taking the cigar from his mouth the proprietor, glancing at me, asked, 'That your daughter?' 'No, my wife. We need a room with a bath.' 'Only got one,' the man said. 'Ain't cheap. It'll cost you three bucks. Two bits more for soap and towels.' "

She laughed and went on to tell me that, after leaving Colorado Springs, they reached Trinidad and set out to make the run over Raton Pass to Sante Fe. It was a bright Sunday, there was little traffic, the road was good and they zoomed along at fifty miles an hour. Fragrant pines hemmed the sinuous two-lane highway over the Rockies. With her husband a quarter of a mile ahead, she increased her speed. Rounding a turn she headed for a narrow bridge. Planks for automobiles lay lengthwise. She throttled down, uncertain which one to take.

She chose the one on the right and got the front wheel onto it, but only momentarily before it rolled off. With her hanging onto the handlebars the machine flipped onto the far side of the bridge and fell on her right leg. Benumbed and in shock, she managed to extricate herself. Her riding breeches were torn and blood was oozing from her right knee.

An automobile stopped. In it were an elderly man and woman. "Are you all right?" the man asked.

"I—I'm—I'm not sure," Gigi stammered.

The woman said, "It's a girl!"

"You must have hit the cattleguard," the man said. "Your wheel got caught in the grating."

"You're bleeding," the woman said. "We'd better get you to a doctor."

"My husband's ahead of me," Gigi said, a hand on her knee to stop the flow of blood.

Dillwyn had seen the accident in his rear-view mirror and turned so quickly that his back tire blew. He came wobbling back, hurriedly extracted a first-aid kit and poured iodine into the wound. Tears cascaded down Gigi's cheeks. On the road near her were two gold pieces, a twenty and a fifty, wedding presents she had been carrying in her watch pocket. "Mad money," Dillwyn said, picking them up. "Is there a doctor in these parts?"

"Yep," the man said. "In Maxwell, up the road a piece. We'll take her."

Dillwyn removed the flat tire of his motorcycle and, carrying it on the handlebar of Gigi's, followed them.

Maxwell was a small, dusty town of unpainted houses and shacks inhabited mostly by Indians.

The only doctor in many miles had a big belly and a wart on his nose. He cut the leg of Gigi's breeches with blunt-nosed scissors and saturated the wound with alcohol. "Anesthetic," he explained.

He ran the end of a suture through the eye of a curved needle and tried several times unsuccessfully to poke it through the skin. He finally managed to sew the gaping wound by using a pair of pliers.

Dillwyn arranged for a mechanic to repair the tire, go back and get his motorcycle and crate them both for shipping.

Gigi ended the episode by saying, "We arrived in Los Angeles and checked into the Alexandria Hotel. That evening the streets were aswarm with people yelling, dancing in the streets and shooting firecrackers. 'This really is the wild, wild West!' I said. Dillwyn said, 'It's Hallowe'en.' "

That was as far as she got about their motorcycling honeymoon before Dillwyn came out and joined us. At once I could see why the innkeeper had asked him if Gigi was his daughter. He looked twice her age. I learned that he was a writer and the brother of Anne Parrish whose *Perennial Bachelor,* published in 1925, and her subsequent books had brought her literary fame. I asked how they came to know Pancho. Dillwyn said that Anne had met her on a cruise around South America and had written her that he and his bride were coming to California. "Pancho was the first person we met when we got to Los Angeles," he said. "She brought us to Laguna and we liked the town so much we came here to live."

At dinner I was not seated near Gigi and after dinner she and Dillwyn left. They did not reappear at Pancho's that weekend and I had no reason to believe I would ever see her again.

I wrote to Mother:

I have met a woman with whom I would like to spend the rest of my life. She is absolutely absolute. The trouble is, she is married. Married women seem to be my propensity. One might assume that I like the danger of adultery or am a born philanderer. Neither of these is true. I am eager to get married, to found a home and family. I want to prove that I can be a worthy husband and father.

With marriage in mind, I have looked at lots of ladies, but until now have not met one who fulfills the physical, personal, intellectual and spiritual image my imagination has sculpted. Having come upon one who does, she is beyond my reach. I couldn't pay her a higher compliment than to say she reminds me of you.

If Gigi had remained in Laguna our trajectories might never again have crossed. But Gordon Pollock arranged for her to get a screen test. It turned out so well, Samuel Goldwyn signed her to a contract and she came to Hollywood. To honor this advent the Pollocks gave a cocktail party to which I was invited. Eager to see her again, I went. After congratulating her, I said, "I prophesy you're headed for stardom."

"You're day-dreaming," she said. "I don't know a thing about acting."

"All you have to do is be yourself. You've got all it takes." Then I said, "I'm afraid I made a bad impression on you when we met in Laguna and it has been troubling me. I didn't tell you about Osbourne and myself because I didn't want you to know that I'm on my uppers. He and I are more like brothers than servant-master. We live together because I can't pay him and he has no other place to go. I tell you this because truth is good for friendship and I want to be your friend."

"Being poor is no disgrace."

"It is in Hollywood. You've heard about the actor at a dinner party who admitted to being out of work. He was not served dessert."

She laughed, amused, and I felt a spark of sympathetic affection. She touched my hand and said, "I was born poor. My parents were Irish immigrants who settled in Somerville, Massachusetts. I was their fifth child. My mother died when I was five, giving birth to her seventh. The baby died, too. I was shunted from one foster home to another. When I was eight and living in Canterbury, New Hampshire, a school mate, Jean Paul, and I became chums. Her parents are Quakers. Though they had six children they adopted me. It was through them I met Dillwyn. He was Daddy's—Mister Paul's—cousin."

The Goldwyn publicists did not delve into her ill-starred childhood; instead, they dwelt on her association with the Parrish family, particularly with Anne Parrish and Dillwyn's cousin Maxfield, the distinguished artist. They also played up Gigi's and Dillwyn's honeymoon, and pictures of her on a motorcycle appeared in newspapers and magazines.

For me to covet Gigi was nonsensical, even idiotic. I had little to offer the beautiful young lady save a song and a loving heart. Over and above that impediment, she was married, had a good job and was on her way to becoming a celebrity. Nevertheless, to me she was the epitome of womankind, the prize of a lifetime, and she kept revolving through my mind.

Knowing my financial plight, she occasionally invited me to dine with her and Dillwyn. I always accepted and took Osbourne to help in the kitchen. During these visits I sensed that, while she was fond of me, Dillwyn considered me a rival. This was understandable because the fact that I adored his wife must have been evident.

At this time my life's tide had fallen to its lowest ebb. I owed the landlady, the utility companies, friends, and the finance company for Osbourne's car and Osbourne himself. I had no job. My future, based on my past, was not bright. I could have papered the wall with manuscript rejections. My clothes looked as if they came from a Salvation Army barrel. My mooching days in Hollywood were running out. I had hoped that *Gun Girl* would establish me as a literary talent. It had not made a ripple. So far as I know, the only ones who read it were a few relatives and friends. The same with *Stunt Man.* It was obvious that, as a free-lance writer, I was a fizzle.

Disillusioned and depressed, I wrote to Martin Dunn, the city editor of the *New York American,* a friend in need, and told him my tale of woe. He promptly replied, offering me a job, salary forty dollars a week. Now all I needed was train fare.

It came from an unlikely source. As I emerged from Bank of America, where I had unsuccessfully tried to obtain a loan, I ran into an erstwhile Detroit bootlegger I had met at a meeting of the Screen Writers' Guild. After seeing the film *Little Caesar,* he had come to Hollywood figuring the movies was a racket he could get into, go legitimate and make a pack of jack. He called himself Max Williams, but that was not his Christian name; it was more like Wolskinski.

"Say," he said, grabbing my arm, "you're just the guy I wanna see. I've written a story that can set this town on its ass, but it needs a little polishin'. How 'bout helpin' me out?"

Under other circumstances, I would have given him the breeze, but it occurred to me that by helping him I might be able to borrow a few bucks. "I don't know that I'll have the time," I said. "I'm leaving town, going to New York."

"When?"

"Soon's I can scratch up the train fare. What is it?—a gangster story?"

"Hell, I ain't gonna tell you if you ain't gonna help me with it."

I laughed. "I'm not going to steal it, for Pete's sake! How far along with it are you?"

"I got a whole outline. Won't take long to smooth it."

"That's fine. If I do this, it'll cost you a hundred dollars."

"Okay. Soon's we sell it."

It was a long shot, but I went with him to his fleabag hotel room to get the manuscript. It was a sheaf of foolscap written with pencil in large letters, about two paragraphs per page.

"Let me read it to you," he said.

"Never mind," I said, having had experiences with budding authors. "I'll take it home and go right to work."

It was entitled *The Mob* and was about a bootlegging war. I thought Warner Brothers might like it, they having produced *Little Caesar;* moreover I had met Darryl Zanuck, who recently had been put in charge of production there. I expanded the story, gave the moll more sequences, added an automobile chase over the Detroit-Windsor Bridge and through the Ford plant, corrected the spelling. Took me a couple of days. While I was clean-typing it Max telephoned me. My phone had been cut off, but I had given him my neighbor's number. He had suddenly become ill, been rushed to Hollywood Hospital where his appendix had been removed. He wanted to know how I was coming. I said I'd finished the piece and was going to take it to Zanuck.

"I hope you sell the son-of-a-bitch. I'm gonna owe the doctor and this hospital more than four hundred bucks."

I took the manuscript to Zanuck's office. He was busy, so I gave it to his secretary. "Tell him," I said, "that the guy who wrote this jewel is in Hollywood Hospital and desperately needs the dough."

People are inclined to pooh-pooh miracles, but a couple of days later the story editor called me. "Say," he said, "Zanuck likes this piece. How much does this guy—what's his name?—Williams—want for it?"

"I think he'll be reasonable," I said. "He's in the hospital and needs the dough to get out. How much does Zanuck think it's worth?"

"He'll give a thousand."

"I'll be right over," I said, and had difficulty putting the receiver back on its hook. For a moment I couldn't breathe. It was as if, like a mendicant monk, I had swallowed my tongue.

I got the check, cashed it and took the money to Max. He was so elated he paid me one hundred and fifty dollars.

Because of the popularity of gangster films at that time, Warner's production of his story was box-office successful and for a while he became one of Hollywood's white-haired boys. When his meteoric rise fizzled he went to Mexico. The last time I heard of him he was bartending in Acapulco.

Before leaving for New York I persuaded the Pollocks to hire Osbourne and dropped by Goldwyn Studios to bid goodbye to Gigi. Dillwyn was usually there when she was working but had left to go to a dentist. She was working in *Roman Scandals*, a musical starring Eddie Cantor, and wearing a harem costume with see-through pantalets. Between takes we were able to converse. "Hollywood hasn't been very good to you," she said. "You should have taken Louella Parsons' offer to get into Metro."

"I couldn't make it as an actor. My heart wouldn't have been in it."

She shrugged. "You aren't going to spend the rest of your life in New York. When're you coming back?"

"Soon's I can. Love the sunshine." I scanned her figure through the see-through costume. "My one regret is: I'm leaving your seductive presence."

She raised a hand to smother a smile and looked around to see if we were being overheard. Then, looking directly into my eyes, she said, "I'm sorry to see you go, but perhaps it's just as well."

"Why do you say that?"

"I think it's best that you get out of my life. If you stay here you might mess it up."

"That I don't want to do. I'd like to share it." The kleig lights went on and she had to go on the set. I said, "I'll always hold you in my heart."

She kissed my cheek, said, *"Au revoir,"* and I watched her go toward the glittering set, feeling that I was seeing her for the last time.

CHAPTER TWENTY-ONE

I WAS SITTING IN THE Super-Chief club car wondering whether or not I could afford to buy a martini and still nourish myself all the way to New York, when Henry Dunn, son-in-law of movie bigwig William Fox, came in with Robert Vignola, a film director. I had known them during my stunting days. In the movie business, nepotism was rife and Henry was its personification. He had married Fox's daughter and had become his secretary. His brother and other members of his family also had jobs at Fox Studio. Henry was short, stout and jowly, had thick lips and used talcum powder to cover his heavily bearded cheeks and chin. It was commonly known that he was homosexual. He had been the nominal producer of the picture I had worked on at Donner Lake. Vignola was an Italian-American who had started his career as an actor and had gotten in the movies by giving handball lessons to Sol Wurtzel, the Fox Studio general manager. By one of those little miracles that occur in the movie business, he had become a director of B films. He had the reputation of being a pederast.

They ordered drinks and asked me to join them. When it came time to pay for the second round, I explained my financial predicament. They not only paid for it but for another as well and took me to dinner. Accepting their generosity put me under some obligation, but I weighed that against going sober and hungry for four days and the prostitute in me prevailed.

During dinner Henry and I talked about the fun we had in the Truckee bordello where the company congregated evenings because liquor was available there. Later, lying in my upper bunk, listening to the clippity-clap of the steel wheels ticking off the miles, I recalled the Donner Party tragedy and again the idea to make a novel of it came to mind. It was a powerful story of man's wanderings. Written well, it could be rewarding, could revive my confidence and renew my moribund pride. I was going to work on *The American,* but that is not where I wanted to spend my life. The compulsion to write books was still in me. While on *The American* I could research the migration era at the New York Public Library, where there is a treasure trove of American history. The sound of the train's wheels reminded me that we were traveling as much as eighty miles an hour over terrain on which covered wagons had averaged fifteen miles a day. Before drifting off to slumber I began choosing characters on whom to structure the story. Gigi would be the heroine and Uncle Billy Wilmerding would be the leader of the caravan . . .

The day after arriving in New York, I went to work on *The American.* My shift started at one o'clock in the afternoon, thus leaving my mornings free to spend in the library. Every morning when that great institution's doors opened I went in to delve in books and records of western migration and stayed until time to go to work. Weekends and evenings before retiring I transcribed the notes.

Fifteen dollars of my first paycheck went to Osbourne for the final payment of his beloved Overland.

The Lindbergh kidnapping, then a year old, was still news and, because I had become acquainted with Lindbergh in Paris, I was assigned to report it. The baby had been abducted March 1, 1932, by a kidnaper who climbed to the second story nursery by ladder and left a note demanding a ransom of $50,000. A little more than a month later the money had been yielded on the promise the child would be delivered. The promise proved false; the baby's dead body was found in a wooded area near the Lindbergh home. The only evidence the police had were the wooden ladder and the serial numbers of the twenty-dollar ransom notes. Every bank and gasoline station in the New York area was given a list of their serial numbers and gas station attendants were repeatedly urged to jot down the automobile license plate number on every twenty-dollar bill received. In September 1933, one ransom bill with a license number inked on it was deposited in a bank on 125th Street. The police were notified and promptly arrested Bruno Richard Hauptmann in his Bronx home. There they found more than $14,000 of the ransom money and learned that a portion of the ladder used in the kidnapping had come from a plank in the attic.

During Hauptmann's sensational trial, I was fascinated by his stolid behavior. Throughout he was impassive, cold, emotionless, showed no regrets, no remorse. Psychiatrists claimed he was Lindbergh's alter-ego, the tail-side of the coin, that he had been drawn to Lindbergh because he was his opposite. It was reasoned that he had chosen to hurt Lindbergh because he resented the flyer's overwhelming acclaim. Hauptmann, too, had done a dangerous stunt. He had worked his way across the Atlantic on a freightship and, having no passport, had jumped ship by hiding under a New York dock for twelve hours, hanging some of that time by his hands.

When I could wheedle complimentary tickets from the newspaper's drama department, I would take Mother to a play. Nan and Walter Huston came to New York that fall to open in *Dodsworth* and we attended the play's opening and the after-performance party at the Ritz-Carlton Hotel. Now and then I corresponded with Gigi and Dillwyn and, through the press, kept track of her movie progress. Irving Cobb, the noted columnist, wrote that she was the most beautiful brunette in Hollywood. She was chosen a WAMPAS "Baby Star" in 1934. WAMPAS was the acronym for Western Association of Motion Picture Advertisers. Once a year its members chose the "Babies" from among the upcoming actresses as the most likely to attain stardom. When her first film, *Roman Scandal,* opened in New York, I sat in the front row.

I wrote congratulating her, and Dillwyn replied suggesting I call on his sister Anne. Since her novel *The Perennial Bachelor,* published in 1925, she had followed it every year with another best-seller. She was not only personally successful, she was married to Charles Corliss, at that time a John Pierpont Morgan partner. They lived in a deluxe apartment on upper Fifth Avenue and, at her invitation, I went there for tea.

Anne was stylishly attired and the apartment was awesomly furnished. I sat in a chair which, she told me, had belonged to Charles Dickens and she in one which had belonged to Theodore Roosevelt. The walls were hung with paintings by Degas, Renoir, Monet, Utrillo, Pissarro and Toulouse-Lautrec. The tea, thin chicken sandwiches and chocolate cakes were served by a maid in a stiffly starched apron and lace cap. The cups were the thinnest porcelain, the doilies crisply ironed.

We talked about writing and she said she was collaborating on a play with Alexander Woollcott. "I'm also thinking of writing a novel about Gigi," she said.

Anne's husband did not appear. Dillwyn had written me that he did not feel comfortable with her literary friends: *He thinks they're too Bohemian.* It was a tranquil, get-acquainted tête-à-tête and Anne was gracious and kind. Financially the Corlisses were out of my league. I did not have the time or money to socialize with them.

During two and a half crammed years, I read hundreds of books about the opening of the West during the 1840s, transcribed reams of notes and laboriously finished the first draft of several chapters of my novel. By the spring of 1935, I had progressed to the point I felt I needed to go to the University of California's Bancroft Library where is housed the outstanding Donner Party lore. I quit my job, bid Mother farewell and set out.

To save money I should have gone directly to Berkeley. I didn't. I went by way of Hollywood. As soon as I had checked into the Knickerbocker Hotel I telephoned the Parrishes. To my delight Gigi answered. Would I come for cocktails?

In the taxi carrying me to the Parrishes' Laurel Canyon house I was troubled about the ethics of what I was doing. Coveting another man's wife breaks the Tenth Commandment and, according to law, Gigi belonged to Dillwyn. She was his portion of life's precious bounty. He had discovered her, had shaped, molded and taught her. She was his masterpiece, a beautiful, bright and provocative woman. Then what was I doing trying to lure her away? As I bounded up the stairway to their front door I said to myself, "You're a good-for-nothing reprobate. You've got no right to do this." I rang the bell.

Gigi opened the door, cried, "Welcome home!" and gave me her hand and offered me a cheek to kiss. She was delectable, a delight.

Dillwyn, coming up behind her, pretended mild enthusiasm saying, "The Penitent returns!" and limply shook my hand.

Intoxicated by the sight of her, I flung my trenchcoat on a chair, reeled to take in the familiar room—the bearskin rug, the shelved books, the phonograph, Dillwyn's painting over the fireplace mantel— and strode ebulliently to the big window which overlooked the city. Aggregates of electric lights were twinkling in the gloaming. "Marvelous!" I exclaimed, turning back to them. "In New York, all I could see out of my window was a brick wall."

"What brings you?" Gigi asked. "Have you come to stay?"

"No. I'm well into my migration book. It has taken me two years to get the characters a couple of hundred miles west of Independence, Missouri, and I've got a long way to go. I need to do more research on the Donner Party. There's a wealth of it in the Bancroft Library at the University of California, so I'm on my way to Berkeley. Just stopped by to say hello."

Dillwyn mixed gin with vermouth. While we were sipping our first martini I related my visit with Anne. "She plans to write a book about your life," I said to Gigi.

"Oh, my God! I hope she doesn't."

"It won't be a biography," I said. "How is your career progressing?"

"I've just finished working with John Barrymore and Carole Lombard in *Twentieth Century*. I was Barrymore's secretary."

I laughed. The Great Profile was famous for his womanizing. "Did he try to seduce you?" I was joking.

"No such luck," she said. "Dillwyn was always there to protect me."

Dillwyn smiled meekly and said, "But she did escape one assignation. Howard Hawks, who directed the picture, took a fancy to her. He told her he thought he could get Columbia, which produced it, to give her a long-term contract. Then he invited her to dinner at his house."

Gigi said, "Jessie, my agent, said Hawks was an important director, and I should go. Timmy and I had a real knock down and drag out fight. I had to take a taxi because he wouldn't take me."

"What happened?" I asked.

"Hawks greeted me at the door and led me to the bar, behind which was his agent, Jerry Something-or-other. Jerry poured us some sherry, and Hawks and I went and stood before the fire. I assumed other guests would appear presently. 'I'm so glad you could come,' Hawks said. 'I want to know all about you. What's this about you coming to California on a motorcycle?'

"I told him that it was ghastly because we started from Delaware at the wrong time, in October, and that it was raining and cold. 'Who's we?' he asked, and from the tone of his voice I sensed he was startled. 'Why, my husband and I,' I said. 'We were on our honeymoon.' Hawks looked at me as if he had never seen me before. 'You mean you're married?' His voice had risen. He stepped away from me, went to the bar and berated Jerry: 'For God's sake! Why didn't you tell me this young lady's married? You know I don't fool around with married girls!' The two of them left the room. I stood in front of the fireplace for some time before Jerry reappeared. He said, 'I'm sorry, Mister Hawks has been called away. I'll take you home,' which he did."

"What about the contract at Columbia?" I asked.

"Mister Cohn offered one, but Jessie wouldn't let me accept it. She said it was for peanuts."

After the third martini I sensed I might be overstaying my welcome and asked to call a taxi.

"Oh," Gigi said, "don't go. Stay for supper. I'll whip up some spaghetti to celebrate your return."

Overjoyed, I said, "I'd be insane to refuse."

She fetched her purse, said, "Timmy darling, would you get us some wine?" and gave him money.

I said, "I'll set the table."

Dillwyn left and Gigi went into the kitchen. I followed her as far as the kitchen doorway and said, "I need to know where the silver is."

She directed me to silverware, place-mats, and napkins. I did not move at once to get them but stood looking at her. She was in profile, engaged in slicing a large onion. I heard the car's engine start and its sounds recede. The ticking of the kitchen clock sounded unusually loud, and when the cuckoo popped out to announce seven o'clock I was startled. There was something emotional, mystical and prophetic about the setting, as if designed for drama.

I said, "The reason I came to Hollywood on the way to Berkeley is because I hoped to see you."

She glanced at me, smiling faintly. There was approval in her eyes. "I wondered if you were ever coming back," she said.

Inexorably drawn, I stepped toward her. It was as if we were following a foreordained script. She put down the knife and onion and turned to me. We embraced and, as if on cue, kissed.

Our parabolas, which had started from distant places and wandered seemingly without design, had joined.

She said, "Remember?—I had a premonition you might complicate my life." We kissed again before she pushed me away saying, "It can never be."

"Why not?"

"I can't leave Dillwyn. He needs me. And there's my career; I can't give that up."

"I'll support you. I'll get a job."

She became busy at the sink, filling a pot with water for the spaghetti. "It's impossible," she said and took the pot to the stove. I went to her and again we embraced. Her head on my shoulder, she said, "It's wonderful to see you again," and then expressed a guilty afterthought. "Better hurry and set the table."

I was sweeping up the pieces of a glass I had dropped when I heard the car drive up, its engine stop and its door slam.

Dillwyn whistled coming up the stairs, doubtless to warn us he had returned. He brought two bottles of Chianti.

During dinner Gigi and I tried to disguise our feelings. We were overly polite, laughed too heartily at each other's remarks and otherwise revealed nervousness. Dillwyn must have felt the current of our emotions, but if he did he gave no sign. I helped with the dishes after dinner "in lieu of Osbourne" and Dillwyn drove me to the Knickerbocker.

Being alone with him was uncomfortable. We did not have much to say to each other and the silences were oppressive. I condemned Howard Hawks for his nefarious behavior, the while thinking that I was the kettle calling the pot black.

Dillwyn said, "In the movie business, I'm sure you know, girls have to go through those situations. The casting couch is one way to fame and fortune."

As we drove up to the hotel, he said, "How long are you going to be here?"

"Leaving tomorrow for Berkeley."

"When you coming back?"

"Don't know. It'll be a while."

"Good luck," he said, and drove away. It was obvious he was glad to be shed of me.

CHAPTER TWENTY-TWO

RIDING NORTH ON THE Greyhound bus, watching the ever-changing scenery slither yonder, I contemplated the situation. Why, I asked, am I so overwhelmed by this lady? She was beautiful, to be sure, was modest, kind, generous and capable; but there was another aspect of her character I could not define. From her came a magnetic intensity which thrilled me. If it was love it was as mysterious and incomprehensible as life itself. Would this lady who has my heart, leave her husband? And if she did, would she then have me? Hardly. I could only offer her adoration, fidelity and a doubtful future. From her point of view, I was a long-odds gamble, an unstable, rootless twenty-seven-year-old, unsuccessful writer without income. My assets were nil. Leaving Dillwyn would burn the bridge to his family's wealth and prestige, and if she did leave him she could take her pick of any number of well-endowed, distinguished and celebrated men. Where, if any, was my common sense? I sorely needed a wife but before I chose one I would have to be able to afford her, would have to be able to propel my end of the seesaw.

From Berkeley I wrote the Parrishes a thank you note and calculatingly included my address.

The Bancroft Library is loaded with lore of western migration, with diaries, letters and books, with newspaper clippings of incidents, tragedies, accidents, mishaps and jokes, and I sought to devour them all. Day after day I assembled data and spent evenings developing the novel. I did not pause for lunch. As I wrote, Gigi's image appeared on almost every page.

I spent an evening with Freddie McNear, a San Franciscan I had known in Hollywood. His family was wealthy from gold mines and he had never worked for a living. Together we had driven to Guaymas, Mexico, over the roughest trail imaginable and had shared other experiences. Through him I obtained access to the California Historical Society library, where, after ransacking the Bancroft, I holed up. Freddie took me to the Bohemian Club for drinks. I offered to pay my share, but he would not permit it. 'You can take me to dinner when you finish your book," he said. "When's that going to be?"

"God knows. I hope this year."

"Seems to me you're putting all your eggs in one basket without assurance that any of them will hatch."

"That's a writer's gamble," I said. "The poor bastard spends years researching and writing a book, then maybe a year or more finding a publisher. Another year will pass before it's published, after which he has to go out and sell the damned thing. He's lucky if he makes a dollar a day."

"Then why do it?"

I shrugged. "Truthfully, I don't know. It's some kind of compulsion, a monkey gnawing at my consciousness. He wants me to structure indelible words full of wisdom and rhythm that will go down though the ages. About the only satisfaction I'll get is seeing my name on a book's cover."

"That's hardly enough."

"James Joyce spent years writing, and almost as long finding a publisher. It was finally published in France by an American, Sylvia Beach, who ran a bookstore. Fortunately for Joyce, the book was banned in the United States and England. Otherwise he might not have earned a franc. In Paris tourists bought it and took it home as a token of sophistication. Whether or not they read it is a moot question. His next book, *Finnegan's Wake,* took him about fifteen years to write and I don't think he ever made any money from it. The only thing that kept him and his family alive throughout his writing life was charity. Wealthy ladies supported him. The one thing every artist needs, he told me, is an angel."

"Why don't you get a job and write in your spare time?"

"If I stop now so will the pioneers I'm writing about. I've got to keep 'em going. Presently they're at Salt Lake. If I leave 'em, they'll die."

"Seems like they've got you by the gonads," Freddie said. "Well, good luck." We clicked glasses before sipping the cabernet.

I HAD BEEN in San Francisco almost a month before I received a letter from Gigi:

> It may interest you to know that there have been some changes here. Dillwyn has gone to New York to visit his sister. He did not want to leave me in the Laurel Canyon house alone, so persuaded our friends Mary Frances Fisher and her husband Alfred to come stay with me. Al is an English instructor at Occidental College and Mary Frances is a fledgling writer. She is working on a book about food during the Depression entitled *How To Cook a Wolf.* They are both darlings. If you're planning to come back to Hollywood I'd love to see you.

I was breathless getting to a telephone. "Does this mean that you and Dillwyn have separated for keeps?"

"Not exactly. It's sort of a trial."

"When's he coming back?"

"I don't know. Not for a while. When're you coming down?"

"I've just about finished up here. I could come this weekend."

"That will be fine. I'll have Em Eff prepare a banquet in your honor. She's a marvelous cook. Are you hungry?"

"For you, yes."

She laughed. "Well, let's not have this call cost you any more. I'll look forward to Saturday." She hung up.

I telephoned the Pollocks, told Mary Ellen I was coming and she said I could stay in their bunkhouse with Osbourne until I could find a permanent abode.

Osbourne came to the bus station in his Overland to pick me up. We embraced with brotherly fervor. Seeing the car I said, "I'm surprised the old lady is still running."

"New engine," he said, grinning proudly.

"Belongs in the Smithsonian."

"They tell me she gets more valuable every year. They don't make 'em anymore. Some day I'm gonna trade her for a Rolls Royce." We had a good laugh.

When I got to the Parrish's house the Fishers were present, so I had to be satisfied with pecking Gigi's cheek.

The Fishers had recently returned to California from France, where Al had taught English in the university in Dijon while M.F. had been engrossed in culinary arts. In time she would become celebrated for her literary writings about food. The "banquet" she prepared turned out to be a salad, the principal ingredients of which were raw onion, mushrooms and okra. It was not to my relish, but to be polite and because I was hungry, I devoured my portion.

While we were with the Fishers there was no opportunity for Gigi and me to speak privately, so after dinner we went for a drive in her convertible. Dillwyn had not taught her to operate the car, so I drove. We went up Laurel Canyon to Mulholland Drive and parked in an uninhabited area overlooking the Los Angeles basin. The city's million multicolored lights sparkled like sequins on a Spanish dancer's skirt. There was no moon, but the sky was awash with stars. As soon as I had turned off the engine a wordless, famishingly intense kissing session began. When finally we paused to profess our pent-up thoughts, I said, "It's more than obvious and natural that I'm trembling to make love to you."

She moved slightly away and said, "This is not the time and place."

"Granted. Could we make a date?"

"Please don't be impatient, John." She enclasped my hand and her touch calmed me. "I have to get used to my new freedom."

I was hypnotized and bewitched, a satyr under the spell of a tantalizing, enrapturing Thais. Whatever she said, I would do. Alone with her, with stars above and shimmering lights below, with the soft air and the faint musical noises of the night, I was in a replica of Heaven. I said, "You are aware that I adore you, that I want to marry you, that I want to live with you for the rest of my life, that I want to take care of you and to share your children."

"All of that will have to wait. I'm not sure that I'll get a divorce. If I do, and assuming it is granted, it'll be a year, according to California law, before I can marry."

"You could get a quickee divorce in Mexico."

"Wouldn't think of it. For the first time in my life I am an independent person. To me it's a fantastic experience and, at least for a while, I don't want to be beholden." She kissed my cheek to take the sting out of the declaration.

"Where does that leave me?"

"We'll have fun together. I know very little about you. The Pollocks tell me that in Paris you were a playboy, that you loved 'em and left 'em. If I get married again, I want it to be for keeps. They tell me you've already been married a couple of times."

"Once," I interrupted. "The other was annulled."

"Well, you've had more than your share of bed-mates. I have had only one."

"How did you come to marry Dillwyn?"

"One summer the Pauls took me and the children to Corea, a fishing village on the Maine coast. While we were there Dillwyn joined us. During the war he had left Harvard to become an ambulance driver in France. He had never had a job, but he and his sister Anne had written and illustrated several children's books. He had an elfish spirit and got along so well with us children that Daddy proposed he come to Canterbury, spend the winter and tutor us. This he did. As a teacher he proved to be permissive. He thought learning should be amusing. 'One learns more quickly when he or she is having a good time,' he told us. When I said I couldn't understand geometry, he took my math book and tossed it into the pot-bellied stove, saying, 'Chances are you'd never use it anyway.'

"One day in the spring, shortly before he was to go home to Delaware, he asked me to go walking with him. I was surprised by his seriousness. We went traipsing through the woods, ostensibly to hunt trailing arbutus. When we were out of sight of the house he stopped.

'I've got something to tell you,' he said. 'I've fallen madly, hopelessly in love with you.'

"I was thunderstruck. I had been aware that he liked me and had been flattered by his attention but was flabbergasted by his declaration. I was thirteen and he was more than twice my age. Moreover, he was beyond my ken intellectually and culturally. I was a child. He could have been my father. 'I want you to marry me,' he said.

"Marry you!" I exclaimed, flustered. "Why, I can't do that! I'm not old enough!

" 'I don't mean right away,' he said quickly, as if I were a bird and might fly away. 'I mean when you grow up—when you're sixteen. Just promise me.'

"I had never made a personal decision, had always been at the command of others. I was secure and happy with the Pauls and not ready to be drawn elsewhere. The thought of leaving them was dismal. Undecided to laugh or cry, I laughed, tapped him on a shoulder, said, 'You're crazy!' and ran. He soon caught me and, struggling playfully, we fell into the snow. He kissed me on the lips.

"When I was almost sixteen I was in Switzerland with the Pauls. He came to get me. I did not feel that I could refuse him. He took me to his mother's home in Delaware where we were married."

"That's quite a story. It explains a lot."

"He has been very kind to me and I really shouldn't leave him. But there's something missing, an emptiness in my life that I want to fill. He hasn't been able to support us. We've had to rely on his sister Anne."

I said, "I assure you I am not the philanderer you've been told, and if you marry me I promise to be faithful."

Her laughter was melodious. "Right now I don't want to marry anyone. I'm supporting myself and I want to be free."

"But you don't want to go through life a grass widow!"

"I prefer merry to grass."

"I can wait. I've been in love with you since I was born and will be as long as I live."

"How would you support me? You're broke."

"I'm hoping the book will make a bundle. It'll take you more than a year to get a divorce," I said, resorting to salesmanship. "Look, if you marry me I promise, my hand on a Bible, to provide you with food, fun, adventure, excitement and a mink coat. To me you are the most beautiful, marvelous and darling woman on earth, and I will devote myself to providing, protecting, adoring and amusing you. Together we will live a wonderful life." I paused and looked at her to see how my pitch was doing. She was smiling. "I've never been truly in love before," I went on, now under full steam.

She laughed at the hyperbole and pressed against me. "You're impossible!"

"It's gospel," I said, and embraced her.

When we parted, I said, "Gigi is not an Irish name. Where did you get it?"

"I was christened Gertrude. My baby brother called me Gigoo and it came from that. I hated the name Gertrude."

"Gigi doesn't suit you. Sounds gaga."

"My middle name's Katherine."

"Well, that's a strong name. You are a Katherine. May I call you that?"

"If it pleases you." She laughed. "Already you're trying to change me."

"I don't want to change anything else. From now on I'm going to call you Katy."

After more kissing, she said, "I'd better be getting home."

I started the engine.

I MOVED INTO the small hotel on Sunset Boulevard where I had lived as a stunt man. As the days rolled into limbo I worked on the novel and scrambled to pay the nine-dollar-a-week rent. Jean Wick sold one of my short stories and for a while this windfall kept me solvent. A couple of times Mother, subscribing to my wails, sent me a few simoleons. With one contribution she wrote:

Accept these few farthings with my love. Sorry I can't send more. Your last letter reads as if you were one the jump ahead of the sheriff. You and I seem to be affected with the same disease. As for me, I am constantly on the lookout for the man in the white coat coming over the hill to take me to the old ladies' poorhouse.

Creating is always a lonely pursuit and more often than not
fraught with parsimony. It seems to me though that, at your age
and experience, you should have climbed out of the poor-man's
pit. You can't go on expecting charity to carry you to the grave in
a silk-lined coffin. Broke as you are, how are you getting along
with the "ideal woman"? According to your chart, you're going
through a black period and it looks as if you'll be some time
coming out of it. Don't get discouraged. Accept gracefully the
aches and pains of misfortune . . .

When Katy was not working I would dine with her and the Fishers.
At other times my nourishment came from a nine-cent quart of milk
which I drank in the grocery store to keep from paying a deposit on the
bottle. Meanwhile, I kept moving the wagon train across the continent,
subconsciously suffering the frustrations, discomforts and calamitous
tribulations of its characters, convinced that the completion and publication of the novel was as essential to me as surviving was to them. I
hoped it would revivify me, raise me in Katy's estimation and make me
some money.

That summer Katy worked in several films, Al Fisher taught English
to the children of Otto Klemperer who had come from Germany to
conduct the Los Angeles Symphony Orchestra, and M.F. taught a
French class. Some weekends I would take a day off and we would all
go to the beach to swim, sun and picnic. Late in July, Katy left with
other WAMPUS "Baby Stars" and a number of celebrities on a
promotional junket. They went by chartered train to Chicago and
Minneapolis and appeared in packed movie palaces. Hedda Hopper
went along as "chaperon." When Katy returned I was delighted to find
her as unblemished, affectionate and radiant as ever.

She said it had been a marvelous experience. "We were wined and
dined, cheered and flattered, honored, admired and besought. It was
unbelievable, like going through fairyland."

The first thing she wanted to do when she got home was to learn to
drive a car. I took time off to teach her. Her motorcycle experience
helped and she learned quickly. However, acquiring a driver's license
brought out a facet of her character I had not suspected. Thereafter
when I was driving she became co-chauffeur. "Look out!—there's a

stop sign!" "You're driving too fast!" "Watch out for that car!" It seems that she had quickly forgotten that I had taught her to drive.

The evening of her birthday in late August I drove her to Malibu to have dinner. Our spirits were bubbling and it seemed that nothing untoward could occur. When she asked me to drive more slowly I did so. Once she said, "As soon as you get behind the wheel the stuntman in you comes out." I was annoyed.

"Haven't you learned," I said, "that a lady shouldn't italicize a man's shortcomings? Don't you know that she should see him in the same state of perfection as he sees himself?"

"Posh!" She followed this expletive by cautioning me about a traffic light which changed as we reached the crossing. I decided to go through the intersection while the light was yellow and thought that I had done so. But presently a police siren howled behind us. My temper rose when I was given a citation, and when, as we went on, Katy said, "I warned you." I was hard pressed to contain my irritability. Thereafter we rode for a while without speaking. I gradually calmed down.

Finally, after begging a pardon for my behavior, I said, "When I'm driving I'd appreciate it if you wouldn't tell me what to do."

"I only tell you what to do when I think I'm being helpful," she said. "I do it for your own good."

"I appreciate your concern, but I am a grown man. I usually know what I am doing."

"Well, I'll try to be quiet while you're driving if, when I'm speaking, you'll not interrupt me to supply a word or phrase. I'll concede that you know how to drive if you'll concede I know how to speak the language."

"When I supply a word," I said, smiling, "I'm simply trying to help you build a vocabulary. Like most women, you're inclined to talk a great deal and sometime you grope for a word. It's then that I—" smiling at her "—kindly supply it. Being a writer, I have a fairly verbose vocabulary."

By now I was joking, but she seized the opportunity to retort: "You may have a verbose vocabulary, but you can't spell for sour apples."

"Touché!" I exclaimed and abruptly both of us burst out laughing.

CHAPTER TWENTY-THREE

ONE EVENING WHEN I arrived at her house, Katy greeted me:
"Guess what?"

"You've been offered a starring role."

"Nope."

"You're pregnant," I was joking.

"Don't be silly. I've hired a lawyer to get a divorce."

I embraced her and danced her around. "Hallelujah! Is Dillwyn protesting?"

"No."

"Is he going to pay half?"

"No. It's my doing."

"How about alimony?"

"If there is any I'll have to pay him. I'm the only one earning anything. And there won't be any distribution of property. About the only thing we own is the Ford, and I bought that with my own money. It'll be a year before it becomes final."

"I will have finished the book by then. We can be married."

"Meanwhile, to keep from starving to death I think you should get a job."

The next morning I telephoned Larry Doyle, my erstwhile collaborator at Universal, who had been hired by Warner Brothers to write a film for Bette Davis.

"Larry," I said, "I'm down to the low common denominator and badly in need of a job. Do you think you can help me get one there at Warners?"

"Have you finished your book?" he asked.

"Not quite, but I'm getting there."

"I don't have much clout in the scenario department. It's alive with relatives of the Brothers. I'm here because my agent is their cousin."

"I'll take any kind of a job. I could be a reader, could write dialog—anything to keep me alive while I finish the book."

With his help the studio hired me as a publicist, salary $50 a week. It was a humiliating come-down, but it was better than nothing. I waited until the day I went to work to telephone Katy.

"Are you sitting down?"

"Yes."

"I've got a job."

"A job!—That's marvelous!—Doing what?"

"I'm a tub-thumper."

"What's that?"

"A press-agent in the publicity department at Warner Brothers."

"You don't seem to be happy."

"It doesn't please me for two reasons—one, it will take up so much of my time, and two, I had hoped to go through this life without writing rubbish, but that's what I'm gonna be doing."

She laughed. "Aristophanes must be turning over in his grave."

MY FIRST assignment was to publicize *The Singing Kid*, starring Al Jolson, then in production. I was to go to the set each day, pick up the petty goings-on of the principals and puff them up. When there were no items of interest, I was to invent some. Even for an actor, Al Jolson was unusually egocentric and reveled in publicity. The first time we met I suggested that he was the greatest entertainer of all time, expecting him to modestly pooh-pooh the overstatement, but he gulped it hungrily.

"Other people have told me that," he said.

"You've probably made more money than any other entertainer in the history of the theater," I went on.

"Yeah, I guess that's true. I've been at it a long time, ever since I was a kid."

"How much would you say you've earned in your lifetime?"

His face pursed, he cogitated. "Oh, seven, maybe eight million."

The wire services carried what I wrote about that interview but Jolson did not like it. He thought it belittled him. "Hell," he said, "I've made more money than that."

Edward G. Robinson was another star in the Warner firmament who loved to see his name in print. He particularly liked us hacks to write about his art collection. Whenever he bought a painting, and he frequently did, he was eager to have it publicized, thinking it enhanced his cultural image. "They are my investments," he would explain. "Hell of a lot more rewarding than buying stocks and bonds." He was prostrated when he and his wife Gladys were divorced and he had to sell much of his collection to settle their estate. His howling may have been heard in the stratosphere.

I enjoyed writing the press book for *The Green Pastures*. The cast was all black. The protagonist, who played De Lawd, reminded me of my friend Brown, except that he was a pious-appearing reprobate who spent much of his time chasing women. Once, when he was needed on the set, Marc Connelly, the co-producer and author of the screenplay, sent me to a hotel in downtown Los Angeles where the actor lived, to get him. I found him in bed with one of the picture's angels. When I brought him in, Connelly admonished him saying, "While you're playing God you'd better mind your morals. The Good Lord won't like being represented by a sinner. He might bring His wrath down on your head."

"Why, man," the actor replied, "I don't believe the Lord Hisself would have turned his back on that gal."

I thought the film might get nation-wide press if I could persuade Aimée Semple McPherson to permit De Lawd to preach in her Four-Square Tabernacle. She had a strong appetite for publicity and, since her sensational disappearing act, whatever she did was newsworthy. I telephoned her. Her voice was soft, intimate and slightly seductive, not at all like the hell-fire-and-damnation oratory she used so effectively from the pulpit. She told me she was intrigued by the idea but would have to submit it to her Board of Deacons for their approval. A couple of days later I went to see her and she reported that the deacons had vetoed it. I think the "Board of Deacons" was her strong-minded mother.

Errol Flynn did not care a damn about publicity, but he got a lot of it because of his weakness for women and carousing. All of the other performers in the Warner stable I worked with knew the value of publicity and cooperated in its production, except Humphrey Bogart.

How Bogart ever attained film stardom is one of those Hollywood miracles. He was of medium height and anything but physically attractive. His face was rather dour. His upper lip which had been injured aboard a Navy ship during World War One, was slightly paralyzed and because of it his speech had a slight lisp. When I went to work at Warners he was acting in low-budget films, usually as a heavy, and had been lucky to get that far. As a stage actor he had had little success in New York. His first break came when he was cast as the gangster in Robert Sherwood's play, *The Petrified Forest,* in which Leslie Howard played the leading role. Warners acquired the play's film rights, hired Howard and intended casting Edward G. Robinson in the gangster role. But Howard threatened to withdraw unless the part was given to Bogart. The studio yielded. The film was a great success and the studio began featuring Bogart in "B" pictures, which is when I came in.

When I introduced myself to him, exuding my dyed-in-the-wool Southern charm, he was brusque. "So you're the news boy," he said sarcastically. "What the hell do you want from me?"

I broadened my already friendly smile and jokingly said, "The public would like to know about your sex life."

I expected him to laugh, but he didn't. He said, "Oh, for Christ's sake!"

"That's a joke," I said. "But I *would* like to know if there's any romance in your life."

"I'm looking for a wife. That do you any good?"

"I'll put an ad in the paper."

He did not think that was funny, either. He said, "Smart ass, eh?"

That is an example of our subsequent conversations. I offered to interview him but we never became friendly. We simply endured each other. Bogart smoked cigarettes incessantly, often lighting one from the butt of another. One day I counted how many cigarettes he smoked— about three packs—and wrote a release, pointing out that without cigarettes actors and actresses would not know what to do with their hands. Bogart did not like it and told me so in strongly articulated words: "Why the hell can't you write something worthwhile, for Christ's sake?"

I was on the set when Mayo Methot came to play a part in a film with him. She and I had a friendly embrace and I introduced her to him. During the making of that film they started a love affair. Subsequently Mayo divorced Percy Morgan and she and Bogart were married. It was not a harmonious mating and lasted only a few years. During World War Two their marital battles were in newspapers almost as often as Ernie Pyle's columns.

IT TOOK A little while to pay my debts but as soon as I had done so I rented a furnished cottage on a steep hillside in the Laurel Canyon area and promptly gave a house-warming party. Friends came with towels, sheets, pillow cases and the like. A practical joker brought a big, fat, dirty old ewe badly in need of shearing. He claimed to have kidnaped her from the Los Angeles stockyards. Attached to her was a pair of knitting needles and a note: *Make your own goddamn blanket!*

Katy brought, for good luck, a cluster of leaves somewhat like a small head of dried lettuce and told me it was a Rose of Jericho. "Would you like to know its Latin name?" she asked. I nodded. "It's Anastatica Hierochuntica." She laughed. "I'm glad you didn't know because it gives me a chance to show off."

"I'm impressed," I said.

"To come alive," she explained, "all it requires is water. Neglected as you see it, it will dry up. But even after a hundred years, if given water, it will thrive again. Thus, it never dies. I brought it to represent my affection for you."

We had one howling time getting rid of the ewe. Because of the steep hill there was no place for her to graze. With a rope around her neck I tied her to a porch support, and while the party was in high gear she slid down the bank and was left dangling. By the time we got to her she had all but strangled. Two of us managed to haul her up and resuscitate her. I telephoned the Society for Prevention of Cruelty to Animals and a truck came and picked her up. The friend who brought her said, "I guess you'll have to sleep cold tonight."

As for the Rose of Jericho, I watered it from time to time, but sometimes forgot. The Mexican girl who came to clean assumed it had died and dumped it in the trash can. I sorely regretted losing it, not only because it had represented Katy's vow of affection but because it seemed to me prima-facie evidence that life is eternal.

Katy had been renting the house where she and the Fishers were living on a month-to-month basis from a woman who owned the master lease and the furniture. When, that fall, Al returned to Occidental to teach and he and Mary Frances moved back to Eagle Rock to be near the college, she was faced with an alternative: buy some furniture and stay where she was or move into a less expensive apartment. She elected to do the latter. When I suggested she move in with me, her response was anything but enthusiastic.

"Oh, my Lord! I can't do that!"

"Why not?"

"It's immoral—that's why not! What would our friends think? The Pauls are going to move out here and what would they think of me? And what would your mother think?"

"Darling," I said, "Queen Victoria is dead."

"Morality isn't."

"But us living together makes good sense. We love each other and can't get married. There's no sense in living in two houses. It's not only more expensive and inconvenient, it's not half as joyful."

She refused and rented a furnished apartment for thirty-five dollars a month. I helped her move. The apartment was a single room with a let-down Murphy bed, a pullman kitchen and a bath. It was in downtown Hollywood. The first time I saw it I said, "This is no place for a beautiful lady to live by herself," hoping she might change her mind. "They're all kinds of knot-heads out there. You've got no protection."

"There's a double lock on the door," she said, and began unpacking.

"Look," I said, still trying, "why do we have to wait until the State of California says we can dwell together? We're grown up. We love each other. Why can't we make a marriage contract right now?—vow to have and to hold from this day forward, for better, for worse, for richer, for poorer, to love and to cherish until death do us part?"

I paused for her reaction. She was frowning. I went on. "We could do that, and I'm sure it would be all right with the Lord."

"It won't be legal," she said. "What we need is a license."

I gave up and went back to my bailiwick. For a while we saw each other infrequently, usually on weekends. Then late one night she telephoned: "Did I waken you?"

"No."

"What are you doing?"

"Driving oxen. Same as always."

"I'm lonesome."

"That makes two of us."

"I've decided I don't like living alone."

"Neither do I."

"I've been thinking about what you said, that it's silly for us to have two homes."

"Well—?"

"My next month's rent is due tomorrow."

"I'll come right over and help you pack," I said, and didn't pause getting under way.

By the time I arrived, she had put her bags, pictures and books in her car. I was so excited, I embraced and kissed her before asking what I could do to help.

She said, "There's a half bottle of bourbon in the kitchen. Let's celebrate." I poured the drinks. We clicked glasses and I toasted. "To everlasting togetherness!" Then I asked, "What made you change your mind?"

"I was unable to sleep, and lying there I thought about us and my future. I am alone and adrift, as I was as a child. I have no family. The few friends I have are not close. The only time in my life I ever felt loved was when I was with the Pauls. 'What,' I asked myself, 'am I going to do with my life? Am I going to stay in Hollywood and hope to make it in the movies or am I going to get away and find a happier life?' Hollywood is full of girls like me. The only interest men have in us is as bed partners. I feel belittled. Just last evening, Jessie Wadsworth asked me to go out with some mucky-muck from General Motors. I refused. She's going to have a fit when she finds out I've decided to live with you. She's going to say I'm ruining my career."

I said, "I wish I could tell you how elated I was when I picked up the phone and heard your voice, and the sensation of joy your words gave me. I almost fell out of bed. If the Good Fairy had offered me a wish it would have been to hear what you said. It was highly dramatic. It said that I was the luckiest man alive, that I was going to live with the most beautiful, gracious, charming, and delightful woman on earth!"

"Whoa!" Katy said, laughing. "Don't overdo it."

I put an arm around her. "I love you with all my heart and will do so as long as I live. I, too, am alone. Like you, as a child I was pushed from place to place. For years I have wanted to have an honest-to-God home. I've wanted to be married to a wonderful woman and have wonderful children."

"You talk as if we were about to be married."

"It is my hope—as soon as the law allows."

"I've said it before and I think it's time to say it again—." She smiled to take the sting out of what she was about to say. "—I've been told that you are unreliable, that you love 'em and leave 'em. If we do get married it has got to be for keeps. I don't want another divorce. If there is one, you'll have to get it; I won't."

"If you marry me there'll be no divorce because I won't give you any reason for one."

We lapped up the liquor and left, she in her car, following me in mine.

It was after two o'clock in the morning when I carried her over the threshold, put her down and said, "Welcome home!"

AFTER KATY had filed for divorce, Dillwyn wrote to Mary Frances Fisher from Delaware, asking her to join him and his mother for a trip to Europe. She accepted the invitation and during their sojourn she and Dillwyn began a love affair. It did not end when they returned, though she rejoined her husband. Dillwyn went back to Switzerland, bought a house near Vevey and invited both M.F. and Al to spend the summer with him. They went. After a few weeks Al found the *maison à trois* uncomfortable and left, whereupon M.F. obtained a divorce and she and Dillwyn were married.

While driving an ambulance in France during World War One, Dillwyn had injured a hip. In Switzerland the hip became tubercular and a leg was amputated. He and M.F. returned to California and Katy and I went to see them. He was pleasant and we thought he was enduring the pain and disability well, but shortly thereafter he ended his life. In a letter to Katy, M.F. wrote: *You were his true love and he was mine.* . . .

CHAPTER TWENTY-FOUR

THAT FALL, Nan and Walter Huston, after a long run in New York, came to Los Angeles with *Dodsworth*. Katy and I attended an evening performance at the Biltmore Theater, after which I took her backstage and introduced her to them. They invited us to join them for supper. Nan told us that *Dodsworth* was to be filmed by Sam Goldwyn, that Walter was to be starred and that Fay Bainter was to play his social-climbing wife. She grimaced before saying, "My part's going to be played by Mary Astor. Goldwyn wants a younger, more glamorous girl." She asked how my book was going and I said I did not have much time for it, that I was working at Warner Brothers as a publicist. "However, I'm getting it done, working on it nights and weekends. I applied for a Guggenheim Fellowship, but was turned down."

"I've got an idea," Walter said. "I'll be your Guggenheim. You can come to work for me, handle my correspondence, be my gofer and finish your novel."

It was a startling invitation and I was overjoyed by the opportunity to escape from Warner's hustling department and become associated with a man for whom I had the strongest esteem and affection. "I'd love it," I said. "When do I start?"

"The play closes in two weeks and Nan and I are going to the mountains. You can come with us."

To me, it was a ten-strike, but on our way home Katy expressed concern. "If you're going to live in the mountains, what about me?"

"Oh, they'll invite you—no question."

"But if I'm going to work in Hollywood, I can't stay up there. Furthermore, they won't want me all the time. It'll be embarrassing because they know we're not married."

"I'll come home weekends," I said, hoping that would reassure her. It didn't.

She said, "I don't like to be dependent on friends."

"It'll only be for a little while—until I finish the book."

"He didn't say anything about salary."

"No, but he'll be fair. It's a great opportunity. I'll be helping him and he'll be helping me." I took a hand off the wheel, clasped one of hers and kissed it. "You are my hope and my happiness, the most marvelous companion on the face of the earth. If it doesn't work out or makes you unhappy, I won't do it."

She ruminated for a while before saying, "I want to do what pleases you."

IT WAS mid-November when the Hustons took me to Running Springs, a hamlet in the San Bernardino Mountains near where their house had been built. On the way up, everything above four thousand feet was mantled in snow. Nan and I told Walter about the fun we'd had in Paris without alluding to our brief romance. While she and I still had strong affection for each other, her marriage had sublimated any sensuality and I thought it would be inappropriate to mention it. When we had exhausted that subject, Nan asked about Katy. From the tone of her inquiry I sensed she disapproved of her. I briefed them on Katy's biography, and Nan said, "Typical movie-star story. Girl comes out of the ghetto into the glitter."

Walter said, "Sounds like Mary Astor. She, too, had a mean father, a German immigrant who molested her. When she was fourteen, according to the story, he sent her out on the street to earn money."

"From what I understand, she's still at it in Hollywood," Nan said, laughing to mitigate the spite.

Addressing me, Walter said, "Your friend Katy and I might be kinfolk. My parents came to Canada from Ireland, and they say everybody from the Emerald Isle is related."

Nan asked, "Are you going to marry her?"

"If she'll have me."

"I don't think you should. You're a writer on your way up. Before you take on responsibilities you should make a name for yourself."

"I don't want to live alone any more," I said. "I've been wanting a home for a long time."

Walter said, "You've got one now."

Nan's brother, Roy Sunderland, was at the Running Springs grocery-post-office. Because it was impractical to use a car, he had come in a caterpillar-tread contraption to carry us through the snow and slush to the house, three miles away. Roy was about fifty, skinny as a plank and somewhat unstable due to a nerve disease which was whispered to have been syphilis. He and his wife, Ray, were caretakers of the Huston place. Walter left his car in the village's only garage, we loaded our luggage onto the snowmobile, piled in and set out. Leaving the highway, we snaked through a cathedral-like forest of gigantic pines, Walter singing his vaudeville songs, *Oh, I Haven't Got The Dough Re Me* and *Why Speak Of It?* I joined in. Our cacophony and the clatter of the Model T engine alarmed wildlife along the way. Squirrels and deer scattered and birds flew off chirping warnings of alarm.

Huston House was high-ceilinged and heavily beamed with, in the living room, a gigantic stone fireplace sized for five-foot logs. Facing the fireplace was a semi-circular, twenty-foot divan, "the passion pit." The dining room was baronial. There was an eight-stool bar. The large kitchen had both electric and wood-burning stoves. An extra-large refrigerator and deep-freezer contained a month's supply of meat, vegetables and fruit, while the pantry housed boxes of canned and packaged foods. There were three major guest rooms, all with baths, and the master bedroom had an adjacent sitting room with fireplace. In the basement was a six-bunk "overflow" room. Ray and Roy lived in small quarters on the far side of the house. I was assigned the guest room which looked over the ice-filled swimming pool and tennis court.

The evening we arrived we stretched the cocktail hour, me bartending, while Ray prepared dinner. After dinner we all helped "do" the dishes, then Walter and I played cribbage and Nan read from her Christian Science textbook.

Save when there were no guests, that was pretty much the evening routine. We would all be in bed by ten o'clock. During the day Walter and I would spend an hour or two on some project, writing letters, reading scripts, in the workshop making furniture or repairing one thing or another. When the weather was good we swept the court, played tennis or went together to Running Springs for mail. Every day I managed to squeeze a few hours to work on my opus.

One day Walter and I decided to try skiing. Both of us were novices. He had done some cross-country and a little downhill for a film, but I hadn't skied since I was at Donner Lake. We clamped on skis and herringboned up a nearby hill to experiment. It was very cold and the snow was crusted. When we got to the top, he elected to go first and set out with a whoop. Because of the trees I soon lost sight of him. Presently from below came a crashing sound, followed almost immediately by his yell: "John!—don't do it!" But the warning came too late; I was under way. The frozen snow made it difficult to avoid the trees. Unable to stop I went by Walter with a whoosh. He had struck a stump, was lying on his side removing his skis. When finally I was able to stop I took off my skis and hurried back to him. He was sitting on the stump. He laughed and said, "Damn near broke my bleedin' neck." Such insouciance was typical. He was bruised, but not badly hurt. We gave up skiing and went back to the workshop.

I had been at Huston House for more than two weeks and, although I wrote Katy every day, was beginning to feel guilty for not seeing her. I asked Nan if I might invite her to come up for the weekend.

"Why, of course," she said.

The only telephone in the area was in the grocery store. When I went to get the mail I called her.

The first thing she said after "Hello," was: "When're you coming home?" She sounded peeved.

"Next week. Walter's got to do a radio show and I'm coming with him. They want you to come up this weekend."

"You mean tomorrow?"

"Yes. Takes about two hours. If you leave at ten o'clock you'll get here for lunch."

"How do I get there?"

"Drive to San Bernardino, then take the main road to Arrowhead and Big Bear. Running Springs is half way between them. I'll be waiting here for you."

"What'll I wear?"

"Something warm. Drive carefully and remember—I don't want to lose you."

"You almost did. It's a good thing you called."

Running Springs had no roadside identifying sign. I was waiting outside the grocery store at eleven o'clock the next morning not wanting her to drive through the village unheralded. Noon came and went before the postmistress called me to the telephone. It was Katy.

She said, "I'm in a gas station somewhere near Yucaipa. I must have missed the Arrowhead turnoff. I've had a hard time getting you on the phone. Sorry I'm late. A man here told me how to come and I'll get there as soon as I can."

About forty-five minutes later she arrived, parked her car in the Running Springs garage and we set out for Huston House hugging each other all the way.

Nan received Katy hospitably, though not with open arms. She was assigned the guest room overlooking the valley. The question of whether or not she would move in with me never came up.

During lunch, Katy related her conversation with a man at White Water: "When I was trying to reach John by telephone, I couldn't remember the name Running Springs. I told the operator I was trying to reach a place that had something to do with water. She suggested White Water and I asked her to try it. A wheezy voice came on: 'White Water Garage.'

"Is this the place where Walter Huston lives?

" 'Who?'

"Walter Huston.

" 'You mean the pitcher actor?'

"Yes.

" 'Don't believe so.'

"You know him, don't you?

" 'Can't say's I do.'

"He lives somewhere around there.

" 'You don't say?'

"He and my husband are supposed to meet me there with a sleigh.

" 'What a what?'

"A sleigh—to take me through the snow to Huston's house.

" 'Snow!—Why, lady, there ain't no snow 'round here. This here's th' desert! Ain't nothin' but sand.' "

Katy related the incident well and won forgiveness for being late. Seeking further approbation, she went into the kitchen after lunch to help Ray with the dishes; but Ray, who resented me as a permanent guest, did not receive her kindly. She testily told her to get out, saying, "I don't need you." Being uncomely and overweight, Ray probably envied Katy's attractiveness.

Roy, on the other hand, was overly friendly. Wherever Katy went he was likely to appear. While Katy was making her bed the next morning he came into the room and said, "Here—let me help you." The bed made, he suddenly seized and kissed her and exclaimed. "Merry Christmas!" though Christmas was weeks away.

Katy told me of the incident and I felt compelled to mention it to Nan. She took it lightly, saying, "Oh, Roy must have gotten carried away. Up here in the mountains he doesn't see many pretty girls. I'll speak to him."

Ray must have heard Nan talking to Roy, because that evening, while we were at the bar before dinner, she came wild-eyed from the kitchen with a shotgun, grabbed Katy's arm and swung her around. "What're you doin' with my husband, you bitch!"

Walter and I hastened to restrain her. Walter took the gun away and said, "Are you out of your mind?!"

"She's been kissin' him!" Ray said, and spat at Katy.

Nan said, "Ray Sunderland! You get yourself back to the kitchen!"

Casting a hateful glance at Katy, Ray went. Walter ascribed her performance to "Mountain Fever."

The next morning I took Katy to her car. As she started the engine she said, "I'm not coming up here again."

I said, "Never say never."

"John, I want you to understand my position. I'm risking my career for you. But the way things are going, I'm in a quandary. I don't know what to do. How can I give up the rest of my life for you and you're not with me?"

"I realize that this is a difficult time for both of us. Please bear with me for a little longer. I promise you it will come out all right. I simply won't fail you."

"I love you," she said, tears in her eyes, and drove away.

WALTER WAS ENGAGED to play *Henry, the Fourth* on radio and managed to get me in the cast. I was to play the bit role of Clarence. In the beginning of rehearsal I spoke several lines, but as we proceeded the script was cut for commercials. When the play was finally broadcast all I had to say was, "Hath the King called?" Though in rehearsal I had repeated the line a dozen times, when I got on the air I flubbed it, saying, "Doth the King call?"

Recounting my botched performance to Katy, Walter said, "Where he dug up 'doth' only God knoweth. He's got to be a genius rewriting Shakespeare."

I HAD WRITTEN Mother that Katy and I were living together while Katy's divorce was being finalized and she had not replied. I got the impression she was displeased. But when Katy got home from Huston House she found Debbie had sent her an oil portrait of me. This gave her an excuse to write her.

Dear Mrs. Lewis:

Your sending me the portrait of John thrills me so that I don't know how to thank you. It and your lovely letter have made me go around with a smile in my heart. I don't know how you could bear to part with the painting and it seems unfair that I should have both it and the original.

I don't like "living in sin" either. I don't like the phrase because I don't feel that we are. Our living without benefit of clergy is more or less a form of cowardice on my part, a sort of "look before you leap." That may be an anachronism, for I'm afraid I've leapt!

John thought you might be bitter about our living together,

but I felt, from what I have heard about you from Elinor and John and from what I know of them, that you must be one of those rare mothers who bring up their children in a "live your own life" policy. I look forward to getting to know you.

I can find no proper words to thank you for the portrait and your affectionate and understanding letter.

This comes with my love,
Katherine

Among those who came from time to time to visit Walter and Nan Huston at Running Springs were Edith and Loyal Davis and Edith's daughter Nancy. Loyal was a celebrated neurological surgeon and had the surgical chair at Northwestern University. Edith, who had worked in the theater with Nan, had married Loyal after divorcing Nancy's father. Nancy was seventeen, very pretty, and Nan thought she was exceptionally talented. While the Davises were there during the summer of 1938, she wrote Mother and asked her to do Nancy's horoscope, giving July 6, 1921 as her birthdate, New York City as the place and 1:18 P.M. as the time.

None of us in our wildest dreams could have foreseen what would happen to Nancy, but Mother's horoscope, dated August 9, 1938, describes a lady who became Mrs. Ronald Reagan, and not only the First Lady of California but the First Lady of the United States.

Here is what Mother prophesied:

Dear Miss Davis:

The beautiful Spica was rising on the eastern horizon at the hour you were born. It is said to bring riches and honors when it is in this position in a chart. Spica is in Libra, so Libra is your rising sun and Venus your "ruler."

Your Sun, Mars, and Mercury are all in Cancer in conjunction with Sirius, another star of first magnitude. As you have three planets (the Sun is a planet) centered around Sirius, its influence should be very marked in your character and in the events of your life. It points to a prominent position in life, with probable voyages.

While the sun was in Cancer at the time of your birth, the

Moon was just entering Leo. This combination of influences—Cancer and Leo—makes you an extremely independent person, and while you are perfectly willing to cooperate with other people you are a true individualist and know exactly how to get your own way. Outside of the Sun and Moon there are several factors in the chart which show determination and persistence in hewing your own destiny. Once you set your head to do or achieve anything you will pursue that ambition until it is fully accomplished if it takes your life-time. You will undoubtedly develop one single purpose in your life that will be paramount to everything else—and once it has become clear to you, you will never let it go.

You should be capable of placating, managing and directing people tactfully, without in the least giving up your own aims or ideas. You are willing to take orders if necessary, but your true aim and object is to give orders to others. You are inherently sure that you know better and can see further than the average person, and you are right, you do and you can.

You should be able to understand exactly the "politics" that go on in personal, social or business life. You have within you an aggressive mental outlook with far ranges of thought. You are modern, original, and inventive. You even tend to be radical, yet your sense or order, form and organization, of older standards of conduct and methods, would prevent you going overboard along revolutionary lines. Your judgment for the most part is excellent.

By no chance could you be called a clinging vine, nor even a "sweet young girl." Yet you should be extremely popular with all sorts of people, young and old. You are a natural leader in whatever sphere you choose to move. Your feeling for art in any form is potent; your sense of balance, proportion, color and tone should show in your appearance, surroundings, words or actions. You look upon elegance and distinction as essential to any success. You should be able to use the theater, moving pictures and radio in some way to forward your own career. You can be subtly or rowdily dramatic when you please; in fact an acute sense of emotional magnetism makes you act precisely and powerfully to dramatize yourself or your purpose.

Friends are extremely important and very fortunate for you, especially if they are older and influential men.

You should go in for a career. A person with your ability could hardly do anything else. You are the executive type. Business should come naturally to you. You are a born publicist. Advertising, movies or politics should bring you fame and wealth. You have everything it takes.

The year 1938 is one of the most important in your life, and between your birthday this year and in 1939 your status, position and outlook may be changed materially. In some way you come out of a long climb upward to reach a new place in the world. The indications are for a more far reaching and revolutionary change in your life than seems possible on the surface.

The next big turning point in your life seems to come in 1940-41 when you could have a love affair that would have an important effect upon your life. It is possible that you will be married in May 1942. However by July 1942 world conditions, finances, family matters, health conditions and your personal ambitions come under a cloud that could last intermittently for some time, and some phases of which might not be finished until the spring of 1947. However, in spite of this cloud (or perhaps because of it) during these years you will make a steady climb to the top, and even by 1946 you can fully expect to receive some very high honors and to have much personal happiness. Also you will have great outer assistance from important persons during that time, and the difficulties you must overcome will give you your BIG chance to show all of your fine and unusual qualities of mind, intelligence, heart and character, and the opportunity to develop into the magnetic executive leader that you are certainly destined to be.

So be prepared to take your place in the larger affairs of the world within the coming years.

Sincerely,
Deborah Lewis

CHAPTER TWENTY-FIVE

N AN AND WALTER moved back to Beverly Hills for the filming of *Dodsworth* and I was able to live at home. Much of
the time Katy was "between pictures," which is Hollywoodeze for
being unemployed; thus we were together a great deal and I was able to
work on the book with consistency. I went to Goldwyn Studios once or
twice a week to deliver or pick up Walter's mail and messages, and
sometimes Katy and I would have dinner with him and Nan.

During the filming, Walter's sister, Margaret Carrington, married
Robert Edmund Jones, the distinguished theatrical designer. She had
been a concert singer and had voice-coached some of America's outstanding actors, including John Barrymore for his performance in
Richard III and *Hamlet.* Her late husband had been a wealthy stock
broker. She had been instrumental in getting Walter, then working in
vaudeville, his first acting job in the legitimate theater by financing the
Brock Pemberton production of Zona Gale's *Mister Pitt,* with the
stipulation that Walter play the title role. While the play itself was not
enthusiastically received and did not have a long run, his performance

was extolled. One reviewer called it "a masterpiece, a flawless characterization." Walter earned another high step up the theatrical ladder by appearing as Ephraim Cabot in Eugene O'Neill's *Desire Under The Elms*. Critics applauded his performance and O'Neill called it "the truest characterization I have ever seen."

While *Dodsworth* was still in production, Margaret offered to underwrite the production of *Othello*, with Walter playing the Moor, and Nan, Desdemona; Robert Edmund Jones would design and direct. Everyone involved became enthused. Max Gordon offered to produce and the play was scheduled to open that winter in New York.

In late September the film *Dodsworth* was finished and the Hustons and I returned to Running Springs. There they spent hours every day, not necessarily with each other, strolling through the house and the hinterland speaking Shakespeare's lines to the rafters and the pines; meanwhile, I worked assiduously to finish my novel.

As I came down to the last pages of the saga, I seemed to be in a trance. In all probability it was spiritual and mental exhaustion. It had been a long and arduous journey over plains, mountains, rivers and desert, up and down canyons through all kinds of weather; it was as if I were coming out of a blizzard onto a verdant meadow warm with sunshine. The last page finished, I got into the Cunningham and raced home to Katy.

It was a momentous occasion and we rejoiced. "Now," I said, "all that has to be done is the final editing and clean-typing."

"You do the editing and I'll do the typing."

"It's a deal! But we can't do it right away. Nan and Walter leave next week for New York to begin rehearsals and they want me to go with them. I said I would if you would come with me. Will you?"

She hesitated, considering the consequences. I went on: "I'm eager to see Max Perkins at Scribner's and sell him our masterpiece."

"How long will we be gone?"

"Rehearsals'll take about a month and there'll be three or four weeks of tryouts before the New York opening. By then your divorce will have become final, we can get married."

She shook her head. "I don't want to get married in New York."

"Why not?"

"It's unromantic, like getting a dog license. If we're going to get married I'd like it to be in a small town, one with an unusual name."

"How about Moose Jaw?"

She laughed. "Where's that?"

"I'm not sure, somewhere in Canada. How about Kalamazoo? It's in Michigan."

"That's out of our way."

"We'll pass through lots of towns with funny names on the way and you can take your pick."

"If we get married I'm going to quit the movie business and you're going to have to support us. Suppose you don't sell the book?"

"If you go with me, I'll sell it. One look at you and any publisher will grab it."

She smiled, then frowned before saying, "Okay," thereby indicating for the first time that she would marry me and we sealed the affirmation with a kiss.

When we set out in late September for New York in her convertible the weather was warm, so we had the top down. It remained beautiful until we reached Rock Springs, Wyoming, where we spent the second night. But the next morning when we got up it was snowing. I hurried to the car to raise the top and sweep its seats. Snow kept falling while we had breakfast and by the time we left the hotel it was coming down so profusely the windshield wipers did not clear it. We had driven about ten miles before the storm turned into a blizzard. The car had no heater and the light sweaters we were wearing were woefully inadequate. Visibility was almost nil and every car, bus and truck was moving cautiously. We were on the major Lincoln Highway and there was lots of traffic. Soon there was an accident, then another; a Greyhound bus had skidded and was across two lanes. Cars slithered off into ditches. Unable to get through the jam of stalled cars, I decided, despite Katy's foreboding, to leave the pavement and take off over the unfenced prairie. We made fair progress, bouncing along, grimly tense and at every bump holding our breaths prayerfully. Presently the rear wheels became stuck; all they would do was whirl. Katy slid over and took the controls and I got out and pushed. My low-cut shoes sank in the snow and at once my socks became soaked. Rocking back and forth, we eventually got the car rolling and back onto the highway. My feet and hands were numb. For long periods we were unable to move. I rarely turned off the engine for fear it would freeze. From time to time I got out and helped push another vehicle out of our way and we were able to move another few yards. My feet became so numb, Katy removed my shoes and socks, dried my feet on her skirt and rubbed them between her hands. Our teeth chattered.

Trying to assuage her anxiety, I said, "This is what happened to the Donner Party. Believe it or not, it happened in late September, just about the same time as now. They came to the top of the Sierra Nevada and were on the verge of the Promised Land when it began to snow. Their animals were exhausted so the emigrants decided to rest until the storm subsided. It snowed for fourteen days and nights and the drifts rose above their heads. They were locked in. Thirty-nine of the eighty-seven died. That's not going to happen to us," I said, faking resolution and cheerfulness. "We've got a hundred horses to pull us through. We're gonna mush on." I looked at her and grinned.

She snuggled closer and put her head on my shoulder. "The horses may run out of gas."

It took us ten hours to go seventy-five miles and reach our first habitation: Wamsutta, a railroad siding, cluster of houses, lodge and grocery store. By now it was dark and still snowing. The hamlet was crowded and the few rooms of the lodge long since had been assigned. Even the half-dozen rocking chairs in its parlor had been rented for the night and people were already occupying them.

Katy and I had eaten only snow since breakfast, so I stood in line at the grocery store to buy edibles. When at last waited on, I asked the grocer if Katy and I could spend the night in his store, saying we'd be grateful to sleep on the floor. To my surprise he invited us to spend the night with him and his wife in their house. They also gave us supper and insisted we sleep in their bed.

I said to them, "You win the prize for being a roadside friend to man!"

During the night Katy and I thawed and the storm subsided. Come morning our hostess gave us a nourishing breakfast and we were able to fill our all-but-empty gas tank and resume our journey.

Trying to make up for lost time, I drove fast through the rest of Wyoming and across Nebraska. In Nebraska the highway bordered the unswerving railroad tracks and I began racing a passenger train. Our speedometer was quivering at ninety when a police car passed us and the policeman flagged us down. He got out of his car, approached us and said, "I see you're from California. Where do you think you're going?"

Lamely, I said, "New York."

"The speed limit in this state is seventy miles an hour," the policeman said, tilting back his trooper's hat. "If you expect to get there I recommend you observe it." With that, he saluted, got back in his car and, with a screeching flourish, drove away.

I sighed, put the Ford in gear and, as we drove on, said, "That's as gentlemanly an example of police work as I've ever experienced."

Katy grinned. "He slowed you down, so he's my friend."

Thereafter, to the trooper's credit, we cruised through Nebraska slightly under seventy-five miles an hour.

As the tires sang their monotonic music, our spirits were high keyed. We were glad to be with each other and I was relieved not to have gotten a citation. We sang, played license-plate poker, read Burma Shave doggerel and commented on the passing scene. We passed a cemetery on the fence of which was a sign: TAKE YOUR TIME. WE CAN WAIT. Grim humor, and as American as *e pluribus unum*. Rolling through the corn-and-hog country, the limitless farmland undulated like a female body by Rubens. Ahead three iridescent crows winged up from a mashed rabbit on the macadam and Katy said, "Crows must be the Negroes of the bird world," and added: "Isn't it strange that the Ten Commandments don't mention racial prejudice?" A black sedan loaded with nuns wearing starched coifs passed us, breaking the speed limit. Katy said, "Must be late for Mass."

In a barnyard was a huge sow surrounded by a litter of piglets all competing for nipples. "Political hangers on," I said. Thus we rolled.

That night in Lincoln we went into the hotel bar for stimulants and sat in a booth. The only other tippler in the place was a tall, cadaverous, hollow-cheeked, tousle-haired man seated at the bar. After we were served he raised his glass to salute us and said, "The threat of doom hangs over us like a thunderhead!" It was a startling gambit and, not wanting to get involved in bottle philosophy, I raised my glass but did not say anything. Presently he came over to us, saying, "God has not given us an inkling of what He has in mind. Perhaps you can tell me." He looked from me to Katy. She shook her head and said, "Haven't the faintest idea."

He continued: "For all man's knowledge of the sciences and all of the recountings of history, despite the labor of preachers and poets, we are all blind as to what the plan is." He looked at Katy. "Is that not true, Miss?"

I said, "You sound woeful, as if you'd fallen from grace."

"I have, sir. Yes, I have. I was a minister of the gospel. I am no more." This piqued my interest. I asked, "What happened?"

"I was Baptist born, Baptist bred and will be a Baptist 'til I die. I would preach my heart out and the congregation would remain as sinful as ever." He drained his glass, said, "Excuse me," and went back to the bar for a refill. After slurping a swallow there, which bobbed his protuberant Adam's apple, he smacked his lips with trance-like relish and returned. "It's obvious," he resumed, sitting down opposite us, "that God wants man to press on for the ultimate truth, even if he destroys himself by doing so. He sends us up one tunnel of ignorance and down another." He leaned forward and put his elbows on the table. "Is that guile on God's part or is it our fault for wanting to know?" It was a hypothetical question and he did not wait for an answer. "And suppose we found out all there is to know, would we become gods?"

"I guess we would," I said, hoping he would conclude the harangue.

After taking another slurp, he said, "Sometimes I wonder if life isn't a practical joke. If it is, the gods must be laughing like hell."

"Humor helps it," Katy said. She and I finished our drinks, bade the crackpot philosopher goodnight and went into the dining room.

CHAPTER TWENTY-SIX

THE HUSTONS WERE ENSCONCED in the Waldorf-Astoria Towers and Katy and I moved into an apartment in the Beaux Arts near the East River. Once settled, we set out to see Mother. She greeted us with high spirits and was affectionate to Katy, whom she was meeting for the first time. I had written her that we planned to be married and had sent her Katy's birthplace and date, asking if she would do her horoscope. While I had little faith in astrology, I thought it would interest Katy.

After the perfunctory greetings, Debbie went to her desk. "You did not send me the time she was born, so I don't vouch for its accuracy." She picked up the chart and looked questioningly at Katy. "Have you any idea?"

"Not the slightest," Katy said.

"Are you an early riser?"

"Yes."

"Are you energetic, by which I mean not lazy."

Katy looked to me for the answer. I said, "She certainly is not lazy."

"I try to keep up with John," Katy said. "He has one speed—wide open."

"Then you must have been born in the morning," Debbie said. "That's the way I've charted it." She consulted the chart. "John asked me to find out how you and he will get along as wife and husband. Well, you're a Virgo and he's a Pisces, so you should do pretty well. Having been born on the opposite sides of the Zodiac should mean you're well balanced. Right now, according to both of your charts, seems to be a fine time in your lives." She paused. "Because you both have been married before, you should know what you're getting into. Each of you needs an anchor. Believe me, going through this life alone is uphill all the way. Just remember, marriage is a union of concordance, of mutual esteem, loyalty and steadfastness. As husband and wife you're going to have to sustain that harmony, to work at it. Unfaithfulness, rancor, bitterness will kill it." She went on at length, preaching advice based on her personal philosophy, and finally said to me: "You wrote that you've finished the book."

"Practically. While we're here I'm hoping to find a publisher. I'm going to Scribner's first. They publish Fitzgerald, Hemingway and Thomas Wolfe."

"It's a good book," Katy said. "It's about nine hundred pages long."

"How long has it taken you to write it?" Debbie asked me.

"Four years."

"How long did it take the wagon train?"

"Six months."

We all chuckled. Debbie said, "Just goes to show that writing books is a hard way to make a living."

Othello had been in rehearsal for a week before Katy and I arrived and there was a severe problem: no actor had been engaged to play Iago, the second most important role.

Many actors had been auditioned for it, but all had been found wanting. Finally, in desperation, Robert Edmund Jones chose Robert Keith to play the part. He came in late and had to memorize the multitudinous lines in a hurry. When the play opened for a tryout in New Haven, Jones decided he was too gentle, too deferential for the part, that he did not exude the necessary evil. G.P. Huntly, who was playing Cassio, suggested Brian Aherne for the part. Aherne had played Shakespearean roles to much acclaim, was tall, handsome and a gifted actor. It happened that he was in England. In his autobiography, *A Proper Job*, Aherne recounts what happened:

> I was following the will-o'-the-wisp over the mountains of North Wales when one night I received a phone call from America. It was Max Gordon, who was in trouble. "Brian," he said, "I've got Walter Huston in *Othello*, directed by his brother-in-law, Robert Edmund Jones. We open in New York in three weeks, and the show is dying on the road. We all agree that everything will be fine if we can replace Iago. Will you rush here, study it fast, and take over in Philly for the week before the New York opening?
>
> I thought of the phrase which, they say, is used by Buckingham Palace to convey a tactful but negative answer. "Oh, Max!" I cried. "That's a lovely idea!—but I'm afraid it might be a little difficult."
>
> A couple of days later . . . I was delighted to meet Douglas Fairbanks, Jr., again in London. As we strolled on the lawn after lunch he asked me, in his usual charming way, what I was up to, and I mentioned the *Othello* offer. He stopped in his tracks, his eyes wide with amazement, then he hit me on the chest, quite hard. "You bloody fool!" he said. "When are you going to get wise to yourself? Get on the phone to Gordon at once and tell him you'll do it! Don't you realize this is one of the great parts of Shakespeare? I'd give my eye teeth to play it. God! How can anybody be so stupid? . . . "
>
> I cabled Max that I would sail two days later . . . I holed up in my cabin to study the part which seemed to me as long as Hamlet, and almost as difficult. Arriving in Washington, I went straight to the National Theater to see the show, and as I sat there my heart sank like a stone. Robert Edmund Jones—Bobby Jones—the greatest designer of them all . . . had done a magnificent production with imaginative scenery and sumptuous costumes, but as a director I knew he had failed. The play was a beautiful, tedious bore, I did not go backstage that night. I went

straight to my hotel room and there came to a hard decision. I would give Iago a bravura performance, with all the flash, fire and humor that I could, and the devil take the hindmost; I was in, and there was nothing else I could do.

Poor Bobby Jones was reduced to despair by my performance and used to leave little notes on my dressing table saying, Brian, Iago is evil, slimy and dark. He must horrify the audience, not fascinate them and make them laugh as you are doing! It is not fair to the play! Walter and his wife, Nan, never complained, never faulted, and helped me in every way they could. We moved to New York where Gordon had booked us into the New Amsterdam, a huge, musical comedy house . . .

First-night audiences always bring the electricity of excitement and it was rife when Katy and I reached our seats. I excused myself and went backstage. Everything was in turmoil. Made-up actors in costume were frenziedly pacing, mumbling their lines.

Entering Walter's dressing room I said, "You don't seem to be nervous."

"Sir," he said, his face and hands smeared with heavy dark-brown make-up, "why should I be nervous? I'm a well-known professional actor." Then grimacing, he said, "That's what Henry Irvine said before excusing himself to vomit." He grinned. I laughed.

I got back to Katy as lights dimmed. The murmur of the sold-out audience subsided. There was a pin-dropping hush. We clasped hands prayerfully. Aware of the great effort that had gone into the production, we fervently wanted the play to succeed.

Walter came through the rich velvet curtain in his magnificent costume and began: "I come no more to make you laugh; things now, that bear a weighty and serious brow, sad, high and working, full of state and woe, such noble scenes as draw the eye to flow, we now present . . . "

I got the flutters, afraid something untoward would happen. But it seemed to proceed exceedingly well. Soon though, I became concerned by Aherne's performance. Although he had played the role for only a week, he was out-acting Walter and electrifying the audience. His Iago was authoritative, zestful, cunning, deceitful, artful and sly. Also, unfortunately, amusing. Words which should have been solemn came from him humorously, causing the audience to titter.

During intermission I went backstage to report to Walter: "They're eating it up."

He was on cloud nine. Adrenalin was bubbling. "I never felt more confident on a stage in my life," he said. "There's applause at the end of every scene."

I did not mention my puzzlement about Aherne. I simply said, "The audience seems to love Brian."

Throughout the performance the response was enthusiastic and, as the final curtain fell, the applause was thunderous. After innumerable curtain calls, many shouts of "Bravo!" and whistling, with people remaining in their seats and shouting for Jones in lieu of the author, it would have seemed idiotic to have judged the play a failure.

With the Hustons and the Joneses, Katy and I repaired to the Ritz-Carlton restaurant for a celebration and to await the reviews. The newspapers came out about two o'clock. Walter chose the tabloid *News* first. Its critic, Burns Mantle, had a precise, four-star system of rating plays and was a quick read. To our surprise and chagrin he was less than lukewarm about the production. He gave it two and a half stars.

Bobby said, "That might be all right for Mantle and the *News*. Let's hear what Brooks Atkinson has to say."

Atkinson, the *Times* critic, was the dean of New York reviewers. His opinion was no more favorable than Mantle's. Besides the setting and costumes, he had liked only Brian's Iago. The reviews in the *Herald-Tribune* and the *World-Telegram* were in accord, praising only Brian's performance.

Margaret asked, "After all the months of hard work, after all the fond care and all the money spent, how could we possibly have produced a turkey?"

"Maybe they think it's Thanksgiving," Walter said to grim laughter.

For his autobiography Aherne wrote:

The headlines were even better for me than I had feared: MISTER AHERNE IN WALTER HUSTON'S OTHELLO—TRIUMPH AND DISASTER AT THE NEW AMSTERDAM THEATER—THE

GREATEST IAGO OF OUR GENERATION. All day I wondered if I should telephone Walter, but what could I say? . . . That evening, as I sat at my dressing table, making up as Iago, I heard steps on the stair; came a knock on my door. In came Walter, fully costumed and ready for the performance. Sitting down, he gave me a sly smile and said with a rueful laugh, "Well, I'm afraid they didn't like me." In that moment we became firm and devoted friends . . .

After three weeks the play closed. I ghost-wrote an article for Walter entitled "Aftermath" for a theatrical magazine:

"I could not escape the clear cry against my performance. The critics did not want me, whom they considered a homespun actor, to put on airs. What made it so hard, I guess, is that *Othello* was my first failure in thirteen years of acting. I had come to believe that as an actor I could do no wrong. There is nothing like a blockbuster failure, such as *Othello*, to destroy that illusion."

Shortly after the play closed, Nan and Walter took off for Running Springs and I went to see Max Perkins, taking Katy, my *raison d'être*, for good luck.

CHAPTER TWENTY-SEVEN

THE SCRIBNER BUILDING is in the high-rent district of Fifth Avenue, a comparatively small but elegant structure sandwiched between higher-risers. The company's bookstore occupied the street level. When Katy and I got there I wanted her to go with me to the editorial office, but she refused, saying, "This is your performance, not mine."

"But you're my *chef d'oeuvre.*"

"Your *chef d'oeuvre* is the manuscript. I'd just be in the way. I'll wait in the bookstore. Good luck." And thither she went.

I went through the building's sanctified doorway and got into the aged, cage-like elevator and pressed button number five. Ascending in the creaky contraption, I thought of the many famous writers who had ridden in it, none with more hopes than I.

The waiting room into which I stepped was lined with varnished, glass-enclosed bookshelves. I felt a sense of familiarity, as if I had been there before. I had read about it in one of Thomas Wolfe's books. There was no receptionist. I glanced at my watch: ten minutes to noon.

I was early. I went to a bookshelf and read the authors' names on the books: S.S. Van Dine, John Galsworthy, Marcia Davenport, Ring Lardner, Marjorie Kinnan Rawlins, Winston Churchill, Alice Longworth. . . .

A middle-aged woman in a tweed suit appeared. "You must be Mister Weld," she said, speaking quietly. "I'm Irma Wykoff, Mister Perkins' secretary. Won't you come in?"

With nervous anticipation, as if stepping onstage as the curtain was about to rise, I followed her into a small room, the windows of which looked out on Fifth Avenue. Seated at a cluttered desk was a slight, rather pale Anglo-Saxon in a much-worn, three-piece suit. It was Maxwell Evarts Perkins and he was wearing a fedora. I would learn that wearing the hat indoors was an eccentricity. It helped his delicate hearing by pushing his ears slightly forward. Miss Wykoff brought me a straight chair. Perkins' pale blue eyes looked up at me, expressing curiosity and cordiality. Without getting up, he said, "Won't you sit down?"

Awe-struck, I said, "Thank you, sir," and did so, saying to myself, "Don't be stupid."

"Bobby Jones tells me you've written a book." He, like Miss Wykoff, spoke quietly, as if in a library reading room. The words came slightly from one side of his mouth and sounded faintly humorous. The way his eyes crinkled supported this impression.

I said, "Yes, sir. It's almost finished. I've got a little more to do."

"Then you didn't bring it with you?"

"No, sir."

"Is it a novel?"

"Yes, sir. It's based on the Donner party incident, a covered wagon story. I'm hoping I can get you to read it."

He smiled. "We do that here."

"It's not my first book. I've written a couple of others. They were published by Robert M. McBride."

"Has McBride seen this one?"

"No, sir."

"Why don't you submit it to them?"

"Frankly, I'd rather have Scribner's publish it."

"Where do you live?"

"In California."

"Bobby Jones tells me you're a friend of Walter Huston."

"I have that honor."

"Then you must have seen his *Othello*."

"Oh, yes, several times." I shook my head.

"Too bad," Perkins said. "How could it have failed?"

"I thought it was fine."

"I didn't see it," Perkins said. "He's a fine actor. I saw *Dodsworth*. He was marvelous."

"Critics thought *Othello* was out of his range," I said, "and maybe they're right. He's a gentle man, too kind and modest to kill. I've never heard him raise his voice in anger."

Perkins consulted his watch, drawing it from a vest pocket. I interpreted that as a signal for the interview to end, so got up. He arose, saying, "It's lunch time," and surprised me by adding, "How about joining me?" I would learn that such gestures were characteristic.

"Why," I said thinking rapidly, "I'd like that very much. But what do I do about the lady who's waiting for me in the bookstore downstairs?"

"We'll take her along," he said, ushering me out the door.

Katy was dressed in a herringbone, Irene suit, a jabot and feathered felt hat. I was button-tight proud to present her. "Miss Parrish," I said, "this is Maxwell Perkins."

She, too, was awed. She said, "How do you do?" respectfully.

Perkins removed his hat, bowed slightly, saying, "I'm enchanted," and turned to me. "I hope your book is as good as she looks."

I grinned.

"It's much better," she said.

"All young women are beautiful," Perkins said. "I should know. I have five daughters."

We went up Fifth Avenue to Fifty-third Street and turned east. Our destination, it turned out, was Cherio's, number Forty-six. Here Perkins was well known. The proprietor, Romolo Cherio, a small, dark-skinned Italian, greeted him deferentially and led us through the bar to a corner table in the dining room. It had a reserved sign on it, which Cherio removed. There, almost every weekday, Perkins sat for lunch, generally with writers, agents and friends, and it had become well known to the literati. A man of regularity, he drank one or two martinis and dined on creamed chicken or guinea hen. That day we each had one martini and a guinea hen.

While we dined I told Perkins about Katy's movie career.

She said, "When I marry John, I'm going to give it up. I'd rather help him."

Perkins smiled, and said, "A writer can use a typist."

"I think writers are more important than actors," she said.

I asked, "Does Scott Fitzgerald's wife type for him?"

"Not much. She's a writer herself. The two of them usually have a secretary."

"How about Hemingway?"

"He's had several wives. I think they've all helped him. But now he's affluent and hires someone."

I told him about working on the *Paris Herald* and he told us about his stint on the *New York Times*. I had read that he had gone to Harvard, so I mentioned that my forefathers had helped found the university, hoping thereby to impress him. He said he remembered Weld Hall and Weld Boathouse on the Charles River. Katy said her former husband, Dillwyn Parrish, had gone to Harvard; and thinking it would help, I said he was the brother of Anne Parrish, thus snatching at any prestigious thread that might heighten his opinion of us. The cliché *It's not what you know, it's who you know* popped into mind. Thus far, Walter Huston and Bobby Jones had helped.

I intrigued Perkins when I told him my mother was the astrologer, Deborah Lewis. "I know it's not a science," he said, "but astrology has always interested me. I have a friend who is an astrologer. Her name is Elizabeth Lemmon. Maybe your mother knows her. She lives in Virginia and every now and then writes and tells me my good fortune She never mentions the bad."

"Mother's like that," I said. "Perhaps all astrologers try to avoid slings of misfortune." We talked about writers and writing, mentioning our favorites.

"Have you ever read Tolstoy's *War and Peace?*" Perkins asked.

Neither of us had. Katy said that her adopted mother, Teedee Paul, had read *Anna Karenina* to her. "The Pauls were Quakers," she said, "and we all lived—quote—the simple life—end quote, by Tolstoy's code."

"In my opinion," Perkins said, "*War and Peace* is the finest novel written in any language. I urge you both to read it. You can learn much from it.

On our way back to his office he bought an afternoon newspaper, glanced at the headlines—turbulence in Europe—tucked it under an arm, saying, "That Hitler—he's a madman!" I asked if he thought there would be a war. "If Hitler keeps fortifying and enlarging Germany there will be. The idiot seems to be determined to exterminate the Jewish race. No moral nation is going to permit that."

As we walked along I told him that Katy and I were about to drive to California and that we planned to marry on the way.

"We want to be married in a small town with an odd name," Katy said.

"There's a town named Ship Bottom on the Jersey coast," Perkins said, and smiled.

We laughed and Katy said, "We were thinking of Chillicothe, Missouri. It's on the way."

Perkins bade us goodbye at the Scribner Building entrance and said, "About your book, do send it to us. We'll have a look."

Being with him had been a memorable experience. He had been gracious, kind and hospitable, a gentleman of the old school. "If nothing comes of it," I said to Katy, "I think we've found a friend." We went into Scribner's bookstore and bought a copy of *War and Peace*. "Max Perkins recommended it," I said to the clerk.

"Oh, yes," she said. "Because of him we sell a lot of them."

Our next stop was at Bloomingdale's where we bought, for eighteen dollars, a platinum wedding ring.

The next morning we set out in the Ford with me singing, "Oh, we're gonna be married, we're gonna be married, we're gonna be married in Chillicothe . . . "

Katy's spirits were equally high. At last we were on the right track, one which led to a bright future, perhaps a glorious one. She said, "Even if Mister Perkins finds the manuscript wanting, he will suggest ways to improve it. If he accepts the book you'll be over the hump and on your way—to the greatness you deserve." I kissed her hand. She went on: "You've done your apprenticeship. Now comes the prize."

"She's already here," I said.

That day we got as far as Everett, Pennsylvania, where we stopped for the night at a ramshackle motel. The next morning we started early and crossed the Mississippi at Hannibal, familiar territory to Katy. We got to Chillicothe about four o'clock in the afternoon, only to find that, it being Saturday, the courthouse was closed. We spent the night there and, not wanting to waste Sunday, drove to Carthage, Missouri, attracted by its classic name. Reaching the town, we drove into a gas station and while the long-faced attendant was filling our tank I told him we were on our way to California and had come to Carthage to get married.

"Won't be able to get a license tomorrow," he said. "Courthouse'll be closed."

"Why? What's the occasion?"

"Holiday. Town's a hundred years old."

My expression revealed disappointment. "That's too bad!" I told him about losing out in Chillicothe.

"Joplin's up the road a piece," he said. "You could get married there tomorrow."

"We wanted to get married here because of the town's historical name." And to show off my erudition, I said, "You know where it got it, don't you?"

"Sure," he said. "Want your oil checked?"

"Please."

Opening the hood he looked me in the eye. "Got it from ancient Carthage in North Africa. That city was founded by Tyranian emigrants led by Elissa about the year 850 B.C. Elissa was known as Dido. She and her followers bought a piece of land on which to build a town, but for the price she and her cohorts were able to pay, they obtained only as much land as could be contained by the skin of an ox." He swallowed and his prominent Adam's apple bobbed up and down. "Dido cut the ox skin into strips narrow enough to extend around a hill and there they built Karthadshat, which became known to the Greeks as Carthage." He withdrew the dipstick, wiped it off with his fingers and shoved it back into the crankcase. "Oil's okay," he said.

Handing him a five dollar bill, I said, "You're sure up on your history."

He nodded. "Teach it in high school. This is my moonlightin' job."

That day we pressed on through Oklahoma. Seminole, Texas, intrigued us, but we also reached it at an inconvenient time. Katy said, "It looks as if Miss Fortune is trying to tell us something."

As we approached Arizona we realized we were running out of real estate. It occurred to us that Phoenix was a singularly appropriate place for our nuptials, we both having risen from the emotional ashes of other marriages. We rolled into the city on the eve of Lincoln's birthday in time to obtain a marriage license. The next morning we found a judge to perform the ceremony in his upstairs office. He was to ride a horse in the holiday parade and was costumed in a ten-gallon hat, an orange shirt, a red handkerchief and spurred cowboy boots. Without removing the hat he greeted us perfunctorily and said, "I don't have much time. Where's your witness?"

"Don't have any," I said.

"Got to have somebody sign the license," he said and went into the hall. At the foot of the stairs an old man was asleep in a chair. "Hey, Walkup, we need you!"

A seam-faced, illiterate Indian came up and from the time he joined us until he left he did not utter a word. The judge wasted no time declaring us husband and wife. He then wrote S. *Walkup* on the witness-line, had the Indian add an X and counter-signed the license.

"As a matter of curiosity," I said, handing him his ten-dollar fee, "what does the Ess in Mister Walkup's name stand for?"

"Search me," the judge said. "Maybe Sam. We named him Walkup because when we need him he has to come up the stairs. Give him a few bucks on your way out."

Katy and I toasted our wedlock with Coca-Colas and lit out for home. "I'm glad we didn't get married in Chillicothe," she said. "Mister Walkup's name wouldn't be on our license."

I had never been so happy. I had a lifetime contract with the woman I adored. Katy was happy, too, though perhaps not so euphorically as I. I had bet on a sure thing, she on a long-shot. With her snuggled close to me, we rode for several miles without speaking, letting the thoughts of the momentous event sift through our minds. Chained together at last and forever, whither would our destinies take us?

She finally broke into the breezy silence by saying, "Now that we're married we should start planning our children."

"It's apropos."

"I'd like to have several," she said. "Dillwyn was sterile, but I didn't know it until Em Eff told me. I'd like our first child to be a boy to carry on your name—" She kissed my neck. "Which I'm sure is going to be famous."

"And I'd like to have a girl as beautiful as you," I said.

CHAPTER TWENTY-EIGHT

Back home, while clean-typing the manuscript, my old type-writer, beaten to a frazzle, foozled. At the shop to which I took it to be repaired, a typing class for children was in session, sponsored by the Remington Company to promote its typewriters. Having for years punched keys with two fingers, I asked the teacher if I might join the class and she rather reluctantly said yes. I promptly handed over the two dollar fee, was assigned a typewriter, a table and a chair and awkwardly started practicing with the children. It was not easy break-ing my old habits, but after two hours I had learned and memorized the fundamentals. From then on it was a matter of practice. The shop-keeper rented me a typewriter to use until mine was repaired and I hurried home to teach Katy.

To my astonishment and delight she quickly became more dexterous and proficient at typing than I. Eager to help me with the book, she managed to clean-type its eight hundred pages. Before posting the manuscript to Max Perkins we both kissed it, uttered a few words to bless it and crossed our fingers. Its publication could exalt us. Its rejection was too horrendous to contemplate.

Leaving the post office, I said, "Aside from your wedding ring, that two dollars I spent for typing lessons is the best investment I ever made."

Weeks went by without word from Scriber's. Every day I went to the mailbox and waited for the postman. He came in a car and was a bearded little man with gleeful gray eyes who wore a baseball cap bearing his name: ZEKE. One day when I told him what I was looking for he said, "Say, I've always wanted to write a book."

"What about?"

"My folks. They're a circus." He chuckled. "Take Aunt Minnie. She's a lulu. Was a trapeze artist. Got married five times. Killed 'em all. Is still lookin'. Then there's Aunt Sadie. She was in the circus, too, bareback rider. Married a contortionist, had triplets. The triplets turned out to be contortionists and ruined the act; there were too many of them. Grandpa Yancy was a gold miner. For fifty years he scratched along Yuba River, died a pauper. Grandma Nellie ran a whorehouse in Marysville, otherwise he'd have starved to death."

"Sounds like a good cast," I said.

"Trouble is, I ain't got time. Got to earn a livin'."

"That's every writer's wail."

A few days later he came by with nothing but junkmail and I said, "I've been thinking about your family. I'm thinking of writing a book about the gold rush. Your grandparents would be good characters. Tell me more about them."

"Grandpa Yancy was a guzzler. Once when he and his buddy, feller named Porky, were in a Mississippi saloon lappin' up the juice, they ran out of money. So Grandpa went out and sold Porky's horse for ten bucks which they spent on more drinks. When Porky sobered up and found out what had happened he had Grandpa put in jail for horse-stealin'. In them days that was the worst crime, next to murder. Grandma had to bail him out by buying th' horse back. Cost her a hundred bucks."

Days when he had nothing for us, Zeke would wave as he drove by and sing out, "No news is good news!" or "Not today! Maybe tomorrow!"

As the days ticked away without a word from Perkins my spirit withered. The fear grew that the effort and years I had put into the book had been in vain. I had envisioned myself an imaginative, creative and capable writer, as good as anyone. It began to look as if that had been self-delusion. Finally in desperation, I wrote Perkins: "I'm sorry to remind you that it has been three months since I sent you a manuscript . . . "

Forthwith came a telegram: "Sorry for the delay. Greatly impressed by the book. Through office error, the manuscript was returned to Jean Wick. Letter follows. Perkins."

Katy's and my spirits flowered like watered roses of Jericho. While there was no promise to publish, the words "greatly impressed" were intoxicating.

The next day the special-delivery letter arrived. It said that those at Scribner's who had read the manuscript were in favor of its publication providing the love story was built up. "That is the novel's backbone," Perkins wrote. "It needs a strong central story." This was mildly disappointing. I had tried to coalesce a cluster of characters into a mural of the western movement and had deliberately avoided stressing any of their stories; moreover, I had rewritten all of the book at least eight times. I wept a little inside, but it did not occur to me to refuse the stipulation. I went to work at once to build up the love story and finished it within a month. Off the pages went to Perkins.

Came another letter from him:

> The scenes you've added are fine and we're pleased with them. However, we believe the book's ending is too abrupt. A reader, like a horse after running a race, needs to go on a little farther to relax and to evaluate what has gone before. Those in your pilgrimage have lived through ordeals of wilderness, desert, mountains and snow; those who survive should be brought down into the California sunshine and given a taste of the good life. As you have it now, their stories end when they get out of the snow . . .

Aware I was learning the rules from a master, I sighed and went back to work. I added a chapter, the manuscript was approved, and Perkins sent me a contract and an advance royalty check for $500. Flustered by excitement, and having faith in Scribner's, I did not read the contract carefully. I skipped almost everything but the royalties clause: ten percent of the retail price up to five thousand copies, twelve-and-a-half percent thereafter. The book was scheduled to be published in March, which was six months away.

Max wrote:

> When the book does come out I think it would be well if you come to New York and assist us in promotion. I also suggest you bring your beautiful wife. She's bound to be a great help . . .

I handed Katy the check. "It's a rainbow day," I said. "Buy yourself something."

"Oh, no," she said. "Let's save it 'til we get to New York."

The book's publication assured it was imperative that I withdraw from the Huston payroll. That would please Katy. She had long wanted us to be self-sufficient. My withdrawal was important for another reason: it was a sad time for Walter and Nan. The failure of *Othello* had not only painfully hurt their egos, they had lost a great deal of money and time.

Katy still worked occasionally, though the jobs she got were minor and of short duration. Now that we were married, what little enthusiasm she had for the movies was waning. What she wanted was children.

We both became concerned that she did not become pregnant, and we went to be examined. My sperm proved generative, but she was found to have fibroid tumors. The gynecologist's prognosis was: they should be removed, which meant the excision of the uterus. She would be barren.

I don't remember a day so fraught with sorrow. Leaving the doctor's office, I tried to console her. Speaking softly, my arm around her, I said, "It's the will of God," trying to hide my own disappointment.

But she was not comforted. She continued to weep silently. "I'm sorry," she said. "I'm sorry for your sake. I'm depriving you."

"Not at all," I whispered. "I have you. You are my child and I am yours. We don't need progeny because we have each other."

We talked about adopting a child, but after considerable discussion agreed not to.

Max Perkins wrote, asking what I intended writing next: "We can't have you flying on one wing." I replied, saying I had done so much research in California history that I should use more of what I had learned, and suggesting a novel about the California gold rush. He approved the idea.

Breathing in and exhaling a deep sigh, I started structuring the story. In beginning the book, the screen of my imagination was foggy. I saw a river, a shack and a couple of men shoveling gravel and sand into a sluice. One was Zeke's Grandpa . . .

Inasmuch as I would be spending upwards of a year writing the book, I again applied, this time sponsored by Perkins, for a Guggenheim Fellowship. The $2,600 grant would ease our financial plight besides which it would be prestigious. When, like the first, it was rejected, Perkins arranged for Scribner's to send me a monthly stipend of $125 advance royalty while I worked on the book.

It's not as much as you would have gotten from Guggenheim, he wrote, but it will help. Sorry we couldn't have scheduled DON'T YOU CRY FOR ME for the Christmas trade . . .

CHAPTER TWENTY-NINE

K ATY AND I WERE IN New York on the publication day of *Don't You Cry For Me.* We found ourselves in a new, exciting, almost paradisical world. Reviews were flattering. The one in the *New York Times* appeared on the front page of its *Book Review* section with the banner headline: AN EPIC TALE OF THE OLD WEST. The reviewer, Fred T. Marsh, judged it:

> A narrative of epic proportions and wealth of detail, this saga of a covered wagon caravan of nearly a hundred years ago is the kind of stuff which epics have been made—the *Book of Exodus,* the *Aeneid,* and the *March of the Ten Thousand.* It is a tremendous achievement, an extraordinary and moving piece of historical realism . . .

Suddenly we were celebrated. Friends lauded me. People I barely knew and acquaintances I had not seen in years telephoned or wrote to congratulate me. One of the broad windows of Scribner's bookstore was filled with copies of the book and my name was bannered over them. In the editorial office Katy and I were greeted by the staff with effusive esteem. Charles Scribner toasted us with champagne, saying, "There's a new star in the literary firmament."

I asked Whitney Darrow, the company's sales manager, if he thought the book would become a best seller.

"There's no way of knowing," he replied. "What makes a best seller is as mysterious as guessing which baby's going to become president of the United States. A book gets caught up in a wave of popularity and suddenly everybody wants to read it."

I asked John Hall Wheelock, the distinguished poet and Scribner editor who had guided my book through the paths of printing, why thousands of people go through the agony of writing books.

He said, "There's no artistic accomplishment comparable to having a book published. It's ego building, like having a monument raised to you in a public square."

The Charles Scribners invited Katy and me to spend a weekend at their home in Far Hills, New Jersey, and, following instructions, we boarded a private club car attached to a train at Hoboken. A black porter in crisp white jacket, his shoes highly polished, was the major domo. At first, realizing we were not club members, he frowned, but when I said that we were guests of Charles Schribner he quickly became benign, ushered us to plush seats and asked what we would like to drink. A number of other men, splendidly groomed, were in the car and four of them were playing bridge.

"We're with the glitterati," I whispered to Katy.

And she said, "Where we belong."

Charlie met us at the Far Hills station and drove us to the family mansion overlooking the winter-bleak, rolling hills. Mrs. Scribner had told Katy we were not expected to dress for dinner so she had not packed an evening dress or my tuxedo. Thus we were surprised and embarrassed when, Katy in her Irene suit and I in tweeds, we joined the Scribners and their other guests before dinner to find the ladies in high regalia and the men wearing black ties. Mrs. Scribner apologized for the misunderstanding, saying by formal she had meant white tie.

I said, jokingly, "In California we only wear white ties in the movies," and everyone laughed, thus relieving the awkward situation.

Despite our inappropriate attire, it proved to be a wonderful evening for us. During dinner Katy, with characteristic modesty, told about her movie experiences and won everyone's esteem by saying, "It's got to be the craziest business in the world!" And I won some point recounting some of my experience as a stunt man.

After dinner we gentlemen retired to the study for brandy and cigars and Charlie told anecdotes about James M. Barrie and John Galsworthy when they were guests at Far Hills. He then made a toast to me, saying, "They have left the literary scene. Let us welcome a newcomer."

BEFORE LEAVING New York to return to California, Katy and I had a session with Max Perkins at the Ritz Bar. It was his habit to stop there for a drink or two on his way home to New Caanan. He arrived with a briefcase loaded with manuscripts. Soon the conversation turned to Thomas Wolfe, who had died the year before of tuberculosis of the brain. Katy asked about his affair with Aline Bernstein. "She was twice his age," Katy said. "What brought them together?"

"I believe it was her infatuation for his literary talent," Max said. "Though older, she was—and still is—a beautiful woman. I think Tom needed an older woman. His mother suckled him until he was five years old and I don't think he ever lost the mammary hunger."

"He was never married?"

"No. I don't know why. He truly needed a wife."

I asked, "How could he and Mrs. Bernstein have carried on that long love affair without her husband knowing?"

"She was a theatrical designer and had a studio away from home. They met while he was writing *Look Homeward, Angel*. She helped him financially and let him live in her studio. After he became successful he severed their association and it almost broke her heart. One evening she came to my office while he was there and threatened to kill herself."

"He wasn't loyal," I said. "Look what he did to you and Scribner's."

Max's blue eyes twinkled and his pale lips formed a slight smile. He did not comment, though he had labored as editor, teacher, coach, friend and surrogate father to help Thomas Wolfe through massive manuscripts over several years, had spent nights and weekends with him listening to his agonizing, trying to balance his prodigality and assuage his brooding. In a fit of pique, Wolfe had left Scribner's and taken his work to Harper's. It had been a classic example of ingratitude.

Max asked how I was progressing with the gold rush book. I told him I had blocked out the first draft.

"I'd like to see it," he said.

"Not yet," I replied. "It's nothing but bare bones. I'll finish it this summer and get it to you before snowfall."

"And what next?"

"I think I'd like to do one about slavery. I've always had a strong sympathy for Negroes."

"If you're going to research slavery," Max said, "you shouldn't go to California. You should go to your native South. There's a treasure trove of slavery lore in the library at the University of North Carolina and I have friends there who can help you. They're the James Boyds. Jim's one of our fine writers and an authority on the Civil War. He lives in Southern Pines. You could spend spring and summer there, research and finish the gold rush book . . . "

And that's what we decided to do.

Walter Huston was in New York, having agreed to appear in William Saroyan's play, *Love's Old Sweet Song*. I went to say goodbye to him and watch a rehearsal. Saroyan invited me to sit with him. He had an unorthodox way of playwriting. He started a situation and then built on it scene by scene while it was in rehearsal. That was the way he had composed *My Heart's in the Highlands* and *The Time of Your Life*. He believed it added spontaneity and freshness to the characters and situations. To the actors, of course, this method was horrendous. Not aware that Saroyan resented advice, I made so bold as to ask why he didn't write the entire play before beginning rehearsal. He looked at me as if I had insulted his mother.

At the lunch break Walter and I went to Jack Dempsey's Restaurant. Dempsey had a photographer take our picture to hang on the wall with other celebrity friends.

"I want it understood," I said to Walter, when we were seated, "that you are my guest."

He grimaced an expression of surprise. "What does that mean?"

"It means I'm paying."

"You've got to be kidding."

"It's a small way to thank you."

"In that case," he said, his forehead unfrowning. "I'll have soup."

We both laughed and ordered corned beef sandwiches and beer.

I said, "I don't think I ever told you that my father died when I was six months old, and all of the time I was growing up I kept looking for someone to fill his place. You have done that. From you I've had paternal friendship. For which I am more than grateful."

He put a hand on the table for me to enclasp. "I have two sons," he said, "both named John."

By the time Katy and I got to Southern Pines, North Carolina, azaleas and dogwood were in bloom. For me, getting back to the romantic South was nostalgically beguiling, and Katy, there for the first time, flowered like a magnolia. The talk of the inhabitants was musical and friendly. We rented a modest cottage and, after shopping for groceries, called on the James Boyds, whose colonial mansion was like a setting in *Gone With The Wind*. Jim was a gentleman of the old school and his charming wife was his compliment. They had invited their neighbors, the Struthers Burts, both noted writers, to meet us. All were friends of Max Perkins. After a few dollops of bourbon and an hour of sparkling talk, Katy and I went back to our abode where we had fried chicken, southern cornbread and a salad of greens. Thomas Wolfe, who had been born and brought up in Asheville, would have described the repast as nameless, wordless, beyond the power of tongue or pen, and I think James Joyce would have described it even more effusively. In a word it was scrumptious.

The next morning we went to the University of North Carolina Library at Chapel Hill, obtained a number of books and arranged to have others sent to us periodically.

Throughout the summer I worked on the gold rush novel and Katy clean-typed the pages as I finished them. We would arise at six-thirty, be at work by eight, pause at noon for lunch, then cease at four to exercise and socialize. The Boyds introduced us to a number of other hospitable residents with whom we played tennis or swam in their pools. In the evenings we researched slavery and made notes.

The gold rush novel *The Pardners,* was finished in mid-September and the manuscript sent to Max Perkins. Within a week he wired us: "Delighted, Scribner's proud to publish."

October first, we took off for California.

CHAPTER THIRTY

O N OUR WAY HOME, while the miles rolled away into the past, we talked of our future. I said we should get out of Hollywood, that we needed a place to live where we could work without social interruptions. I said I had always wanted to live near the ocean and Katy suggested Laguna Beach.

"That would be ideal," I said. "But what about your career?"

"If they want me, they'll find me. Anyway, I'd rather help you."

Househunting in the Laguna area, we were drawn to a real estate office by a sign written in chalk on a blackboard: BEACHFRONT HOUSE FOR SALE, $4,500.

The realtor drove us down a narrow lane leading toward the ocean. At its dead-end, and set half-way down the cliff, was a box-like, three-story, stucco house, its flat roof sloping toward sand and rocks below. A rickety wooden stairway led to a door pitifully in need of paint. The screen door was awry.

Looking at the house from the top of the stairs, Katy raised her hands and exclaimed, "Oh no!"

I took her arm, saying, "Inasmuch as we're here we might as well have a look."

"It's a fixer-upper," the agent said, which was as obvious as the sunshine.

We went down the shaky staircase and into the kitchen. There was no stove and the sink was filthy. But when we entered the living room our opinions changed dramatically. We were astonished by the spectacular views from the four large, plate-glass windows. Two of them framed the Pacific and those on either side looked onto beaches seventy feet below. The fireplace was full of ashes and ash dust was on the plankwood floor. There were two rooms downstairs and beneath them was a basement with a dirt floor.

Back upstairs, I said, "Marvelous location."

Katy, as enthusiastic as I, clutched my arm and said, "We can fix it!"

The realtor explained that the woman who owned the house was about to lose it because she could not make the mortgage payments. She owed $2,500 and the bank was about to foreclose.

I asked, "When does the foreclosure take place?"

"Within forty-five days, take or give a few."

"If it hasn't sold by then," I said, "we'll take over the mortgage, give the owner five hundred dollars and pay your commission. How much will that be?"

"A hundred and fifty," the realtor said.

I signed a note to that effect, we rented a cottage nearby and I went to work on the slavery book.

As I wrote, the house kept breaking into my thoughts. Katy and I acutely needed a home of our own, a place to work, to plant and nurture our roots. For years I had hoped to own a beach house, even a shack, where I could swim. It had been a dream, a wish, and I had come to think it never would come to be. There it was. Would we get it?

The day before the foreclosure the telephone rang. It was the realtor. He said, "You've bought a house."

We had hit the jackpot. It was a bonanza! We whooped and hollered and hugged and kissed and laughed and cried. We were going to have a home of our own, a place from which we did not have to move, a shelter from storms and a haven from adversity, a place where Katy could reign and embellish, where I could work and we could play.

Not taking time to spruce up, we hurried to the realtor's office to sign the papers, then to the bank to assume the mortgage. We took possession in early February of that fateful year, 1941. It was raining. I mean in torrents. The roof and unputtied windows leaked and we used every towel, bucket, pan and pot we could muster to keep from being inundated. It rained all night and we got little sleep, but in the morning the skies cleared, the sun rose and we jumped out of bed to revel in the beauty of the world. On the horizon of the blue Pacific were Santa Catalina and San Clemente Islands. Just below a school of dolphins swam by, seeming to smile and say "Hello." On a salient of rock a man was fishing. Beyond him several pelicans glided southward.

We worked day and night to clean and put the place in order. A carpenter-friend, whom Katy had known when she and Dillwyn lived in Laguna, came to help. Within a few days the windows were reputtied, the roof repaired and Katy had painted the entrance door. The carpenter and I built bookshelves on either side of the fireplace. Katy made drapes. We polished the living room floor and spruced up the garden. Before dark every afternoon we would scramble down the cliff to stroll on the beach. The Pacific was too cold for swimming but the sunsets were dazzling. We would skim pebbles, play tag, talk to the sandpipers, gulls and pelicans and glow in our good fortune. Meanwhile the world continued to spin on its wobbly axis and the dark clouds over Europe were drifting our way. Mother got a touch of fame that year by prophesying in the July issue of *American Astrology* that a war between the United States and Japan would begin in the mid-Pacific on December 7.

By the time her prediction came true I had finished the slavery book and had started a novel about a neurological surgeon based on the life of our friend, Loyal Davis, Nancy Reagan's step-father.

With our country at war, it was obligatory that I do what I could to help win it. The draft board classified me, aged thirty-six, as too old to be a foot soldier, so I wrote Bill Donovan, whom I had known in New York, asking to join his covert organization. I was sent numerous forms which I quickly filled out and sent back to Washington. Either I wasn't wanted or they were lost in the shuffle. I received no reply.

Meanwhile our friend, Max Miller, author of the best-selling *I Cover the Waterfront,* who lived in La Jolla, came calling with Ernie

Pyle, the columnist. Max wanted Ernie to see our "hangover" house.
Ernie wrote a column about their visit:

> On our way to Los Angeles, Max Miller and I told spinach jokes
> and got around to more serious questions of what each of us was
> going to do, personally, about the war in lieu of continuing to
> write our respective brands of deathless literature.
>
> It wound up we were both in a quandary, didn't know what
> we should do, probably couldn't do it if we tried, and got exactly
> nowhere with our problem. "I thought maybe you'd have an
> answer," Max said. "But I guess it's the halt leading the
> blind . . . "
>
> It being a literary day, we stopped in South Laguna to see
> another author, John Weld. We stayed a couple of hours and we
> all praised each other to the skies. It was wonderful. John Weld
> writes semi-historical novels. I don't doubt that some day his
> name will carry great respect. He and his wife Katy live in one of
> the most spectacular houses you ever saw. It is a cottage perched
> on a shelf halfway down the high perpendicular cliff that rises
> smack out of the Pacific . . .

I asked Max and Ernie for suggestions as to what I might do in the war
effort and learned they were in the same predicament. Max said, "I'm
working at Consolidated-Vultee in San Diego, but I was in the Navy
toward the end of World War One and I'm thinking of going back in."

Ernie said, "I guess I'll become a war correspondent and go where the
action is."

"You might come to Consolidated and go to work," Max said to me.
"They build B-24 bombers and Pee Bee Wye flying boats. They need all
the help they can get."

A few days later I went to San Diego, Max introduced me to the head
of Consolidated-Vultee's public relations office, and I became editor of
the company's house organ, *The Consolidated News*. I would have
preferred a more requisite role in the worldwide drama, but was assured
the *News* was important to the company's 40,000 employees. Max
rejoined the navy to write a number of books about its actions and Ernie
went on to become famous for his dispatches as a war chronicler.

CHAPTER THIRTY-ONE

For everyone it was the end of an era. Just as I was getting a beam of literary fame and seemed on the way to becoming the next Scribner star, I stopped writing and lost the impetus. Working weekends, I did manage to finish the doctor book, but did so without giving it the rewriting it should have had. Scribner's published it, but the book was not widely reviewed and did not sell well.

Not long after I went to work for Consolidated-Vultee, Henry Ford got a contract to build B-24s in Michigan. He and his minions came to San Diego and hired as many people from Convair as the company could spare. Through some whim of fate, I was one of them.

That I agreed to work for Henry Ford was ironical. I had met him in Cherbourg, France, in the early Thirties, having been sent by the *Paris Herald* to interview him on his arrival in Europe for the first time since his "Peace Ship" fiasco in 1915. I was the only newsman to greet him when, at daybreak, he debarked from the *Europa*. Falling in beside him as he strolled along with his wife and several cohorts, I identified myself but before I could ask about his European plans, he said, "I don't want to talk to you."

I was dumbfounded. "But I've been here all night waiting to welcome you," I said.

"You news fellows always misquote me."

"Well, give me a chance to quote you properly."

He did not reply. He and his party climbed into two Lincoln limousines. He rolled up the window, thereby separating me, and was driven away, headed for Paris.

Since meeting him in Cherbourg, I had harbored a grudge. But with a war to be fought, I swallowed the ill will and Katy and I took off on that long drive to Dearborn, Michigan.

Shortly after I got on the Ford payroll, Henry Ford II came to work for the company. His father, Edsel, recently deceased, had been the company's president; now Old Henry was back in command. The War Production Board was having difficulties with the stubborn, eighty-year-old industrialist and, because the company was family owned and vitally important to the war effort, it had arranged for Young Henry to leave the Navy, hoping he would be able to control his grandfather.

It was a benumbing assignment for the twenty-six-year-old, whose grandfather was notoriously independent and perverse. The old man had such little faith in his grandson that when Young Henry arrived at the Dearborn headquarters he was not given a desk. Add to that, the old man's body-guard, Harry Bennett, was furtively running the company and regarded Henry as a spoiled child.

Bennett, the company's bête noir, was thick-skinned, insensitive, power-loving, tough, gruff, ungracious and cocky. He had been something of a prize-fighter before getting a job in the Rouge Plant and had caught Henry Ford's fancy by knocking down a rambunctious employee. Ford made him his body-guard and the company's police chief. These were important jobs because the old man was fraught with paradoxes and qualms; he imagined diverse plots against him and other members of his family, particularly his grandchildren. As Ford's body-guard, Bennett also became his chauffeur. He would pick him up early in the morning at *Fair Lane,* the Ford's mansion, be with him throughout the day and take him home in the evening. When one wanted to reach Henry Ford one had to go through Bennett.

It did not take long after I went to work in the company's main office building for me to learn of Bennett's power. His office, fifty feet long and about twenty feet wide, was in the basement. At the far end was his desk. On the wall at the other end was a target. It was his habit to punctuate his conversations by shooting pellets at it. He wielded his power indiscriminately. He was a member of the Board of Directors, the meetings of which the old man rarely attended. When important decisions needed resolution Bennett would leave the meeting to "talk to Mister Ford." He would then return to say, "Mister Ford says to do it this way." Whether or not he had actually conferred with the old man was moot. It was generally thought that he had not bothered to do so, that the decisions were his own. Everyone in the company, including the directors, were fearful of him because, through the old man, he had power to fire anyone.

Soon after he arrived, Young Henry spoke to his grandfather about Bennett and the old man said, "Don't talk to me about Harry. I can trust him."

Young Henry finally got an office and a desk down the hall from mine, and we, both newcomers, became friends. We discussed his role in the company and the Bennett situation.

I said, "You should fire the son of a bitch."

"I can't," he said. "If I try to do that grandfather might fire me."

I also became friendly with Jack Davis, vice president of sales and advertising. Jack had been with the company for a long time and had been close to Edsel Ford. A couple of years before, in a conflict with Bennett, he had been demoted and sent to work in California. On the advice of his mother, Young Henry brought Davis back. The three of us—Young Henry, Jack Davis and I—became a coterie conspiring to get rid of Bennett.

Bennett must have heard rumors to that effect because one of his goons came to my office and, without preliminaries, said, "Mister Bennett has heard that you told someone at the Athletic Club he was on his way out. If he sees you in the hall he'll knock your teeth down your throat." Without waiting for a response, he left.

It took me a few brooding minutes to decide what to do. I could confront Bennett forthwith and rebut the rumor, or forget it. I rather welcomed the opportunity to do the former. It would be interesting to see what Bennett would do. He could fire me, but he couldn't do that without cause.

I went to his office. Guards were at desks on either side of the door. "What chew wanna see him 'bout?" one of them asked.

"Private matter," I said, with the tone of "It's none of your damn business."

"He ain't in."

"Then give him this message. I understand he wants to knock my block off. Tell him I'm available in my office from nine to five." Both guards snorted as I turned to go.

I did not hear from Bennett, but a few weeks later while Katy and I were playing golf with Jack Davis someone came out of the pro-shop and called me to the telephone. It was John Bugas, former head of the FBI office in Detroit, who had been hired by Bennett to be the company's personnel director.

"I want to see you," Bugas said.

"When?"

"Right now."

"I'm on vacation," I said. "Can't we discuss it over the telephone?"

"No. You'll have to come in."

"I don't know that I can get there before closing time."

"I'll wait."

I drove to Dearborn. Bugas was in an office next to Bennett's. He was not cordial. He said, "You've overstayed your vacation time."

"What do you mean?"

"You haven't been here a year. You only get one week's vacation. You're into your second."

"I got permission for the extra week."

"From whom?"

"John Thompson." Thompson was head of public relations.

"He says he didn't give it. You're fired."

"By whom?"

Bugas avoided the question. "Company policy."

I left him and went to say goodbye to Young Henry. As I related what had occurred, he became angrier by the word. Both of us realized I was being fired to undermine him.

Finally he said, "Do you want to go?"

"Frankly, no," I replied. "Besides the world war, there's an important war going on here and I'd like to stay until both are resolved."

Henry thought about this for a spell, then said, "Tell you what you do. Go to New York and open a public relations office." The next morning I left. Katy stayed to pack and would follow me.

In New York I leased a suite of offices in Rockefeller Center, hired a secretary and an assistant and went to work repairing one of the old man's broken fences: boycott by Jews of Ford cars and trucks. One of my first acts was to persuade the company to donate $25,000 to the Jewish Welfare Fund. Thereto the Ford Motor Company had never contributed to any Jewish charity.

Shortly thereafter the Young Henry-Harry Bennett feud ended. Jack Davis learned from the captain of one of the company's Great Lakes ships that Mr. Ford was showing signs of senility. He had gone with the captain on a voyage to northern Michigan to pick up iron and coal. "I think the boss has lost his marbles," the captain told Jack. "He couldn't remember what day it was." Davis passed this remark to Young Henry and suggested the time had come to fire Bennett.

Young Henry, still fearful of what his unpredictable grandfather would do, did so. He then trepidatiously went to inform his grandfather of what he had done. To his surprise the old man took it calmly. "Well, now," he said, "I guess Harry's back where he started."

Bennett was far from "back where he started." During his thirty years at Ford he had managed to acquire a fortune. He had a two-towered "castle" near Ann Arbor, an elaborate home on Grosse Isle, a cottage on Lake St. Clair, a camp on the Huron River, and a ranch in Desert Hot Springs, California, to which, when he left Ford, he repaired and where he eventually died.

World War Two and the Ford-Bennett war ended about the same time. Soon thereafter I resigned from the company and Katy and I hied back to our snuggery in South Laguna. Max Perkins petitioned me to get back to book writing and I agreed to compose a California trilogy: *The Mission, The Ranch* and *The Town.* I eventually wrote *The Missionary,* but, because I became involved in doing other things, it took me several years. I have yet to write the other two.

This could be the end of our story, but there is another adventure that should be told. Having never had a honeymoon, Katy and I decided to take a trip around the world on freight ships. To help finance the venture we decided to make a film of it.

"We'll call it *Freightboat Around the World*," I said.

"What'll I do? Hitchhike?"

"You'll enhance every sequence. When we get to Egypt you'll climb a pyramid and talk to the Sphinx."

She made a wry face. "What'll I say to him?"

"Oh, the usual—'What do you know, Joe? How're the kids?' "

She laughed, "Sounds like fun."

I took lessons in cinematography, bought a sixteen-millimeter camera, a sound recorder, lighting equipment and thirty thousand feet of film. Katy and I researched the countries we planned to visit and I wrote a narrative outline. Passage on freighters proved difficult to schedule and obtain, but through our friend, Victor Andrews, a gentleman orange farmer who also lives in Laguna Beach, we managed to book on several lines for the entire circumnavigation. Victor had influence in shipping because much of his fruit was shipped to the Far East. To Katy's and my delight, he and his wife June, a concert singer of the highest quality, decided to go with us. Our first voyage was to be to Hong Kong by way of Japan on the *Laust Maersk,* a vessel of the Danish Maersk Line. Our expedition was to be a lark.

It proved to be that and more.

CHAPTER THIRTY-TWO

AT THE SAN PEDRO DOCK, her lines dangling from the boom, the *Laust Maersk* was beautiful, even in the late January rain. Thick-coated a light blue, her prow rose majestically from the bilgeous water as if she were disdainful of it. The only uncomely thing about her was her name. She had been christened for a member of the Danish family which owned her, and because the name was difficult to pronounce one of our friends dubbed her *Lost,* that being, he thought, a humorous sobriquet. It proved to be prophetic.

June, Victor, Katy and I climbed the gangplank followed by a horde of friends laden with bottles, flowers and baskets of fruit who had come to bid us bon voyage. The ship's master, Svend Kjerulf, was not aboard. The chief steward, Mr. Simonsen, a pale, bald, pot-bellied Dane, greeted us graciously, helped decorate the main salon with flowers and proceeded to uncork a few of the bottles. He introduced his wife, a rather pretty, aging blond, and explained that it was the policy of the Maersk Line to permit wives of officers, in the interest of marital relations, to accompany their husbands from time to time. Hardly had she been introduced before she began telling Katy how vehemently she hated the sea. "I only come along," she said, "to keep my husband out of mischief. There's not a man aboard who doesn't have a girl in every port."

By the time Captain Kjerulf came aboard we passengers and our friends had several sheets to the wind, and the good captain himself, who had been celebrating ashore with expatriot countrymen, was well underway. A short, stocky, florid-faced Dane, he over-apologized for being late. The *Laust* had been scheduled to sail at five o'clock but her lines were not cast off until after six. It was still raining and a strong wind had come up. "Don't worry," the captain said in a toast to the four of us, his only passengers, "we'll make up the lost time by noon tomorrow. We'll just add an extra turn to the screw."

As it turned out, we never did make up that lost hour. Due to the storms encountered, the *Laust Maersk* was two-and-a-half days late approaching Japan.

Mr. Simonsen delayed dinner until the ship had cleared the breakwater so the captain, whose duty was to be on the bridge when leaving or entering a port, could join us for the repast. Dinner was excellent: hot, thick, well-seasoned soup, fish, several meats, four or five vegetables and, for dessert, Baked Alaska. There were also two kinds of freshly baked bread and a variety of cheeses and fruits. Throughout the meal the captain saw to it that Jimmy, the skinny Macaoan dining steward, kept the wine glasses filled. He also had him remove the floral arrangements from the salon tables and set them on deck, saying, "According to the weather report, we're headed into a strong sea." Then, smiling, he said, "You may not know, it's a sailor's superstition that flowers on a ship are bad luck."

Victor outlined our itinerary. We were to leave the *Laust* at Yokohama and, after several days photographing in Japan, rejoin her at Kobe. From Hong Kong we planned to fly to Bangkok and thence to Singapore, where we were booked to board another ship for Malaya, Ceylon and India. A third ship was to take us from Bombay to Kenya and around South Africa to the Mediterranean. (The Suez Canal was closed.) From Genoa we were booked on an Italian liner to Panama and ultimately back to Los Angeles.

Mention of the Italian ship elicited Captain Kjerulf's disdain. He said that, since the sinking of the Italian liner *Andria Doria* by the Swedish vessel *Stockholm*, he would be apprehensive about traveling on an Italian vessel. "Italians are not the world's best sailors," he declared. "The tragedy of the *Andria Doria* was due to bad seamanship." He explained that the Italian liner, westbound and approaching the Ambrose Lightship on the way to New York, had been rammed and sunk by the Swedish ship traveling eastward. The crux of the disaster, he said, lay in the *Andria Doria* turning to port and the *Stockholm* turning to starboard. "They got their signals mixed," he said. "Had both turned to starboard or to port they would have avoided each other. I have a book about that accident. You may want to read it."

During the night the weather worsened. At breakfast the next morning Katy's coffee sloshed into her lap. Two of the vases of flowers on deck tipped over and slid into the dining salon. Jimmy quickly brought towels, muttering "plenny lough." As he spoke, the *Laust* took another deep wallow and dishes on the dining table went onto the deck.

Captain Kjerulf joined us for lunch, bringing a copy of *Collision Course*, the book about the *Andria Doria* sinking. "Everywhere I look at the chart," he said, "there is the eye of a storm. Normally we would follow the great circle route, that being the shortest way, but I've turned us further south. It will take longer, but I'm hoping it will be more comfortable."

Katy said, "I'm beginning to wonder why they named it the Pacific." The captain shook his head and grinned. "It can be a bastard."

As the days ticked on, the storms grew in intensity. With ropes knotted around our waists and tied to railings, Victor steadied me while I photographed the tumultuous sea. Waves fifty feet high engulfed the ship. Now the stern would rise, the screw would emerge and the *Laust* would shake and shudder like a drenched dog. Meanwhile furious winds and torrential rains lashed at her. The sea became so rough Captain Kjerulf reduced the speed to five knots. "I'm afraid if we stay at fifteen she might break in two," he told us. "In all my more than thirty years at sea I've never experienced such a pattern of storms. And there is no relief in sight."

The best times were the pre-dinner cocktail sessions with the officers. After dinner in the lounge we played word games or sang a Scandinavian diversion called Nextasong, in which everyone in turn sings a song.

We crossed the International Date Line on the anything-but-pacific ocean January 28, which means we skipped that day. It was to have been Captain Kjerulf's birthday. He was fifty-five, but admitted to only fifty-four, calling it his leap-backward year. To commemorate the occasion, June wrote a parody to *I Am the Captain of the Pinafore*, which we all sang to him by way of celebration:

> For he is the Captain of our ship *Laust Maersk*,
> And a right fine Captain, too.
> He is very, very good, and be it understood
> He commands a real fine crew.
> His birthday was on the twenty-eighth,
> But we lost that day at sea.
> Oh, he's a dear, and he's younger by a year!
> So raise your glass and quench your thirst
> To the jolly Captain of the great *Laust Maersk!*
> Give three cheers and let's all say,
> Happy, happy, on your lost birthday!

The morning of the fourteenth day the weather began to clear and for the first time we caught glimpses of blue sky, enough now and then to make a pair of breeches for the proverbial wide-assed Dutchman. Our first glimpse of civilization was of two Japanese fishing boats, rusty tubs which looked woefully inadequate as they glided eastward up great swells and plunged precariously into deep troughs. Captain Kjerulf, intending to reach Yokohama that evening, drove the *Laust* through the lessening waves at top speed. By four o'clock the glorious sun broke through the clouds, its brilliance backlighting the purple jagged skyline of Japan. It remained numbingly cold as Victor and I made the most of the breathtaking scene by photographing the deck-hands against it as they prepared the ship for unloading. To have the exposed film ready for mailing, I wrapped fourteen reels, mostly storm footage, in water-tight paper and addressed the package to the processors in Hollywood.

By five o'clock it was dark and we passengers as usual gathered with a few of the officers in the main lounge for cocktails. All of us were in high spirits at the prospect of ending the grueling voyage. As the ship's clock struck four bells—six o'clock—Jimmy announced dinner. Mrs.

Simonsen joined us at the dining table. Captain Kjerulf was on the bridge.

Lightheartedly jesting, we had progressed through the soup and fish courses when we were arrested by a short blast of the ship's whistle. It was followed almost immediately by two seemingly angry blasts. The First Officer sprang to his feet, hastily muttering an apology and saying, "I'm needed on deck!"

Shortly after he left the dining room there was an horrendous sound of crunching steel and the ship shuddered. Some of us at the table were toppled onto the deck and by the time we got to our feet the throb of the engines had ceased and the lights were out. For a moment all was terrifyingly still and quiet. Within seconds came the piercing, chilling sound of mouth-blown whistles and men's frantic voices shouting. We heard Mr. Simonsen's voice holler, "Get your life jackets!"

Getting to our feet, June, Victor, Katy and I joined hands and, with June uttering a short prayer, groped our way through the darkness to our cabins. Katy and I donned overcoats and I helped her slip into and adjust her life jacket. I then ducked into one but in haste did not tie the belt. By the time we got outside in the almost freezing cold there was intense activity. Men carrying flashlights were running hither and yon shouting. We hurried toward our lifeboat station but before we reached it a crewman warned us not to go any further; his flashlight revealed that both starboard lifeboats had been sheared away. In the light's ray we saw the First Mate and others administering to a crewman who had been crushed in the accident and was soaking in blood. The officer was filling a hypodermic needle from a small bottle. Already the *Laust* was listing.

To lessen Katy's apprehension, I clasped her hand and said, "Don't worry, darling. Even if the ship is badly damaged there are watertight compartments which can be closed off. They will keep her afloat indefinitely. At the very worst it will take hours, if not days for her to sink; and by that time all of us will be removed to another vessel. After all," I pointed out, "we are but a few miles from Yokohama."

In the far distance we could see a string of lights flickering on the horizon and were to learn it was seventeen miles to Yokohama. What had happened was: the *Laust* had been struck by the prow of another freighter, precisely as had the *Andria Doria,* and had been peeled open as if she were a tin can. Immediately tons of water had engulfed the engine room, throttling the power plant; hence the lack of electricity for lights, to close the bulkheads, to launch a lifeboat or to send wireless messages.

I left Katy to join Victor and a dozen crewmen who were trying to manually launch one of the portside lifeboats. To concert our powers, the crewmen were counting in Danish; but strain as we did the boat was too heavy for us to lift off its davits. Still we kept gruntingly, frantically trying, a lifeboat being our only hope to avoid the icy water. Meanwhile June's beautiful voice was singing "The Lord's Prayer." The words rose and fell, wafted by the wind. Unable to launch a lifeboat, we abandoned it.

I found Katy and Mrs. Simonsen. The Chief Steward's wife stood shivering in a dress, her arms tucked under her breasts, her teeth chattering. She was without life jacket or overcoat. There was a menacing din: dangling blocks banging against booms, the thump and clatter of objects falling as the listing increased, the sound of running feet and the shouts of men. Katy, screaming to be heard, was urging Mrs. Simonsen to fetch a coat.

"I don't want to go back in there!" Mrs. Simonsen said sobbing.

"I'll get you one," Katy said, and left us.

I put my life jacket over Mrs. Simonsen's head and tied it down. One of the crewmen had opened a locker and was tossing life jackets overboard. I snatched one of the last ones and ducked into it, but again did not fasten it.

Mrs. Simonsen, her teeth chattering, said, "We're going to sink," matter-of-factly, as if she were an oracle.

"Oh, no!" I hollered. "Not this big ship!"

"I always knew something like this was going to happen," she said and burst out crying. "I tried to get George into some other kind of work." I put a comforting arm around her shivering shoulders and she sobbed, "Where is George?"

Aloud I said, "He's busy," and to myself: *"How the hell would I know?"*

Katy returned with her cherished fur coat. Meanwhile the listing had increased and it was necessary to hold onto the railing to keep one's balance; even so, she managed to get the heavy coat over Mrs. Simonsen's thin shoulders and the life preserver. Three flares whistled furiously upward through the cold air and exploded overhead, then drifted down, glowing like pink flowers, their light suffusing the area with an eerie sheen.

Pointing to the long string of glimmering lights on the horizon, I said, "That must be Yokohama."

Katy said, "Looks like a long way to swim."

Mrs. Simonsen wailed, "I wonder if we'll ever get there."

By now the frantic activities on deck had ceased and presently footsteps clattered down the companionway behind us. It was Captain Kjerulf. In great haste he pulled me to one side and whispered, "It's hopeless. Abandon ship!" and scurried away.

At first I did not get the full import of the message. Abandon ship? How? Where? What should we do? When the horrible meaning penetrated I thought of the film I had shot. It was in our cabin, all marvelous footage of storms wrapped for mailing.

"The film!" I exclaimed to Katy, "I've got to get it!"

She caught my arm. By now the ship was listing badly. "Don't leave me!" she begged.

"Be right back," I said and jerked away. As I entered the superstructure I heard the terrifying tumbling of furniture, glassware, bottles, dishes and cargo. A chair had fallen against the stateroom door, but I managed to force my way in and crawl on my hands and knees to reach the built-in desk.

The film and packet of letters to be mailed, were in a drawer. I stuffed the letters into an overcoat pocket and spent precious moments trying to force the package of film into the pocket on the other side. The untied life jacket kept getting in the way. The package proved too large, so I tucked it under an arm and slid back to the door. Groping frantically among the luggage, I found a camera in its case, seized it by the handle and stumbled back through the darkness, one foot trodding the deck, the other the superstructure. In the faint light of the still-burning flares I saw Katy and Mrs. Simonsen hanging onto the ship's railing directly above me. Thought of us getting into the cold water shrank my testicles. I put the camera between my feet and the package of film between my thighs and braced myself.

"Katy!" I cried. "The ship's sinking! We've got to leave her. Let go!"

The two women dropped simultaneously. I attempted to break their falls but their weights upset me and the three of us collapsed in a heap under the stairway. Camera and film went askew. By now the ship's stern was under water and her bow was rising. As we scrambled, trying to get to our feet, it seemed that we were about to be engulfed by a gigantic wave; actually the ship was on her way down. I gave Katy a push to help her clear the stairway, then grasped Mrs. Simonsen's hand; but the water closed over us and she was wrenched away. In the split second before the sea swallowed me I took a deep breath, all I could inhale, well aware it might be my last.

At once I started swimming to clear the cul-de-sac but after several thrashings discovered I was making no progress. At first I thought it was the suction of the ship's sinking that was retarding me, but it proved to be the life jacket. Having neglected to fasten it, one of its corks had become wedged in the stairway. I back-treaded and ducked out of the jacket. Now again when I tried to swim I was hindered. The opening through which I was trying to go was too narrow. Again I backed away, and took another tack. By now my ears had begun to ache. I swam furiously, with all of my strength and dexterity, acutely aware that I was within the grasp of death.

It is a proverb that those moments which precede death are likely to be filled with images of one's past, and so it was with me. The sinking ship was sucking me through that tiny orifice which is the exit from the world. During the brief interval of consciousness a myriad remembrances and reflections spun through my mind. I wanted to take with me as many memories as I could conjure and to review my misjudgments and mistakes.

During the first of those watery moments I continued to swim furiously, flailing and kicking, impeded by the soaked overcoat; but it soon became evident that I was making little progress and that my chances of survival were decreasing with every stroke.

Suddenly something uncommon occurred; it was as if a spring in me had snapped. The cold water had something to do with it. Euphoria set in. Chest pains and ear pains ceased. I felt exalted. I was not floundering in water; I was afloat in rarefied air. One moment I had been clinging maniacally to life and in a split second was welcoming death as a long-sought friend.

I thought that man goes through life concerned with oncoming time, and suddenly it occurred to me that I had no future. Whatever happened thenceforth was no concern of mine. Like chalk hieroglyphics on a blackboard, all of my obligations and responsibilities were being wiped away; intentions and aspirations were being sucked down a drain. It was a glorious feeling. I was truly free. My only regret in bidding the world goodbye was that I would not have the joy of being with Katy. I wondered how she would fare in the perilous world I was leaving and fervently hoped she would survive and live happily. My core shrank at the thought she, too, might be drowning. It would be a bitter miscarriage of justice to deny the world her beauty, grace, courage and kindness. Although realizing it probably was futile, because I had little credit with God, I prayed for her deliverance. . . .

CHAPTER THIRTY-THREE

WHILE THE *Laust* was in her inexorable stern-first dive, Katy, swimming furiously, managed to clear an obstruction and pop into the cold air. The flares burning on the surface gave the choppy, black water the look of crinkled oilcloth. After her first indraft of air she began calling my name, shrieking it frantically into the wind. She struggled to shed her life jacket, intending to go to my assistance, but before she could do so she was seized by the chief engineer and third mate and pulled aboard an oil-drum raft. On the raft were seven crew members, including the seaman who had been crushed in the collision. As she was being lifted aboard she screamed protestingly: "My husband! He's drowning! He's gone down with the ship!" and wrestled to get back into the water. Her captors did not release her, so she resumed screaming my name, her frenzied voice thin against the moan of the wind.

Other members of the forty-five-man crew, including the captain, had left the doomed vessel before she bellied up, sliding down her hull. June and Victor had tumbled across the deck and into the water. June had never learned to swim but the life jacket sustained her and Victor began pushing her in the direction of the miles-away string of lights. Hearing Katy's cries they changed course and reached the raft.

In blissful euphoria, having accepted death, I resumed mentally meandering. I ran through the pattern of my life, appraised my character and sought the forces which had motivated me. One was a hunger for affection and another had been a yearning for fame. I had always sought to be liked and respected. I had always hoped that, once I left the earth, I would be remembered kindly. Now surprisingly these yearnings were gone. Gone also were responsibilities and obligations. Looking back at my tapestry of experience, I had enjoyed more than my share of laughter, but my outstanding stroke of good fortune had been latching onto Katy. It dawned on me that nothing, neither achievement nor riches nor fame could have brought me such happiness.

My maternal grandmother had been helpful. She had pounded into me the importance of integrity, that it is the basis for respect, that respect is the core of affection, and that affection is the nucleus of love. While I had not liked the repetitiveness of her teaching, I appreciated her wisdom.

From my mother I had learned the value of independence. At the time she untied the apron strings, I had not understood her motive. I thought I had been abandoned. It was not until years later, after I had wandered the world alone, that she told me: "I didn't know what to do about a boy, which is why I sent you to others. Meanwhile I had to educate your sister. When the time came to do both I had to let you go."

From James Joyce I had learned tenacity and how to scrounge. Both, in my struggle to stay alive, had stood me in good stead.

Walter Huston had been a past master of kindness, generosity and good humor and had taught me their values.

I learned perception and awareness, as well as grace and gallantry from Max Perkins.

But it was from Katy that I learned fidelity. She had encouraged me, had worked tirelessly for me and had followed me courageously.

I seemed to have been under water for an interminable time, although for me now there was no time. Overlapping scenes raced through my mind, the sequences not in succession. I was reliving experiences at an incredible pace, while natural reflexes were causing me to flail upward as a beheaded chicken keeps flapping its wings.

Suddenly my head popped out of water. I opened my mouth and my lungs sucked in a surfeit of what I thought was heavenly air. I was confused. I thought I had passed into the next world, but this one was very like the one I had just left. The same pink flares suffused the watery darkness, stars were overhead and I smelled the odor of oil. Was it possible that I could be back in the world of the living? . . .

I heard Katy's vibrant voice shrieking my name. Was I dreaming? Was it truly she? Had she drowned, too, and were we both somewhere across the Styx? Alive or dead I was overjoyed at the prospect of finding her.

I opened my mouth to shout, "Here I am!" and a splash of oil slick hit the back of my throat. Coughing and spitting, as if alive, I began swimming in the direction of her voice. I became aware that my left leg was numb. Reaching the raft, it was obvious that I was back among the living. Seven aboard were huddled around the crunched crewman to keep him warm. Body weights were such that all were sitting in water, the temperature of which was forty degrees. The wind-chill factor was well below freezing. Katy helped me squeeze in beside her.

"Oh, Johnny," she said, hugging me joyfully, "I thought I'd lost you!"

"You almost did."

"Are you all right?"

"I don't know yet." There was an excruciating charley-horse pain in my left leg. The third mate's pencil flashlight revealed a severe wound above the ankle. In my thrashing it must have been cut by the ship's crushed steel. Cold as I was, the wound was oozing blood. Removing her stockings Katy tied tourniquets above and below my knee and June slipped off her silk taffeta petticoat and with it wrapped the ankle.

There was talk.

"What hit us?"

"A ship."

"Then where is it?"

"Why don't they put down a lifeboat?"

"Why don't they shine a light?"

"Why don't they help us?"

"Takes a long time for a big ship to stop and turn around," the third mate said.

From time to time, to let the blood flow, Katy would unknot and re-knot the stockings, first one and then the other. Snuggled against her, I said, "I used to think people placed too much value on life. I've changed my mind."

She tightened her embrace. "This would be a strange place for us to die."

"I guess the Lord wasn't ready for us."

For a long time no one said anything. The theme was: grin and bear it; save your energy for daylight. It was not the time for humor or complaining.

We sat in water, shivering and teeth chattering for more than an hour before the light of a red lantern pierced the darkness and we heard the sound of an oar. The third mate signaled an SOS with his tiny flashlight and shouted, "Ahoy!" his voice full of hope.

Presently into our faint halo came a sculled skiff bearing two Japanese men. There were attempts at verbal intelligence. We learned they were from a tanker nearby and had been attracted by the flares. They gave us a line and laboriously began sculling.

The raft was so overloaded and low in the water it took almost an hour to reach the fifty-ton, rusty ship.

The only way to get aboard was by the rungs of a ladder inset into the sloping hull. The injured crewman was pushed up first, then the dripping ladies. When it came my turn I, unable to use my wounded leg, sat on Victor's broad shoulders and, thanks to him, we made the difficult climb together. All of us, with the exception of the mangled crewman who was taken to a cabin, were crowded into the warm wheelhouse. Katy found a shallow shelf near the red-hot stove where I lay down. As if in answer to a prayer, a tanker crewman brought us steaming tea in beautiful porcelain cups. Soon the body heat and the lack of oxygen caused the captain to open a window and let in the cold but fresh air.

During the three hours it took to reach Kawasaki, the nearest port, Katy stood next to me, loosening and tightening the tourniquet. A message to authorities that we were aboard was sent and, when the ship docked, panel trucks were waiting to take us to the American Hospital in Yokohama. We rode the bumpy roads on a steel floor, my head in Katy's lap, and arrived near midnight. A young Japanese physician with an Irish name, Ohara, worked diligently without success to save the life of the badly injured crewman, then shortly before daybreak he got to my leg. He did what he could to repair the wound, sewed it up and applied a cast. When I came out of the anesthesia, he half-apologized for the job he had done, saying, "I get my surgeon's certificate in two weeks."

While I was in the operating room Katy was interviewed by an Overseas Radio reporter from the Far Eastern Network and was still awake when I was put to bed. She sat down beside me, still in shock.

"The doctor says he doesn't know how you're going to come out of this mess," she said. "He says we won't know for a month, when the cast should come off. Meanwhile, what are we going to do?"

I was coming out of the anesthesia. "Go on," I mumbled.

"With your leg in a cast and all of our equipment gone? Our passports, money . . . "

"We'll re-outfit, do what we set out to do."

We learned that the *Laust Maersk* had been struck by an American freighter, the *Alcoa Pioneer* which had returned to Yokohama with a *Laust* lifeboat on its bow. Besides the crushed seaman, four other *Laust* crewmen had lost their lives. When the collision occurred the captain of the *Alcoa* ship had not been on the bridge and the Japanese court that assessed the accident ruled he was primarily to blame.

During my convalescence, Katy wrote to my mother:

By our standards the American Hospital here in Yokohama is pretty shabby, but the treatment we are receiving is first class. Japanese nurses, to use the vernacular, are dolls—self-effacing, kind and generous. There is a big American community here (a U.S. naval base) and many of our countrymen have sent us fruit, flowers, candy and clothing. Our rooms are like Salvation Army thrift stores. Few of the garments fit us and, attired in them, June and I look like ladies from the pickle boat. But we're all grateful to have them. They will stand us in good stead until we get to Hong Kong. The clothes we can buy here won't fit us and that goes particularly for the shoes. Japanese feet are considerably smaller than ours.

The U.S. consul in Yokohoma personally brought us new passports and, after recuperating for three days, Katy and the Andrews went shopping and bought film and the only sixteen millimeter camera in the Navy PX. After five days I was discharged from the hospital, my leg in a cast, and the four of us hied to Tokyo to film the home life of a Sumo wrestler, one of the important sequences of our scenario.

With me hobbling, we spent three weeks in Japan. We shot sequences in Tokyo, Yokosuka and Mount Fugi, went by bullet train to Gifu, where we photographed a sequence of cormorant fishing for which the town is famous, then on to Nara, Nagoya, Kyoto, Osaka where we filmed shrines, statues of Buddhist temples, girls diving for pearls, people planting rice, a tea farm, geishas gilding their lily-like faces, a kimono factory, a cherry blossom festival, the Imperial Palace and a Kabuki performance.

In Hong Kong, with the help of the British authorities, we photographed the island, its peak, the ferry, Kowloon, the refugee ghetto settlements on the hillsides and at the then tightly closed Chinese border.

We photographed for a week in Bangkok.

I had targeted Singapore as the place to have the cast removed. We arrived there too late in the afternoon to find a doctor, but the next morning I was at a clinic's door when it opened. I had been advised to have the incubus removed after thirty days; then I would know whether or not Ohara's surgery had been successful. When the doctor finally, after considerable snipping, got the plaster off, neither he nor I was prepared for the shocking thinness of my leg. "Seems like your calf has gone to pasture," he said, making light of what to me was a calamity. "See if you can raise your foot." I could not. "Get up and let's see you walk."

I stood up, and when I lifted the injured leg the foot dangled; it just hung there. I had to flip it to put it on its sole.

The doctor sat looking at the leg for a while, then said, "Apparently the muscles and tendons, and perhaps the nerves have been severed. They'll have to be stretched and rejoined. I'm sorry to tell you that there's no one here capable of doing that operation. Where do you live?"

"We're on our way around the world. We're going on to Ceylon and Egypt, then to Lebanon and Greece."

"There's an American hospital in Beirut. I suggest you go there as soon as you can. In the meantime, you'll need something to hold up your toe when you walk." He sent the nurse for an elastic and an eyelet-screw. The latter he screwed into the tip of my shoe, slipped the elastic through the eye and tied its ends around my leg below the knee. Now I was able to walk without the foot dropping.

"Sorry," the doctor said, "but that's the best I can do."

Katy, June and Victor were waiting for me in the lobby when I got back to the hotel. Katy cried, "Look! He's walking!"

I lifted a trouser leg and showed the elastic. "The doctor said my leg has to be reconstructed. There's no one here who can do it. He suggests I go as soon as I can to the American Hospital in Beirut."

Victor said, "I have more bad news. Our freighter, the *Leoville,* which is going to take us to Egypt, is due to sail tomorrow; but before we get aboard we've got to get Egyptian visas. We have to prove we're not Jewish. The closest Egyptian consulate is in Kuala Lumpur. I've talked with the captain of the *Leoville* and he has agreed that the three of you can get aboard while I go by train to Kuala Lumpur and get the visas. I'll join the ship at Port Swettenham."

"Can't you fly?" I asked.

"There's a war on. Malaya's aswarm with communist guerrillas and all flights have been canceled. Even trains are having trouble getting through. One is leaving tonight and I'm going to be on it."

June said, "I don't want him to go. It's too dangerous."

"If I don't we'll not get aboard the *Leoville.*"

"I'll go," I said.

"Not with that leg," Katy said.

That evening, June, Katy and I escorted our hero, Victor, to the railroad station. He carried our four passports in a brand new money-belt strapped around his midriff. Although it was a good bet he would not spend much time sleeping, he gave the porter ten dollars and got a berth in the one sleeping car. All of us had our fingers crossed as the train pulled away.

The next day June, Katy and I boarded the *Leoville.*

When the ship reached Port Swettenham and Victor was not there, June was sure he had been killed. But the next day he arrived in a taxi full of excitement and waving our passports. The first thing we wanted to know was how he made out on the train. "Didn't sleep a wink," he said.

"Was there any shooting?"

"I heard some, but the train was not held up. The reason I'm late is, when I arrived in Kuala Lumpur it was Ramadan, and the Egyptian consulate was closed."

"What about proof we're not Jews?"

"I swore on the Koran that we are Christians and gave the clerk twenty bucks. He stamped the passports."

During the five days the ship remained in Port Swettenham we managed to photograph a Chinese funeral, a rubber plantation, a tin mine and scenes in the jungle. The next stop was Pinang, a vacation resort where we photographed the unique railway, the race course, a rice plantation and a maharajah's palace. We then went across the Strait of Malacca and spent several days at Belawan, where we were not allowed to go ashore because we had no visas.

Meanwhile I was having trouble with my leg. By the time we got to Colombo, the capital of Ceylon (now Sri Lanka) Katy was adamant that we fly to Beirut and have it operated. I did not want to pass up Egypt, but she insisted the leg was more important. The Andrews agreed. However, we were unable to fly directly to Beirut so went there by way of Bombay and Cairo. Victor was also eager to get to Lebanon, the land of his forefathers.

The neurologist I consulted at the American Hospital was a big-chested, swarthy man with black curly hair and five o'clock shadow. He examined my injured leg, needle-pricking it and the foot for nerve damage and muscular response. Finally he asked, "When did you say the accident happened?"

"February 5th."

"That's more than two months ago. The severed muscles and tendons have shrunk. It isn't going to be easy to get them back together, but it should be done right away."

"Can you do it?" I asked hopefully.

"I have never done such an operation. Where do you live?"

"California."

"If I were you I would get on a plane tomorrow. You'll find surgeons there who can do it."

I was benumbed; it was as if I had been kicked in the solar plexus. While I was listlessly pulling the sock over my limp foot Katy said, "I'll make reservations." I hardly heard her. She helped me up, I paid the doctor his fee and we went to a travel agency.

The next morning we bid the Andrews goodbye and took off for home; they stayed on to visit his relatives.

Changing planes in New York, it took us twenty hours to reach Los Angeles. There we telephoned our friend, Dr. Loyal Davis, in Chicago. After discussing the injury he recommended Dr. Cameron Hall, an orthopedic surgeon, to perform the operation. Dr. Hall did so in the UCLA Hospital. It took him more than four hours to stretch the severed muscles and tendons sufficiently for them to be joined. When I came out of the anesthesia he apologized, saying he had not been able to restructure all of the nerves. "I couldn't find some of them," he said.

A week after getting out of the hospital I became ill and had to go back, this time with streptococcus. Eventually I recovered and, after weeks of therapy and exercise, I was able to walk naturally.

Meanwhile I had edited the film, written and timed the narration and committed it to memory. Katy and I took off to narrate it in auditoriums across the country. Because *Freightboat Around the World* proved successful, we produced others: *Beirut to Baghdad, Magic Carpet to Persia, Modern Turkey, Ireland From A Gypsy Caravan, Coronation of the King of Tonga,* and *The Basque Sheepherder.* Two of the films won Best Documentary of the Year awards.

ENVOI

I N   T R A N S C R I B I N G these experiences I have skipped a multitude of misadventures and contretemps and have not confessed a number of my impieties and transgressions. Were I given life again, I would not marry Josephine Butterly or Elizabeth Bumiller. Doing so was unfair to them and stupid of me. I've often wondered whether I did wrong in dropping out of Auburn. Many boys and girls work their ways through college and I think if I had been encouraged I would have done so.

What of importance have I learned from my adventures and peregrinations? I have learned the most important rule of all: to do unto others . . .

I've learned that, in speaking, the wisest way is to tell the truth, whereas in writing one has the poetic license to embellish facts to make a good story.

I've learned that, for a man, the key to happiness is a loving woman.

Gertrude Katherine McElroy Paul Parrish Weld is the key to my joy and delight. Considering the distance between us when she was born and the thousands of people we passed before we met, it had to be a machination of fate that we found each other. The sinking of the *Laust Maersk* solidified our union. That brush with death made us realize the fragility and brevity of life and how much we needed each other.

We were in Puerto Vallarta visiting John Huston shortly before he died and came upon a tall palm tree. From its roots to the fronds a flowering vine encircled its trunk with an endearing embrace. It was a statue of Katy and me.

While we were there John asked me, "Did you ever tell Dad about your affair with Nan?"

I said, "Of course not."